Gershom Scholem

Studies in German-Jewish Cultural History and Literature
Editor: Paul Mendes-Flohr

Franz Rosenzweig Minerva Research Center
Hebrew University of Jerusalem
Established in 1990 at The Hebrew University of Jerusalem, the Franz Rosenzweig
Minerva Research Center is funded by the Minerva Foundation, Munich, and the
Ministry of Research and Technology of the Federal Republic of Germany.
Named after the German-Jewish philosopher Franz Rosenzweig (1886–1929), whose
life and work are deemed emblematic of the German-Jewish cultural legacy, the Center
seeks to honor the cultural achievements of German-speaking Jewry from the Middle
Ages until the Shoah, and its subsequent reconstruction. Through its ramified research
projects, the Center also endeavors to examine the "culture of modernity" through the
prism of German-Jewish cultural and literary history.

FRONTISPIECE. SCHOLEM in his apartment in Jerusalem, mid-1920s. Photo by Erich Brauer. Courtesy of the family.

Gershom Scholem

AN INTELLECTUAL BIOGRAPHY

Amir Engel

The University of Chicago Press   CHICAGO & LONDON

The University of Chicago Press, Chicago 60637
The University of Chicago Press, Ltd., London
© 2017 by The University of Chicago
Published 2017.
Printed in the United States of America

26 25 24 23 22 21 20 19 18 17   1 2 3 4 5

ISBN-13: 978-0-226-42863-5 (cloth)
ISBN-13: 978-0-226-42877-2 (e-book)
DOI: 10.7208/chicago/9780226428772.001.0001

Library of Congress Cataloging-in-Publication Data
Names: Engel, Amir, author.
Title: Gershom Scholem : an intellectual biography / Amir Engel.
Other titles: Studies in German-Jewish cultural history and literature (Chicago, Ill.)
Description: Chicago : The University of Chicago Press, 2017. | Series: Studies in
German-Jewish cultural history and literature / Franz Rosenzweig Minerva
Research Center, Hebrew University of Jerusalem
Identifiers: LCCN 2016019388 | ISBN 9780226428635 (cloth : alk. paper) |
ISBN 9780226428772 (e-book)
Subjects: LCSH: Scholem, Gershom, 1897–1982. | Jewish scholars—
Germany—Biography. | Jewish scholars—Israel—Biography. | Zionism—History—
20th century. | Mysticism—Judaism.
Classification: LCC BM755.S295 E54 2017 | DDC 296.092 [B] —dc23
LC record available at https://lccn.loc.gov/2016019388

♾ This paper meets the requirements of ANSI/NISO Z39.48-1992
(Permanence of Paper).

To Ayelet

CONTENTS

ILLUSTRATIONS

ACKNOWLEDGMENTS

I have often imagined myself writing these lines. One day, I repeatedly thought, I will finally reach the position from which I will formally thank those who helped me throughout the long journey of writing. It was a way for me to enjoy the friendship and support I received long before the hard work was done. Now, after imagining this section so often and for such a long time, committing these words to writing feels surreal. The following is therefore only a gesture, a token of the deep sense of gratitude I feel.

To the degree that I have become, in the process of writing this book, a writer, I have Amir Eshel to thank. I am grateful for his support, wisdom, and friendship. I thank every one of the many people who taught me essential lessons along the way. Thank you, Hans Ulrich Gumbrecht, Russell Berman, Charlotte Fonrobert, David Biale, Daniel Weidner, Bernhard Greiner, Christoph Schmidt, Carola Hilfrich, and Joseph Dan. In different ways, they have all offered me deep insights, pushed me to think deeper and write better, and supplied me with the most valuable assets one can have on a long journey: hope and good faith. I am grateful to be surrounded by brilliant and inspiring friends, including Iris Idelson-Shein, Ofer Ashkenazi, Elad Lapidot, Assaf Sharon, and Stephan Steiner. I thank my teachers, colleagues, and friends in Frankfurt am Main, Christian Wiese, Raphael Gross, Shmuel Feiner, Miriam Thulin, Vera Bronn, Grażyna Jurewicz, Ottfried Fraisse, Eva Kaminski, Ulrike Kleinecke, Ansgar Martins, Stefan Vogt, and Tilmann Gempp-Friedrich, for giving me a place to call home. I am thankful for the financial support provided to me by the Mellon Foundation and the Leo Baeck Fellowship. I am thankful to Daniel Wildmann and Roland Hain, who run the Leo Baeck Fellowship

Programme of the Studienstiftung des deutschen Volkes and the Leo Baeck Institute London. I thank Jammie Nathan, Rivka Shveiky, and Zmira Reuveni and the National Library of Israel for their help with reproducing images from the Scholem archive.

Several people have touched my heart with unexpected kindness and generosity. I thank Avner Greenberg and Harvey Shoolman. I owe a special debt of gratitude to Paul Mendes-Flohr, whose actual kindness exceeds even the reputation he has garnered. At the University of Chicago Press I thank T. David Brent and Ellen Kladky for their support and help. I am thankful to Susan Tarcov for her diligent assistance with preparing the manuscript.

I thank my mother Avital—a humanist in the deepest sense of the word—for instilling in me the love of culture. I thank my father, Avner—an engineer by training but a historian at heart—for introducing me to the art of storytelling. I thank Rachel, Ofer, Yonatan, and Michael Engel as well as Simha F. Landau. I thank Alia and Arielle Engel for being playful, charming, beautiful, demanding, and generous companions. I can hardly imagine anything as fulfilling as seeing them grow and as exciting as the anticipation of things to come. And lastly, I thank Ayelet N. Landau. I become a better person every day through her companionship and love and through my continuous efforts to reciprocate in a similar coin. This book is dedicated to her.

CHAPTER 1

The Stories of Gershom Scholem

In my opinion, my scientific endeavor should be discussed according to its stated objectives, not according to its hidden meanings.

GERSHOM SCHOLEM TO BARUCH KURZWEIL, 1959

Gershom Scholem (1897–1982) occupies a central role in our intellectual imagination. The foremost scholar of Jewish mysticism, Scholem was an intellectual giant, "the creator of an academic discipline," in Martin Buber's often quoted assertion,[1] and among the most influential scholars of the previous century. Yet despite his charismatic personality and the many books and articles he wrote, there is something about him that remains mysterious and never fully exposed. Hans Jonas, one of Scholem's close friends and an influential philosopher, reflected in his memoir on what one might have expected to be a fundamental aspect of Scholem's worldview. Was Scholem a religious Jew, in any sense of the word? Jonas noted: "We were completely puzzled about this question."[2] This, Jonas added, "remains one of the unanswered Scholem Enigmas."[3] The irksome presence of such a "Scholem Enigma" surfaced again in a column written in the daily *Ha'aretz* by one of Scholem's closest students and friends, Joseph Weiss, on the occasion of Scholem's fiftieth birthday.[4] In

1. On this issue see also Daniel Abrams, "Defining Modern Academic Scholarship: Gershom Scholem and the Establishment of a New (?) Discipline," *Journal of Jewish Thought and Philosophy* 9, no. 2 (December 1, 2000): 267–302.

2. Hans Jonas, *Memoirs*, ed. Christian Wiese, trans. Krishna Winston (Lebanon, NH: University Press of New England, 2008), 166–67. For more on Hans Jonas's relation to and understanding of Scholem see Christian Wiese, *The Life and Thought of Hans Jonas: Jewish Dimensions* (Lebanon, NH: University Press of New England, 2007), 36–67.

3. Jonas, *Memoirs*, 167.

4. For more on the relations between Gershom Scholem and Joseph Weiss see Noam Zadoff,

FIGURE 1.1. Scholem at his desk in his apartment in Jerusalem, 1934. Courtesy of The National Library of Israel, Jerusalem.

this column Weiss noted that Scholem's concealment technique was "akin to that of some medieval painter-artists, whose likeness is depicted in the background of their paintings."[5] In his works, Scholem brought to life an array of intriguing characters, among which are Sabbatai Zevi, Nathan of Gaza, and Rabbi Isaac Luria. If Weiss is correct, Scholem hid his own portrait among these men, but where exactly? It is frustratingly hard to say. As Rolf Tiedemann, one of the first and most influential Walter Benjamin scholars, noted, Scholem was "the ultimate authority, only that one could not quite say an authority on what."[6]

---

ed., *Gershom Scholem and Joseph Weiss: Correspondence 1949–1964* (in Hebrew) (Jerusalem: Carmel, 2012).

5. See Joseph Weiss, "Gershom Scholem is Fifty" (in Hebrew), *Ha'aretz*, November 28, 1947. The recurring references to this column in contemporary studies suggest the centrality of the riddle surrounding the figure of Scholem. See Noam Zadoff, "The Awl and the Sack: Joseph Weiss, Baruch Kurzweil and the Historical Vocation of Gershom Scholem," in *History as a Vocation: Essays for Moshe Zimmermann's Sixtieth Birthday*, ed. Noam Zadoff, Yotam Hotam, and Matthias Schmidt (Jerusalem: Magnes Press, 2008), 73–78.

6. "Er war die uneingeschränkter Autorität, ohne dass man so recht hätte sagen können: Autorität wofür." Rolf Tiedemann, "Erinnerung an Scholem," in Gershom Scholem, *Walter*

Many prominent scholars have written about Gershom Scholem. David Biale's *Gershom Scholem: Kabbalah and Counter-history* has set the standard interpretation for some of Scholem's most important and difficult concepts and ideas.[7] A great number of scholarly articles, book chapters, and a handful of other important books have added essential dimensions to the understanding of his life and his work, and they will be discussed in more detail shortly. Nevertheless, I will argue, the scholarly spotlight on Scholem has not yet lifted the shadow that obscures his image. Scholem is still an enigma today, just as he was for Jonas, Weiss, and Tiedemann about half a century ago. Indeed, it often seems that the overall impression many scholars had while working on this topic is rather similar to the one keenly formulated by David Myers in his book on Jewish historiography. In the closing lines of his discussion on Scholem, Myers notes: "One often gets the sense when studying Scholem's life and work that he took a certain delight in throwing critics off his trail, offering clues in various directions before retracting them at random."[8]

Who was Gerhard (Gershom) Scholem? He never claimed to be anything more than a historian of Jewish mysticism, yet he clearly was.[9] Why then did Scholem become so much more than a historian of the Kabbalah and an expert on obscure Jewish texts? Or alternatively, how could an expert on a decidedly limited field of knowledge become so influential and well-known? These are the questions this book sets out to explore.

In this book I strive to shed new light on the enigma of Gershom Scholem by telling the story of his evolvement over and against the existential questions that he faced throughout his life. I argue that in order to discuss Scholem and understand his confrontation with the fundamental questions of modernity one must follow at least two interrelated yet distinct sequences of events, two plotlines, as it were. The first thread follows the events that made up Scholem's life, his biography, and the second is his historiography, his narrative of Jewish mystical tradition and its role in the creation of the modern Jewish nation.

Gershom Scholem was born in 1897 in Berlin to a middle-class Jewish family and soon became enthralled by the questions and dilemmas of Jewish life

Benjamin und sein Engel: Vierzehn Aufsätze und kleine Beiträge (Frankfurt am Main: Suhrkamp, 1983), 212.

7. David Biale, *Gershom Scholem: Kabbalah and Counter-history* (Cambridge: Harvard University Press, 1979); hereafter *Counter-history*.

8. David N. Myers, *Re-inventing the Jewish Past: European Jewish Intellectuals and the Zionist Return to History* (New York: Oxford University Press, 1995), 175.

9. For more on Scholem's self-perception as a historian, see Elisabeth Hamacher, *Gershom Scholem und die allgemeine Religionsgeschichte* (Berlin: Walter de Gruyter, 1999), 49–72.

in the modern world. He was a devout Zionist and a political activist already at the age of sixteen. In 1923, Scholem immigrated to Palestine, then a mandate of the British Empire. There, he became a key member of a fringe Zionist organization that advocated the creation of a binational—Jewish-Arab—solution in Palestine. In 1925, he became a lecturer at the newly founded Hebrew University and eventually a key figure in Israeli academic and intellectual circles. Scholem himself recounted the story of his life in a memoir[10] titled *From Berlin to Jerusalem*, which leaves many of the story's most intriguing details and events undisclosed.

In order to gain a better understanding of Scholem's evolvement over and against the fundamental questions of modernity, it is necessary to discuss the main modus of his thought, that is, the story that Scholem himself told through his work as a scholar. For much of his long and industrious life, Scholem wrote about, discussed, and expanded the study of Jewish mysticism. The groundbreaking work he undertook in this field made him a famous man. Scholem's study of the Kabbalah is a vast, complex, and multifaceted edifice. Several scholars have offered a typology for Scholem's works,[11] and a bibliography of his writings was published as a separate volume already during his lifetime.[12] Any attempt to succinctly organize them is a daunting challenge; nevertheless, the discussion in this book focuses on what seems to be the fundamental aspect of this phenomenal accomplishment: Scholem's historiography. Beyond other important aspects of his life's achievements, it is Scholem's historiography of Jewish mysticism, I argue, that serves as the distinct core of his bibliographical, philological, and phenomenological writings.[13]

---

10. The book *From Berlin to Jerusalem* is often referred to by scholars as Gershom Scholem's autobiography. However, because it describes in detail only a rather limited period of Scholem's life, I find the term memoir more fitting and I will use it throughout. See Gershom Scholem, *From Berlin to Jerusalem: Memories of My Youth* (New York: Schocken, 1980).

11. Eliezer Schweid, for example, differentiates between Scholem's "bibliographical and philological" works, his books "dealing with larger subjects," essays "devoted to phenomenological analysis," and essays about "contemporary issues." See *Judaism and Mysticism according to Gershom Scholem: A Critical Analysis and Programmatic Discussion*, trans. David Avraham Weiner (Atlanta: Scholars Press, 1985), 11. See also Moshe Idel, *Kabbalah: New Perspectives* (New Haven: Yale University Press, 1990), 11.

12. Moshe Catane, ed., *Bibliography of the Writings of Gershom Scholem: Presented to Gershom Scholem on the Occasion of His Eightieth Birthday* (Jerusalem: Magnes Press, 1977).

13. This observation is similar to the one made by Joseph Dan. See "Gershom Scholem's Historical System," in his *On Gershom Scholem: A Dozen Studies* (in Hebrew) (Jerusalem: Shazar, 2010), 15.

It is, indeed, his revolutionary metanarrative of the Jewish people, laid out most comprehensively in his magisterial work *Major Trends in Jewish Mysticism*, that serves as the fundament for most of Scholem's other discoveries. In this book, Scholem describes, among other things, the events that led from the Spanish expulsion of 1492, through the formation of the Lurianic Kabbalah in Safed in the sixteenth century, to the explosion of the Sabbatean heretical movement on the plane of history, the repercussions of which, Scholem argued, were felt well into the eighteenth century in, among others, the Hasidic movement. This sequence of interrelated events, Scholem furthermore claimed, decisively shaped Judaism and Jewish life in the modern era. It is this narrative too—Scholem's history of modern Judaism from the Spanish expulsion until the fall of the Hasidic movement—that is discussed in the following chapters.

The two central plots—Scholem's life story and his historiography—are intertwined. For, as I show, Scholem's singular scholarly work is deeply rooted in his no less exceptional life story. Some scholars may find this suggestion inadequate to describe the work of this towering figure. But like that of many other scholars and intellectuals, Scholem's scholarly research is underpinned by assumptions and beliefs developed in reaction to events, problems, and dilemmas that he encountered in the world around him. Like many others, Scholem often sought to comprehend and further explain the social situation in which he lived by uncovering its historical foundations even if he never explicitly claimed to do so. Therefore, as in the cases of other authors, any attempt to understand Scholem's work must take account of the events and dilemmas in the context of which they were created.

*

The choice to discuss Scholem's life and work as intertwined stories is part of a continuous, albeit not always explicit, argument about its very nature and value. Indeed, the question why Scholem is still read today, and what relevance he still bears, permeates scholarly discussion just as the "Scholem enigma" once troubled Scholem's personal friends. Thus, for instance, in a 1992 article dedicated to Scholem, Amos Funkenstein writes that the fact that Scholem's work has an echo "in other fields . . . both within and beyond the pale of Jewish studies is . . . astounding if not paradoxical."[14] Not long after concluding

14. Amos Funkenstein, "Gershom Scholem: Charisma, 'Kairos' and the Messianic Dialectic," *History and Memory* 4, no. 1 (1992): 124.

his voluminous study on Scholem's work,[15] and almost fifteen years after Funkenstein's article, Daniel Weidner raised the same problem. Taking
Scholem to be "one of the most important representatives of 20th century Jewish thought" as well as "a major spokesman for Jewishness" is, Weidner con-
tends, "a little surprising, considering that his main works are historiographical, consisting of a rather specialized research on the Kabbalah and its role in
Jewish history." Indeed, he concludes, "the deeper importance of Scholem's
oeuvre remains vague."[16]

These are keen observations. Ostensibly at least, Scholem never wrote anything that could appeal to a wide audience. One is hard-pressed to find, among
his several hundreds of publications, any even remotely systematic discussion
of issues in general philosophy, politics, film, art, literature, or world history.
The few comments he did make on such issues were most often given in interviews.[17] Moreover, as Weidner and others have argued, the overwhelming
majority of Scholem's work concerns a relatively narrow corpus within the
vast field Jewish studies.[18] And yet his life and works have also been studied
by leading literary scholars, such as Harold Bloom, Robert Alter, and Andreas
Kilcher, historians like Steven Aschheim and David Biale, and philosophers
such as Paul Mendes Flohr and Nathan Rotenstreich, who together created
a rather complex if not complicated image. In its entirety, the literature on
Scholem casts him, as David Myers noted, in "a myriad of functions: philologist, historian, philosopher, publicist, and Zionist theoretician and critic, not
to mention his erstwhile career as a serious student of mathematics."[19] There
is therefore a certain peculiarity in Scholem's position in the contemporary
cultural imagination. The fact is that although he was predominantly a scholar
of Jewish lore, his impact is felt well beyond his narrow field and is evident
in a plethora of cultural fields, both within Israeli academia and outside of it.
How is that possible?

15. Daniel Weidner, *Gershom Scholem: Politisches, esoterisches und historiographisches Schreiben* (Munich: Wilhelm Fink Verlag, 2003).

16. Daniel Weidner, "Reading Gershom Scholem," *Jewish Quarterly Review* 96, no. 2 (2006): 203.

17. See, for example, "Dan Miron Interviews Gershom Scholem on S. Y. Agnon," in *Continuity and Revolt: Gershom Scholem in Interview and Dialogue*, ed. Avraham Shapira (Tel Aviv: Am Oved, 1994), 65–87.

18. This observation serves as a cornerstone of Eliezer Schweid's critique of Scholem. See *Judaism and Mysticism*, 33–49.

19. Myers, *Re-inventing the Jewish Past*, 153.

One solution may be that Jewish mysticism has a much wider relevance than one would assume. However, in light of the vast changes that have taken place within the field of Kabbalah studies over the past few decades, this solution appears unlikely. Indeed, the publication of Moshe Idel's book *Kabbalah: New Perspectives* in 1988 paved the way for the reexamination of Scholem's historical and philological methods.[20] Among other issues, Idel's book contains a powerful critique of Scholem's methodologies in the study of the Jewish mysticism and calls attention to new methods and facets of Jewish mysticism neglected by Scholem. Idel's study was followed by others, and the result was a paradigm shift that moved the field of Kabbalah studies slowly beyond the methods laid down by its founding father. The continuous stream of scholarly work published in the last decade alone introduces new voices and approaches in the study of Kabbalistic literature.[21] These transformations should have made Scholem's project obsolete, but they did not.

Scholarly fascination with Scholem endures and has perhaps even intensified. Many of his books are still in circulation, and the past few decades have seen a continuous stream of publications, workshops, and lectures about Scholem and his scholarly work as well as the reissuing of some of Scholem's less-known essays.[22] Joseph Dan's observation from 1997 seems therefore still relevant today: "It is not the question of whether Scholem has been correct in one or another of his scholarly conclusions. Today he is a classic of Jewish

20. Idel, *Kabbalah: New Perspectives*.

21. For an overview of these transformations see Boaz Huss, "A New Age in the Study of Jewish Mysticism" (in Hebrew), *Theory and Criticism* 27 (Fall 2006): 246–53. Concrete examples are numerous; I will restrict myself therefore to four: Elliot R. Wolfson, *Along the Path: Studies in Kabbalistic Myth, Symbolism, and Hermeneutics* (Albany: SUNY Press, 1995); Haviva Pedaya, *Walking through Trauma: Rituals of Movement in Jewish Myth, Mysticism, and History* (in Hebrew) (Tel Aviv: Resling, 2011); Boaz Huss, *Like the Radiance of the Sky: Chapters in the Reception History of the Zohar and the Construction of Its Symbolic Value* (in Hebrew) (Jerusalem: Mosad Bialik, 2008); Yehuda Liebes, *Studies in the Zohar* (Albany: SUNY Press, 1993).

22. Proof of the continuous interest in Scholem and the way he is canonized can be gleaned from the republication of his 1948 essay about the history of the Star of David both in Hebrew and in German. The essay was republished in 2009 in Hebrew as an expanded, reedited, and carefully designed hardcover book by the Museum of Art in Ein-Harod. This volume includes also several short essays about Scholem and his work. In 2010 a German translation was reissued by the Jüdischer Verlag, again as a well-crafted hardcover publication that includes a thoughtful afterword by Gerold Neckar. Scholem's scholarship was also republished in Gershom Scholem, *Lurianic Kabbalah: Collected Studies*, ed. Daniel Abrams (Los Angeles: Cherub Press, 2008); Gershom Scholem, *The Latest Phase: Essays on Hasidism*, ed. David Assaf and Esther Liebes (Tel Aviv: Am Oved, 2008).

studies . . . Some essential aspects of his achievements are beyond . . . detailed discussions and reevaluations."[23] Dan's observation offers a succinct and, I would add, accurate account of a general scholarly sentiment surrounding the image of Scholem and his work. But the problem remains unsolved. One may ask about these "essential aspects" that render Scholem such a pillar of Jewish and Israeli culture beyond "the question of whether Scholem has been correct in one or another of his scholarly conclusions." What are they and where are they to be found? Again, it is frustratingly difficult to say.

The attempt to explain the peculiarity of Scholem's position in the cultural imagination constitutes a defining aspect in the existing approaches to Scholem's oeuvre. The general consensus among scholars seems to be that Scholem is widely read despite his narrow field of expertise and the changes within it primarily because from the depths of Jewish mysticism, of Judaism, or even of the past in general, he excavated some kernel of unyielding philosophical truth. Even if the precise content of this truth is an issue of debate, two major trends emerge from the diverse body of literature that seeks to probe the inner meaning of Scholem's writings. Some scholars, such as Baruch Kurzweil, Amos Funkenstein, Christoph Schmidt, and Benjamin Lazier, have understood Scholem's discoveries to pertain to his Zionist worldview. [24] Despite the differences between them, they all argue that Scholem found in the history of Jewish mysticism a certain precursor, model, or paradigm that could serve the spiritual, ideological, or political needs of the emerging body politic of the Jewish people in the twentieth century. Other scholars, such as David Biale, Robert Alter, and Stephan Moses, maintain that Scholem excavated a much larger and more general idea that touches upon the very foundations of knowledge in the modern period.[25] Significantly, these two interpretive possibilities do not necessarily exclude one another and are at times even found in the literature in conjunction. In what follows, I seek to call both these interpretations

23. Joseph Dan, "Gershom Scholem: Between Mysticism and Scholarship," *Germanic Review: Literature, Culture, Theory* 72, no. 1 (1997): 4.

24. See Baruch Kurzweil, "Remarks on 'Shabbtai Sevi,'" in *In the Struggle for the Values of Judaism* (Tel Aviv: Schocken, 1969), 134–99; Christoph Schmidt, "Der häretische Imperativ," *Zeitschrift für Religions- und Geistesgeschichte* 50, no. 1 (1998): 61–83; Benjamin Lazier, *God Interrupted: Heresy and the European Imagination between the World Wars* (Princeton: Princeton University Press, 2008), 139–45.

25. Biale, *Counter-history*; Robert Alter, *Necessary Angels: Tradition and Modernity in Kafka, Benjamin, and Scholem* (Cambridge: Harvard University Press, 1991); Stéphane Moses, *The Angel of History: Rosenzweig, Benjamin, Scholem* (Stanford: Stanford University Press, 2009), 129–81.

of Scholem into question, but first let us focus a narrow lens on each, beginning with what may be called the Zionist paradigm.

Most attempts to substantiate an essential link between Scholem's Zionism and his work on the Kabbalah concentrate on his studies of Sabbatai Zevi and the Sabbatean movement. The assumption underlying this paradigm is that the heretical Sabbatean movement, which, ostensibly at least, forced Jews onto the plain of world history, served Scholem to prove that Zionism has a precedent within the innermost folds of Jewish history. Perhaps the most succinct and direct formulation of this position is given by Amos Funkenstein who argues: "In Scholem's eyes the Sabbatean movement (and its later developments) was . . . a prefiguration of Zionism."[26] The reasons and the intricacies of this argument will be explored in detail in the fifth chapter below, which is devoted to Scholem's study of the Sabbatean movement. Here it will suffice to note that this position was formulated already during Scholem's lifetime (by Baruch Kurzweil), and endures in some of the most recent scholarship on Scholem.[27] That the relation between Zionism and Sabbateanism is one of the most recurring themes in the literature on Scholem is hardly surprising. The tension between the national project of the Jews and the religious history of Judaism is the topic of a heated debate that does not appear to be dissipating any time in the foreseeable future.[28] In the context of this debate, Scholem's views on Sabbateanism seem alive and relevant.

The second position on the inner meaning of Scholem's writings is more daring, more general, and for this reason somewhat more difficult to formulate. A poignant example of this position is offered by Eliezer Schweid, who, in a highly critical evaluation, writes that Scholem "regarded mysticism as the source from which Jewish religion regenerates itself."[29] In the Hebrew original Schweid uses the rather peculiar term *luz* to denote the word "source" and continues with a short sentence, omitted from the English translation of the book, stating that, for Scholem, mysticism was the essence (*atzmut*) and all

26. Funkenstein, "Gershom Scholem," 133.

27. The first to have made this point is probably Baruch Kurzweil, who was one of Scholem's most fierce critics. See "Remarks on 'Shabbtai Sevi.'" For a more recent formulation see, e.g., Lazier, *God Interrupted*, 139–45.

28. The literature on this issue is vast. See, for example, Aviezer Ravitzky, *Messianism, Zionism, and Jewish Religious Radicalism* (Chicago: University of Chicago Press, 1996); Shmuel Almog, Jehuda Reinharz, and Anita Shapira, eds., *Zionism and Religion* (Hanover, NH: University Press of New England, 1998).

29. Schweid, *Judaism and Mysticism*, 21.

the rest was vessels (*kelim*) or costumes (*malbushim*).[30] These words have
obvious Kabbalistic connotations, and thus Schweid's choice is anything but
coincidental. Indeed, this formulation strongly suggests that Scholem's reading of the Kabbalah is, in and of itself, a mystical act, conjuring Real Presence
from the texts of times past.[31]

A no less bold yet somewhat more specific formulation of Scholem's "revelation" lays emphasis on his understanding and interpretation of language.
Scholem wrote considerably about the question of interpretation, meaning,
and translation in the Kabbalah and beyond.[32] He was especially preoccupied
with issues in the philosophy of language around the end of the First World
War, while in close contact with Walter Benjamin. It is indeed no coincidence
that much of the literature that discusses Scholem's theory of language does
so in conjunction with Benjamin's works.[33] In the most general terms, the argument offered regarding Scholem's thinking on language is that he found in
the Kabbalah a principle of commentary that goes radically beyond the "original meaning" of the interpreted text. Thus the "Kabbalistic" interpretation of
a text may expose a hidden meaning that could transform or even reverse the
overall or apparent "meaning" or effect of that text. In his deeply perceptive
study on Kafka, Benjamin, and Scholem, Robert Alter expresses the idea with
the following words: "Scholem's argument is to propose that commentary,

30. ראה במיסטיקה את הלוז ממנו מתחדשת הדת היהודית. היא העצמות וכל היתר כלים או ג"ש"
מלבושים." In Eliezer Schweid, *Judaism and Mysticism according to Gershom Scholem* (in Hebrew) (Jerusalem: Magnes Press, 1983), 6.

31. Interestingly, much of Schweid's scathing review of Scholem is based precisely on this
premise, arguing that Scholem has, for spiritual reasons, disregarded and subsequently deval-
ued essential elements of the Jewish religious sources and substantial aspects of Jewish history. However, in a strange move, Schweid concedes that perhaps after all this is not the case.
"Scholem himself" Schweid notes, "was not entirely sure whether his judgment was correct."
Schweid, *Judaism and Mysticism*, 21. In other words, even as Schweid criticizes Scholem for his
understanding of mysticism, he also acknowledges that this formulation of Scholem's thinking
does not always quite characterize Scholem's work. Rather than Scholem's not trusting his own
judgment, I would suggest the possibility that Schweid mischaracterizes it.

32. See, for example, Gershom Scholem, "The Name of God and the Linguistic Theory of
the Kabbalah," trans. Simon Pleasance, *Diogenes* 20, no. 79 (September 1, 1972): 59–80; Gershom Scholem, "Tradition and New Creation in the Ritual of the Kabbalists," in *On the Kabbalah and Its Symbolism* (Jerusalem: Schocken, 1996), 158–204.

33. See, for example, Eric Jacobson, *Metaphysics of the Profane: The Political Theology of
Walter Benjamin and Gershom Scholem* (New York: Columbia University Press, 2003); Gil
Anidjar, *"Our Place in Al-Andalus": Kabbalah, Philosophy, Literature in Arab Jewish Letters*
(Stanford: Stanford University Press, 2002), 102–65; Biale, *Counter-history*, 86–89.

which presents itself as a mere supplement to the text or extension or illumination of it, is actually an explosive force for change."[34] Scholem, it is thus argued, discovered that as it draws the innermost aspects of the text to the fore, mystical commentary has the power to pull the text inside out and transform it. This formulation positions Scholem as something of a Jewish Paul de Man. For indeed Scholem, according to Alter, found in the Kabbalah a disruptive system of reading, and it is this that makes him interesting and relevant to this day.

Perhaps the most insightful and complex position on this issue was formulated by David Biale in his hugely influential book *Gershom Scholem: Kabbalah and Counter-history*. For Biale, the determinate aspect of Scholem's achievement is a radical concept of historiography. It might be helpful to describe it in relation to Alter's interpretation. Namely, what Alter describes as Scholem's philosophy of language, Biale attributes to his concept of historiography. Scholem, according to Biale, found in the Kabbalah a notion of historical interpretation that turns history inside out and thus offers a new path into the future. Biale names this kind of historiography "counter-history," defining it as "the theory that there is a continuing dialectic between the exoteric and a subterranean tradition [and that] true history lies beneath the surface and often contradicts the assumptions of the normative tradition."[35] Biale's notion of counterhistory, like many other observations he made in this book, has acquired a dominant position amongst Scholem scholars. This favored position owes itself not only to the interpretive strength of his reading of Scholem, but also to the fact that Scholem's concept of historiography touches upon more general questions about knowledge, as well as questions of politics in the narrow sense. As Biale also argues, it is precisely in his historiography that Scholem allows himself to address the tensions between the historical past and the political future more directly than anywhere in his literary corpus.

Though they vary considerably from one another, all the above-mentioned approaches share a specific understanding of Scholem's achievement and thus also express a certain position about his continuous importance. They all suggest, whether explicitly or implicitly, that Scholem found something of lasting meaning or relevance in the Kabbalah. They all thus attribute, explicitly or implicitly, Scholem's claim to posterity to this finding. And yet there are several problematic elements in this account of Scholem's enduring appeal. Most important, it mischaracterizes the basic impulse of Scholem's writing.

34. Alter, *Necessary Angels*, 86.
35. Biale, *Counter-history*, 195.

Scholem never developed a systematic philosophy of history, language, or politics. He never composed a systematic theological work. Throughout his long and extremely productive career, Scholem wrote many thousands of pages about Jewish mysticism, and yet not once in all this vast corpus of works do we find much more than traces of explicit discussions of the fundamental concepts, ultimate objectives, or the unyielding truths he found in the Kabbalah. The Zionist paradigm is in a similar predicament, for indeed Scholem hardly ever drew explicit conclusions from his studies of Sabbateanism to Zionism. Therefore, the scholarly approaches listed above depend, to a large extent, on hints, casual references, fragments, short testimonies, and most important on the creativity of conjuncture and analysis.

Any attempt to read Scholem as a philosopher of history or of language entails, ipso facto, certain intertextual leaps and anachronistic interpretations. In discussing the key concept of his work Biale, for example, readily acknowledges this fact. "Since Scholem has not articulated systematically his philosophy of history, we must turn to a number of theoreticians whose ideas are demonstrably similar to Scholem's and with whose work he was familiar, even if we cannot establish a precise pattern of influence."[36] Eliezer Schweid takes another route. He criticizes Scholem for ascribing a mystical meaning to the Kabbalah, but also notes that Scholem was never quite sure whether his judgment about the role of mysticism in Judaism was correct.[37] Be that as it may, in order to discuss a particular concept in Scholem's oeuvre, scholars must seek clues and collect ideas across his publications in texts that were written in different time periods and for different ends.[38]

All these apparent methodological problems notwithstanding, the outcome of these readings may still be valid. Indeed, if Scholem's works are mined for their philosophical ore, then it might matter little when, where, and why each single text was produced. One might argue furthermore that Scholem concealed his ultimate goal, the meaning he gave to the basic terms he used, and the reality he found within Jewish lore. It is indeed possible, for example, that

36. Ibid.

37. See note 31 above.

38. The examples are numerous, but David Biale's discussion of Scholem's concepts in his book is informative. For example, in a chapter dedicated to elucidating Scholem's concept of 'Messianism,' Biale makes use of sources that span several decades and includes an analysis of Scholem's published articles, lectures, and newspaper columns that were written for different audiences, delivered in three languages, and published (or delivered) on three different continents. See *Counter-history*, 148–70.

after many years working on secret and esoteric texts, something of the tendency to concealment rubbed off on Scholem and became an essential feature of his own writing. Be that as it may, the idea that there is something secretive about Scholem's writing is often alluded to in the literature. Idel, for example, wrote that "Scholem saw himself as a rediscoverer of the *lost key* of kabbalistic material and also of some historical events" (emphasis added).[39] Some scholars suggest that he was a mystic himself or that he had mystical inclinations.[40] And the great literary scholar Harold Bloom argued that "Scholem, who worked behind the mask of a historian, was the secret theologian of Jewish Gnosis of our time . . . very rarely did he take this mask off."[41] To be sure, this understanding of Scholem is somewhat romantic, but it is not logically impossible.

The mystical understanding of Scholem's works is supported by several key texts, most importantly by a two-page letter he wrote to Salman Schocken in 1937 titled "A Candid Word about the True Motives of My Kabbalistic Studies." The letter was first published by David Biale in his *Gershom Scholem: Kabbalah and Counter-history*, which makes extensive interpretive use of this document.[42] In this letter, Scholem indeed clearly states his yearning for some kind of "beyond," explaining that he "arrived at the intention of writing not the history but the metaphysics of the Kabbalah."[43] In another oft-cited and suggestive section of the letter, Scholem writes: "[T]he mountain, the corpus of facts, needs no key at all; only the misty wall of history, which hangs around it, must be penetrated. To penetrate it was the task I set to myself."[44] With the metaphor of the fog-shrouded mountain, Scholem discusses his desire to find an inner stability (the mountain of facts), which exists within the contingency and partiality of the historical circumstance (the misty wall of history). This powerful image, which is but one example of several expressions of metaphysical yearning, supports the reading of Scholem's work as essentially

39. Moshe Idel, *Old Worlds, New Mirrors: On Jewish Mysticism and Twentieth-Century Thought* (Philadelphia: University of Pennsylvania Press, 2010), 117.

40. This curious position received an almost canonical stature in the literature. See for example Dan, "Gershom Scholem: Between Mysticism and Scholarship," 123–40; Schweid, *Judaism and Mysticism*, 37; Boaz Huss, "Ask No Questions: Gershom Scholem and the Study of Contemporary Jewish Mysticism," *Modern Judaism* 25, no. 2 (2005): 142.

41. Harold Bloom, "Scholem: Unhistorischer oder jüdischer Gnostizismus," in *Babylon, Beiträge zur jüdische Gegenwart* 1 (1984): 70–83, 70.

42. The entire letter appears both in the original German and in English translation in David Biale's book. All citations from the letter are from this book. See *Counter-history*, 74–76.

43. Ibid., 75.

44. Ibid., 75–76.

philosophical.[45] It bolsters the impression that a deeper truth lurks behind the respectable façade of Scholem's seemingly dry historical analysis.

And yet in discussions of Scholem's famous letter to Schocken, the somewhat tentative tone that Scholem employs goes often unnoticed. Scholem expresses here not only his desire to reach some metaphysical depth in his study of the Kabbalah but also caution, even skepticism. In fact, the entire letter is written in the past tense and describes not the insights of the forty-year-old scholar who wrote it but the perspective of a young man entering a new field of inquiry almost twenty years earlier. "I knew what I was doing," Scholem says at the very beginning of his letter, "only it seems to me now that I imagined my undertaking to be much too easy." This key sentence introduces a gap between the "described I" of the letter and the "narrating I," which is maintained throughout the text and charges it with irony. A careful reading of the letter thus reveals that Scholem discusses here what he at one time had hoped to find in the Kabbalah and not what he eventually found it to be. This seemingly unimportant sentence points at the difference. In fact, he goes so far as to admit that his investigations turned out to be much more difficult than he at first expected. But he says absolutely nothing about whether or not the rest of his expectations were in fact met.

One may want therefore to know: Did Scholem eventually penetrate the mist? Did he summit the mountain? The letter seems to indicate that Scholem could not answer these questions because he himself was still unsure. Indeed, it seems immensely telling that in his letter, Scholem echoes these very questions with a question of his own. "Will I get stuck in the mist," he asks, "will I, so to say, suffer a 'professorial death'?"[46] In his letter, Scholem offers no answer. Thus, it would indeed seem that two decades after he started studying the Kabbalah, Scholem was not yet able to say for sure whether or not a mountain would appear beyond the fog. A more satisfying answer cannot be found anywhere in Scholem's academic writings, in his letters, or in his diaries. It may indeed be that Scholem was never quite sure about the mountain. In any

45. See also Peter Schäfer, " 'Die Philologie der Kabbala ist nur eine Projektion auf eine Fläche': Gershom Scholem über die wahren Absichten seines Kabbalastudiums," *Jewish Studies Quarterly* 5, no. 1 (1998): 1–25; Andreas B. Kilcher, "Philology as Kabbalah," in *Kabbalah and Modernity: Interpretations, Transformations, Adaptations*, ed. Boaz Hus, Marco Pasi, and Kocku Von Stuckrad (Leiden: Brill, 2010), esp. 20–26; David Biale, "Gershom Scholem's Ten Unhistorical Aphorisms on Kabbalah: Text and Commentary," *Modern Judaism* 5, no. 1 (February 1, 1985): 67–93. Bloom, "Scholem: Unhistorischer oder jüdischer Gnostizismus."
46. Biale, *Counter-history*, 76.

case, the evident difference between the perspective of the young man and the voice of the mature historian reflecting on his past seems of essential importance to the understanding of this letter. Also the self-doubt and the fear of "professorial death" seem material.[47] While discussing his intentions, Scholem clearly expresses uncertainty about the outcome of his project and distances himself from the "described I" of the letter.

Scholars tend to ignore the differences between Scholem's terse and often cryptic declarations of intent, many of which he penned as a young man, and his voluminous writings, which he published later in his life. Some commentators seem simply to assume that Scholem's reflections on philology and his thoughts on the metaphysics of history aptly represent his actual philological and historiographical work, which was mostly produced later in his life. If this were the case, if Scholem had found any metaphysical truths in the Kabbalah, we would probably find their echo in the five-hundred-page book that is titled simply *Kabbalah* and that he published at the age of seventy-seven.[48] But this book, which consists of Scholem's contribution to the *Encyclopedia Judaica*, makes no such claims. Rather, it consists of a detailed and carefully analyzed historical discussion. It is, to be sure, an excellent source for students in the field of Kabbalah studies, but it remains mostly unfamiliar to other readers. In any case, what could have been Scholem's final word on the issue to which he dedicated his life has nothing to say about metaphysics and has thus received very little scholarly attention, if any.

This is hardly unusual in Scholem's oeuvre. Nowhere in the almost fifty years of prolific writings that followed the letter to Schocken does Scholem mention again the misty mountain or his quest through the historical fog. To a certain extent therefore the doubts he expressed in this letter may very well have been corroborated. To be sure, Scholem never died a professorial death. He was brilliant and industrious to the last. But it is possible that his youthful objective, to reach the mountain of facts through the mist of history, slowly transformed, thus becoming not less inspirational but possibly more mundane. Instead of taking Scholem's letter as conclusive evidence, I would like to suggest that it is important to carefully distinguish between what Scholem said he wanted to do and what he actually did.

47. Some scholars played down the importance of this statement. See, for example, Steven M. Wasserstrom, *Religion after Religion* (Princeton: Princeton University Press, 1999), 32; Paul R. Mendes-Flohr, "Introductory Essay: The Quest of the Philologist," in *Gershom Scholem: The Man and His Work*, ed. Paul R. Mendes-Flohr (Albany: SUNY Press, 1994), 20.

48. Gershom Scholem, *Kabbalah* (Jerusalem: Keter, 1974).

Against the position that Scholem found in the Kabbalah some inner truth but never explicitly described it, one could also argue that Scholem never found any truth beyond what historiography or philology may produce. In writing the history of the Sabbatean messianic movement, for example, Scholem may have been aiming to distill some timeless notion of messianism, expose the universality of Zionism, or offer a complex philosophy of history or language. But he never stated that these were indeed his objectives, he never worked out the metaphysics of Sabbateanism, nor did he conceptualize its relation to Zionism, and therefore it is impossible to determine if these studies do in fact have a deeper, undisclosed meaning.

In the reading of Scholem suggested here, I approach his writings from a perspective different from that of the scholars mentioned above. I take him at his word, assuming that any "hidden meanings," if those exist, lie almost completely beyond the reach of the interpreter. Scholem's writings, I claim in short, must be studied according to their explicit intentions, not according to some occult meaning.

Beyond ascribing to Scholem positions he hardly ever stated, reading Scholem as a philosopher, a mystic, or a theologian entails yet another difficulty. By claiming that Scholem found within the Kabbalah some metaphysical truth, it is assumed, inter alia, that the Kabbalah entails such a metaphysical core. However, Jewish mysticism appears to be much less a definite object than a voluminous corpus of highly complex, dense, and mysterious texts that were written in different times and places. It does not seem likely, in other words, that one may take the mighty creation called "Jewish mysticism" and reduce it to a specific set of metaphysical truths. It is even less likely that Scholem might have done so. The foremost scholar of Jewish mysticism was extremely cautious when he needed to define the subject matter of his lifelong study. As noted above, he hardly ever committed to any specific set of internal metaphysical truths, principles, or even concepts, only to their historical reality. He might have known too much about Jewish mysticism to do otherwise. Be that as it may, one fact cannot be contested: in hundreds of publications Scholem discussed the history of the Kabbalah and offered philological studies of specific manuscripts and texts, while he hardly ever committed himself to any one underlying metaphysical truth. This fact serves as the motto for the present study.

To recapitulate, the literature on Scholem is replete with discussions about how Scholem excavated from ostensibly old and forgotten texts a kernel of truth, be it a philosophy of history, a theory of language, a notion of Zionism, a concept of messianism, or an idea of the Jewish mystic. These discussions,

I argue, seem to be based on a doubly flawed methodology. First, the search for the philosophical underpinning of Scholem's work does not quite represent Scholem's oeuvre but rather shifts the emphasis from his historiographical work to other, marginal aspects of his writing, such as the two-page letter to Schocken. I suggest in contrast that these aspects should be given their due place within Scholem's substantially larger literary achievement and that the focus should return to Scholem's historiography. Second, I argue that the assumptions needed in order to make a claim about Scholem's metaphysical discoveries are unlikely. It is difficult to accept that Scholem understood Jewish mysticism as a given object in which truths can be found. Attributing Scholem's status as cultural giant to this search for meaning furthermore entails the assumption that he adequately understood the secret lore of Judaism. Admittedly, it is at times difficult to say how exactly Scholem understood the Kabbalah, but his writings strongly suggest that he took it to be primarily a historical phenomenon.

All this, however, is not to suggest that Scholem made no use of theoretical constructions, concepts, methods, or theories. Whether he explicitly discussed them or not, Scholem, like any historian, made extensive use of a specific subset of concepts and methods. The existing analyses of Scholem's concepts and ideas are therefore not wrong. Scholem did have a certain concept of history or of language. And he did employ a certain understanding of the terms 'myth' and 'symbol.' Furthermore, I do not suggest that scholars who point at a deep and abiding similarity between Scholem's methods and concepts and those he ascribed to the Kabbalah are ill-informed. Biale, in other words, is quite right to suggest that "the similarity between Scholem's own theological formulations and those he ascribes to the kabbalah seems to be too striking to be coincidental."[49] In short, the notion that led scholars to assume that Scholem is something of a Kabbalist—namely, his use of Kabbalistic tropes in his historical study—is not a figment of the imagination.

Rather than question the validity of the existing scholarship, I seek to question the causality that is implied in it. I wish to ask, in other words, not if Scholem had a "counterhistory" but whether he indeed found it in the Kabbalah. Similarly, I wish to ask not whether Scholem had a concept of 'messianism' or of 'myth' but rather if it would be accurate to argue that he uncovered these concepts in the texts of the Jewish mystical tradition. Thus, I wish to question the proposition that the unveiling of certain metaphysical or philosophical truths, concepts, and principles indeed best represents Scholem's

49. Biale, *Counter-history*, 101.

achievements. For the reasons discussed above, such a proposition does not seem to me to be convincing.

In contrast to the literature discussed here, I argue that Scholem did not discover a deeper philosophical truth or method in the given object called "Jewish mysticism." I rather argue that he organized pliable textual materials according to his already given concepts. In other words, Scholem's major achievement lies not in his discovery but in his creation. Rather than finding the truth of the Kabbalah, he molded the vast literature of Jewish mystical lore into narratives, indeed stories, that entail new truths. And it is therefore these stories that should command our attention.

This suggestion goes beyond the relatively widely accepted insights about the essential similarities between historiography and literature.[50] I argue that in his effort to organize, elucidate, and explicate the Kabbalah, Scholem (re)created it. Indeed, I argue, it is for this (re)creation that he is remembered so far beyond the confines of his field. In other words, Scholem is remembered not because he ventured where no man has gone before and returned, but because he was able to create out of the many thousands of cryptic manuscripts and strange books an image of the world we could never have imagined before him. In the following chapters I wish to depict him, therefore, not as an explorer but as a poet.

This suggestion might be taken by some as an affront. After all, Scholem's claim to truth was serious and absolute. He was a historian of singular integrity, and his meticulous work was meant to be anything but fictional. But the suggestion to read Scholem as a writer does not, in fact, diminish his claim to truth but rather expands it. It is often suggested that in their fiction authors come to touch the truth, illuminate it, and bring it to the fore in ways unavailable to authors of nonfiction. One can find this idea expressed throughout the cultural history of the West. In this context, however, one example should suffice. In his much-debated book *How Fiction Works*, James Wood argues thus:

> We are likely to think about the desire to be truthful about life—the desire to produce art that accurately sees "the way things are"—as a universal literary motive and project, the broad central motive of the novel and the drama: what James . . . calls "the firm ground of fiction, through which indeed there curled the blue river of truth" . . . And in our reading lives, every day, we come across that blue river of truth curling somewhere; we encounter scenes and moments

50. Most notably Hayden White, *Metahistory: The Historical Imagination in Nineteenth-Century Europe* (Baltimore: John Hopkins University Press, 1975), esp. 1–42.

and perfectly placed words in fiction and poetry, in film and drama, which strike us with their truth, which shake habit's house to its foundation.[51]

Truth, in other words, is an essential aspect of fiction. And it is this kind of truth that Scholem created with his work.

Yet, beyond a general search for truth there is another, more specific role allotted to literature that may help describe Scholem's prose even closer. I refer here to what Amir Eshel terms "futurity." "Futurity" he argues, "marks the potential of literature to widen the language and to expand the pool of idioms we employ in making sense of what has occurred while imagining whom we may become."[52] In other words, futurity is the capacity of literature to rethink past events (often past catastrophes) in a way that opens up new possibilities to think the future. Interestingly, the notion of futurity is introduced in Eshel's study through a reading of a lecture that was given by one of Israel's leading authors, David Grossman. In the lecture, titled "Writing in the Dark," Grossman reflects on the role of the writing of fiction in Israel's violent political present: "I write and the world does not close on me. It does not grow smaller. It moves in the direction of what is open, future, possible."[53] The act of writing has therefore a distinct ethical value, and it is imaginative and forward-looking. In order to express this idea Grossman makes use of a somewhat peculiar term: *tikkun*. In the creation of fiction, the writer, he says, weaves "a shapeless web, which nonetheless has immense power to shape the world and create a world, the power to give words to the mute and to bring about tikkun—'repair'—in the deepest kabbalistic sense of the word."[54]

We need not be experts on the Kabbalah to understand what Grossman is telling us here. And we need not be experts in Jewish mysticism to understand the point Eshel is making by quoting this beautiful passage. We need to have merely a rudimentary, even secondhand familiarity with Scholem's work to understand the value both Grossman and Eshel attach to literature. Literature, they argue, is a form of *tikkun*, that is, a mending of the world.

In this context, the question whether or not Scholem's historical observations were accurate is of secondary importance. For in fact, through the concept of *tikkun*, Scholem's work transcends the debate about historical accuracy,

51. James Wood, *How Fiction Works* (London: Jonathan Cape, 2008), 183–84.

52. Amir Eshel, *Futurity: Contemporary Literature and the Quest for the Past* (Chicago: University of Chicago Press, 2013), 5.

53. Quoted from ibid., 3.

54. Ibid.

lodges itself in James's blue river of truth, and makes itself available for future speculations. For this action, I argue, for his futurity, Scholem's influence is felt so far beyond the confines of his academic discipline and the paradigm shifts within it. In his writing, Scholem shaped the vast corpus of the Kabbalah into forms that inform the way we may think of the future. He did so, naturally, with the power of the specific concepts and ideas with which he approached the historical texts. However, this achievement does not lie with concepts. As we shall see here, and as Biale and others have already shown, the concepts that Scholem used—such as myth, symbol, or mysticism—were not uniquely his. Scholem indeed often discussed his theoretical framework rather clearly.[55] And he accordingly devoted very limited resources to developing it, and it does not seem that he was interested in developing it further. Rather, Scholem made use of these concepts in order to create a new literature, that is, to (re)tell the history of Jewish mysticism in a way never told before.

In his historiography and his biographical texts Scholem weaved the old and the new, the esoteric and the political, the personal and the social in order to create narratives, indeed stories. In doing so he made something new. None of Scholem's stories could have been told before him, and it is his unique perspective on past and present that created a new way to think of the future. Indeed, in his stories, I argue, Scholem offered a "widening of the language" and an "expansion of the pool" of idioms available for thinking about "whom we may become." And this is why he is remembered. In this context, therefore, Scholem's own painstaking philological endeavors paved the path for a new truth, a new vocabulary, and a new, future-directed way of thinking. His works, indeed his stories, gave rise to something never before imagined. It is not the other way around. It is therefore not the concepts that Scholem used—his notions of, for example, myth, messianism, or Zionism—that will command our attention in the following chapters. Rather, it is Scholem's stories that are here important.

*

55. Thus, for example, in his introduction to his monumental *Major Trends in Jewish Mysticism* Scholem makes explicit use of a number of scholars, including Charles Bennet, Friedrich Creuzer, and Rufus Jones. See Gershom Scholem, *Major Trends in Jewish Mysticism* (New York: Schocken Books, 1995), 1–39. See also my own article on the subject: Amir Engel, "Gershom Scholems 'Kabbala und Mythos' jenseits deutsch-jüdischer Romantik," in *Gershom Scholem in Deutschland: Zwischen Seelenverwandtschaft und Sprachlosigkeit*, ed. Gerold Necker, Elke Morlok, and Matthias Morgenstern (Tübingen: Mohr Siebeck, 2014), 203–19.

Scholem's unique literary powers have previously been noted by scholars. Rolf Tiedemann, who knew Scholem personally, noted them with great sensitivity. In an essay titled "Memories of Scholem" he recounts, for instance, their initial acquaintance at the Institute for Social Research in Frankfurt, where he was a student. Tiedemann, one of the first Benjamin scholars, and Scholem had their first meeting in Max Horkheimer's office in sight of a Paul Klee painting. "What followed," Tiedemann recounts, "started off as an exam and quickly evolved into storytelling [*Erzählen*]. Scholem was a great teacher who was in no way limited to his field . . . but as a story-teller [*Erzähler*] he was unmatched."[56] It was from Scholem's mouth that Tiedemann first heard about Benjamin's life and his relations, and, more important, about his early philosophy, which was unknown at the time. Even in his eighties, Tiedemann notes, Scholem had complete command of his memory, and he was at his best when he was telling stories. "Even though I was not his student [*Schüler*], I owe so much to Scholem the teacher, but first and foremost I learned from him when he told stories [*wenn er erzählte*]."[57]

A more systematic approach to Scholem's literary production was undertaken by Daniel Weidner in his 2003 book *Gershom Scholem: politisches, esoterisches und historiographisches Schreiben* (Gershom Scholem: Political, Esoteric, and Historiographical Writings). As the title suggests, Weidner offers a study of Scholem's work, which, he argues, is constituted of different modes of writing. Weidner concludes that the secret to Scholem's lasting and abiding influence is to be found there, in his writings: "Scholem's writing unfolds not continuously like the richness of a speech but breaks down time and again through moments of silence. These breakdowns constitute the pithiness of Scholem's text."[58] Weidner then goes on to discuss Scholem's unique employment of irony in the horizon of Georg Lukács's constitutive work *The Theory of the Novel*. He furthermore discusses Scholem's intertextuality, a term also taken from literary scholarship. Weidner also argues that there are two essential motivations that drive Scholem's writing: Zionism and his concept of 'tradition.'[59]

Weidner's conclusions about Scholem's writing constitute, to a certain degree, the initial impetus of the present work. Like Weidner I see Scholem,

56. Tiedemann, "Erinnerung an Scholem," 211.

57. Ibid., 212.

58. Weidner, *Gershom Scholem: Politisches, esoterisches und historiographisches Schreiben*, 415.

59. Ibid., 416.

first and foremost, as a writer of prose, and, like him, I will employ methods of literary scholarship. I also accept his observation about Scholem's motivations. Indeed, as Weidner argues, "One must take Scholem's political intention seriously."[60] However, this book departs from Weidner's approach in one fundamental aspect. Whereas Weidner sees three different avenues in Scholem's textual production (namely, the political, the esoteric, and the historiographical), I see two stories, namely, Scholem's life and the story he told through the historiography. It may seem that the difference is merely technical, but this is not the case. By separating the political from the esoteric and the historiographic, Weidner fails to see how the different facets of Scholem's writings constitute a larger narrative. When told together, I argue, Scholem's stories complete each other and create a larger whole. This is the ultimate objective of this book.

There are, of course, certain consequences in describing Scholem in terms of his stories. This approach places the actual subject matter of Scholem's work well beyond reach. The following chapters will restrict themselves almost exclusively to Scholem's version of the Kabbalah and will hardly mention the Kabbalah at all. They will also use the term Jewish mysticism and Kabbalah interchangeably, despite the problems this may raise among scholars of the Jewish occult.[61] Thus, the difference between the "Kabbalah itself" and Scholem's version of it—a heated topic of debate among scholars of Jewish mysticism—lies largely beyond the scope of this study. This book, it should be clear, is emphatically not a book about the Kabbalah or about Jewish mysticism. And it therefore cannot take a stand on the debates within the field of Jewish mysticism studies regarding Scholem's accuracy, or regarding any other issue pertaining to Jewish secret lore. Rather than a book about Jewish mysticism, this is a book about Gershom Scholem, a twentieth-century German-Jewish and Israeli author and political activist.

Of course, telling Scholem's stories is different from writing his biography. This books aims to place Scholem's history in the context of his life story and, in turn, to put his life story in its own historical context. It seeks therefore to discuss the intellectual production of one man, but through this discussion it hopes also to touch the political, cultural, and social moment in which he lived. In order to do so, this book leaves certain aspects of Scholem's life beyond its purview. Rather than striving to account for Scholem's actions, friendships, collaborations, and disputes in their entirety, and rather than discussing his

60. Ibid.
61. Boaz Huss, "The Mystification of the Kabbalah," *Pe'amim*, no. 110 (Winter 1997): 9–30.

entire oeuvre, this book seeks to account for Scholem's unique literary and political projects and thus gain a better understanding of the man, his work, and the era in which he operated.

By adopting this method of reading, this book aligns itself with another important trend in the scholarship about Scholem. As we have seen, David Biale, Daniel Weidner, Joseph Dan, Moshe Idel, Robert Alter, Amos Funkenstein, and quite a few other scholars sought to locate the reasons for Scholem's peculiar position in contemporary culture by analyzing primarily his writings on the Kabbalah. But to some scholars, Scholem is not so much a unique thinker as a fascinating case in the study of wider historical concerns. In his book *Scholem, Arendt, Klemperer*, Steven Aschheim for example argues: "Taken collectively they yield a mosaic, a kind of composite portrait of the turbulent history of German Jews in the twentieth century."[62] For Aschheim, in other words, Scholem is less an objective and more the means to an end. Another example would be Shalom Ratsabi's book about the "radical circle in Brith Shalom."[63] The central concern of this study is the group's work toward reconciliation in Palestine, to which Scholem contributed. The most thorough and fascinating study of this kind is probably Noam Zadoff's *From Berlin to Jerusalem and Back: Gershom Scholem between Israel and Germany*.[64] In his biographical study Zadoff seeks to illuminate, as the title of the book suggests, Scholem's figure "as it stands between Israel and Germany—the two polls he himself considered as central when writing his autobiography."[65]

These works illuminate Scholem's figure from different perspectives and have proven invaluable to the present study. But by taking Scholem to represent, first and foremost, a larger historical concern—whether it is German Jewish history, history of Zionism, or the cultural tensions between Germany and Israel—Zadoff, Aschheim, and Ratsabi concern themselves with Scholem's actions and not with the intricacies of his writings on Jewish mysticism. It is for this reason that they refrain from a sustained analysis of Scholem's historiography and Kabbalah studies, which constitute so much of his oeuvre.

62. Steven E. Aschheim, *Scholem, Arendt, Klemperer: Intimate Chronicles in Turbulent Times* (Bloomington: Indiana University Press, 2001), 3.

63. Shalom Ratsabi, *Between Zionism and Judaism: The Radical Circle in Brith Shalom, 1925–1933* (Leiden: Brill, 2002).

64. Noam Zadoff, *From Berlin to Jerusalem and Back: Gershom Scholem between Israel and Germany* (in Hebrew) (Jerusalem: Carmel, 2015).

65. Ibid., 15.

This book thus aims to overcome a gap that exists in Scholem scholarship and joins a small number of works that have sought to take a similar path.[66] On the one hand it offers a study of Scholem's biography and benefits from the historiographical studies about him. On the other hand, it offers a reading of his Kabbalah historical studies and benefits from the more conceptual approach to Scholem's writings on the Kabbalah. But here these writings are taken to be not philosophy or metaphysics but literature. As narratives, Scholem's works may be understood in the cultural context in which they were written. Understood one against the other, furthermore, Scholem's two stories—his biography and his historiography—open a new perspective on Scholem and a unique window onto some of the fundamental questions and problems of the first half of the twentieth century in central Europe and in Israel/Palestine.

*

Scholem's two stories shed light on his person, his understanding of the Kabbalah, and the reasons he is known so far beyond the confines of his academic field. However, the choice to tell Scholem's life and work as stories entails a certain important drawback. Stories tend to seek some kind of resolution; in Scholem's case one would be hard-pressed to find such a definite ending. While it is rather clear where these stories start, their endings are somewhat obscure. In both his life and his work, the ending leaves one with more questions than definite answers.

The beginnings of Scholem's stories are clear. His biographical story starts when, as a young Jewish man living in a modern acculturated society in Berlin before and during the First World War, he embarked on a search for spiritual solutions for Jewish life. Scholem's historiographical story starts with the transformation of the Kabbalah from an elite intellectual preoccupation into an ideology of the masses that took place with the rise of Lurianic Kabbalah in the sixteenth century as a result of the Spanish expulsion of 1492. Upon deeper scrutiny, one may see how Scholem also sketches the prehistory

66. There are several scholars whose work is situated on the crux between an analytic study of Scholem and a historical one. Most prominent in this third category are Elisabeth Hamacher, who seeks to read Scholem's studies in the context of a fairly new academic discipline, the comparative study of the history of religions (*die allgemeine Religionsgeschichte*), which was formed in German universities around the turn of the twentieth century, and Steven Wasserstrom, who places Scholem in the more recent circle of the Eranos conferences. See Hamacher, *Gershom Scholem und die allgemeine Religionsgeschichte*; Wasserstrom, *Religion after Religion*.

of these stories. The beginnings of Scholem's stories and their prehistorical sources are discussed in detail in the second and third chapters. The third chapter also shows how the historiographical story of beginning is entrenched in the biographical one. It shows that both as a young man in Berlin and in his later writing on the Kabbalah of Isaac Luria, Scholem was preoccupied by the question of exile and invested in the power of myth. The fourth and fifth chapters discuss a process of disillusionment. Neither the Lurianic myth of exile nor Scholem's personal homecoming provided him the kind of relief he had hoped for. The fourth chapter discusses Scholem's immigration to Palestine and his terrible disappointment in the direction Zionism took in the land of Israel. And the fifth chapter discusses the Sabbatean debacle, a story about a messiah who failed his believers. It is no coincidence, I argue, that Scholem undertook the study of Sabbateanism when he was under the weight of complete disappointment with the Zionist project in Palestine.

Then, sometime in the late 1930s and early 1940s, the story ends. Scholem submitted to a mainstream view of Zionism, and his historiography slowly transformed. Scholem never discussed openly how and why this happened. In search of clues, the sixth chapter of this book follows several threads and documents that lead well into the 1950s and even the 1960s. The book thus ends in a conundrum. From a political standpoint Scholem failed, and the ensuing events in Palestine could not have been to his liking. He tried to warn against them shortly after first setting foot in the land in 1923. But all his efforts notwithstanding, he accepted the mainstream position and was proud of the State of Israel. He was to become the most famous Israeli public intellectual. This complex and partial resolution is also apparent in Scholem's historiography. At the end, the Jewish people are described as a splintered and confused entity with an unclear path forward. Scholem offers no concrete answers. He lived for many more years and enjoyed an immensely productive and successful career, but his attempts to find a solution to Jewish existence through his work and action disappeared from sight. Thus, Scholem's stories never reach resolution. They never solve the problems they set forth but rather dissipate of their own volition. Nevertheless, I contend, they are worth telling.

CHAPTER 2

Writing the Myth of Exile: In Search of Political Rejuvenation, 1913–1918

Back then, . . . I regarded myself as standing, through and through, at the highest spiritual level: Orthodoxy . . . half a year later I was with Buber. Now I am with myself, no, on the way to me.

[Damals . . . hielt (ich) mich für durchaus auf der höchsten geistigen Warte stehen: der Orthodoxie . . . Nach einem halben Jahr war ich bei Buber. Jetzt bin ich bei mir, nein, auf dem Weg zu mir.]

GERSHOM SCHOLEM, personal diary, December 20, 1915

More than two generations have elapsed since the publication of Gershom Scholem's memoir, titled *From Berlin to Jerusalem*, and the events depicted therein require a few words of introduction. Gerhard Scholem was born in 1897 in Berlin to an urban, acculturated, well-to-do Jewish family. At around age fourteen, he experienced what he would later call a "Jewish awakening."[1] For much of his young adulthood Scholem actively participated in the discussions of the Zionist youth movements in Berlin. During this period he struggled to envision a better, more harmonious future for the Jewish people. After a formative period together with his friend Walter Benjamin in Bern, Scholem returned to Germany where he started his lifelong endeavor: a systematic philological and historical study of Jewish mysticism. In October 1923, Scholem immigrated to Palestine, where he was first a librarian and then a lecturer in the newly founded institute for Jewish studies, later to become the Hebrew University in Jerusalem. Scholem's memoir ends at this point. This fact would

1. Scholem, *From Berlin to Jerusalem*, 36–60.

seem to suggest that the odyssey that started in 1897 in Berlin ended in Jerusalem in 1925, with the founding of the Hebrew University. Scholem died in Jerusalem in February 1982 and is considered, to this day, one of the most important Israeli public intellectuals and the founder of the academic discipline of Kabbalah studies.

Scholem falls squarely into the category that some scholars have called "postassimilatory" German Jews.[2] Like Scholem, many young men and women of Scholem's age sought to replace the ethos of belonging or "assimilation" in which they grew up and to create instead a sense of Jewish particularity. In *From Berlin to Jerusalem* the tension between Jewish particularity and integration is vividly represented in the relation between Scholem and his father. Scholem depicts his father, Arthur, as everything he wanted to reject. A paradigmatic example of the first generation of Jewish emancipation in Germany,[3] a successful businessman and a German gentleman, Arthur Scholem is portrayed as having only a rudimentary relation to a Jewish heritage, identity, or past. On the eve of the Sabbath, Scholem recounts in one often quoted section, his father would light his cigar with the Shabbat candle in a "deliberate mockery of the ritual."[4]

Scholem's desire to break free from everything his father represented is echoed already in the title of his memoir. Preferring Jerusalem to Berlin, as the title suggests, amounted to far more than choosing one place rather than another. 'Jerusalem,' in this context, represents not only the cradle of the Kingdom of King David but also the promise of a renewed Judaism. It is a destination that reverberates with hope for a better Jewish existence after two millennia of exile,

2. There is a vast literature on this moment in German Jewish history. See, for example, Shulamit Volkov, *Germans, Jews, and Antisemites: Trials in Emancipation* (Cambridge: Cambridge University Press, 2006), 256–87; Shulamit Volkov, "Jüdische Assimilation und Eigenart im wilhelminischen Deutschland," *Geschichte und Gesellschaft* 9 (1983): 331–48; Paul R. Mendes-Flohr, "Fin de Siecle Orientalism, the Ostjuden and the Aesthetics of Jewish Self-Affirmation," in *Divided Passions: Jewish Intellectuals and the Experience of Modernity* (Detroit: Wayne State University Press, 1991), 77–132; Steven E. Aschheim, *Brothers and Strangers: The East European Jew in German and German Jewish Consciousness, 1800–1923* (Madison: University of Wisconsin Press, 1982) 3–32; Paul R. Mendes-Flohr, "New Trends in Jewish Thought," in *German-Jewish History in Modern Times*, vol. 3: *Integration in Dispute, 1871–1918*, ed. Michael A. Meyer (New York: Columbia University Press, 1998), 336–59; Michael Brenner, *The Renaissance of Jewish Culture in Weimar Germany* (New Haven: Yale University Press, 1998), 1–35.

3. For more, see George L. Mosse, *German Jews beyond Judaism* (Cincinnati, OH: Hebrew Union College Press, 1997), esp. 1–20.

4. Scholem, *From Berlin to Jerusalem*, 10.

physical persecution, and spiritual stagnation. Alternatively, 'Berlin' represents here exile in its most unadulterated form. When Scholem wrote his memoir, after the Holocaust, the name alone shimmered with a terrible and palpable threat to Jewish life. In this formulation, therefore, 'Berlin' and 'Jerusalem' confront each other as extreme opposites, offering radically different options to Jews and Judaism. They represent the choice of the son against that of his father or of a Jewish "postassimilatory" ideology of the turn of the century against an ideology of acculturation and integration that was prevalent before then.

The phrase "From Berlin to Jerusalem" became something of a catchphrase for a certain historical insight and a certain existential choice. But by portraying such a stark opposition between Berlin and Jerusalem, Scholem's memoir forces upon its reader the perspective of the eighty-year-old author, the professor of Jewish mysticism from Jerusalem. In hindsight, the path from Berlin to Jerusalem was inevitable. But growing up, the young Scholem could not have known that Jerusalem would become a home, or that Berlin would transform so radically. From his youthful perspective, life was a combination of irresolvable dilemmas and unfulfilled hopes. Even the Kabbalah, which would become his life's passion, was at this point utterly obscure to him. Scholem's personal diaries, which he wrote with varying degrees of assiduousness between the ages of sixteen and twenty-six, prove this precise point. As these diaries make clear, the young Gerhard Scholem knew only that he wanted to be a Jew in the fullest and most authentic sense. He felt also that somehow Judaism needed to be renewed, rethought, and rediscovered in order to serve as a viable option for young men and women like himself. The more critical question—how exactly are these projects to be undertaken?—stayed largely beyond his reach.

It seemed to Scholem that the ideological and organizational mantle for the momentous project of renewing Judaism would be provided by Zionism. But again, beyond a general yearning to revive a declining nation, it was not entirely clear what Zionism actually meant. It must be emphasized again that from the perspective of the elderly Israeli professor, this question had more or less been resolved. But the young Scholem feverishly engaged himself in formulating and reformulating the ultimate objective of his Zionism. How could Zionism confront the problems of a nation that had been banished by God from its land? What constituted the vision of the ideal Zion or the ideal Jerusalem? How was it to become a reality? How did one earn the right to be a 'Zionist' in this sense, to partake in the project of recreating the Jewish people? Most important, what was the unique role of the lone individual, Scholem, in this grand project of renewing Judaism through Zionism, and of creating 'Zion'? As a young man, Scholem's answers were tentative at best.

This, of course, does not mean that the answers Scholem offered are unimportant or uninteresting. As Arnold Eisen observed in his book *Galut*, "Imagination of homecoming . . . proceeds through over-vivid contrasts with exile."[5] To the young Scholem, in other words, 'Zion' was not so much a concrete place as a vision or an idea about hope and spiritual renewal that stemmed from his reality in exile. Scholem's Zionist visions, perhaps unsurprisingly, embodied everything that the reality of Berlin did not provide. 'Zion' thus became a canvas onto which the confused and frustrated young man projected his desires and needs. As we shall see, all that Scholem considered to be out of joint, arbitrary or wrong in Berlin was transformed into a vision of a place in which everything was in order and comfortably at home.

Scholem's particular turn to Judaism was more hesitant and less direct than is indicated by the formula "from Berlin to Jerusalem." Scholem's Zionism, in other words, must therefore be understood as a search for answers. Moreover, this search must be understood as an instance of a wider phenomenon that emerged throughout Europe at that time and was particularly evident in Germany around the turn of the century. As Jay H. Geller notes, "it is impossible to understand Scholem without his German background and enduring relationship to Berlin."[6] Indeed, in his search for particularity and authenticity, Scholem was hardly unique. The yearning for spiritual truth, social rejuvenation, and a place to call 'home' was prevalent among men and women in urban middle-class settings who reached adulthood shortly before the outbreak of the First World War.[7] Many of the young men and women of this class joined the youth movements, believing that the young people were yet untainted by social institutions and obsolete norms and for this reason were capable of building a new, harmonious society from the bottom up.[8] As we shall see, Scholem's Zionism belongs to this context. It drew upon common sources, upon a prevalent critique of modernity and visions of superhumans, which reach back to German idealism, early German romanticism, and neo-romantic thought. As much as Scholem's specific variety of sources and

5. Arnold M. Eisen, *Galut: Modern Jewish Reflection on Homelessness and Homecoming* (Bloomington: Indiana University Press, 1986), xvii.

6. Jay Howard Geller, "From Berlin and Jerusalem: On the Germanness of Gershom Scholem," *Journal of Religious History* 35 (2011): 212.

7. See Robert Wohl, *The Generation of 1914* (Cambridge: Harvard University Press, 1979).

8. See, for example, John Alexander Williams, *Turning to Nature in Germany: Hiking, Nudism, and Conservation, 1900–1940* (Stanford: Stanford University Press, 2007); Wohl, *Generation of 1914*; Walter Laqueur, *Young Germany: A History of the German Youth Movement* (New Brunswick, NJ: Transaction Publishers, 1962).

insights was unique and proved to be fruitful, his image of 'Zion' was largely a product of his time and his place. As Steven Aschheim already observed, "the intensity of Scholem's commitments, the passion of his engagements, cannot be understood outside this generationally distinctive setting."[9]

Beyond a general sense of yearning, the one concept that best describes Scholem's preoccupation with questions of rejuvenation and spirituality is the concept of 'myth.' In the modern German tradition, the idea of the 'myth' has a rich and intensely complex heritage, which cannot be discussed here in detail. In principle, however, it was understood as an engine for spiritual and/or of national renewal, and a location of collective and personal imagination and creativity.[10] That the concept of myth played an essential role in the work of the older scholar of mysticism is patently apparent and discussed by several scholars.[11] What has received relatively less attention is the fact that Scholem was enamored of this concept well before he started his systematic studies of Jewish mysticism. To Scholem, the Kabbalah was a Jewish myth par excellence, and he adopted the methodologies and concepts for the study of this myth from a specific German scholarly tradition, which itself bore a complex relationship to the German discourse on myth.[12] Indeed, long before he described the myth of the Kabbalah, Scholem wanted to become a writer of myths. And although he knew little about the Jewish mystical tradition at the time, he felt certain that he ought to dedicate himself to composing a Jewish myth for the sake of the spiritual renewal of his people.

This, then, is the starting point for the endeavor to reveal the roots of Scholem's search for myth and to offer a more systematic background to Scholem's *From Berlin to Jerusalem*. The basis for Scholem's Kabbalah studies and the roots of his Zionism and world-renowned historical analysis of

9. Aschheim, *Scholem, Arendt, Klemperer*, 11.

10. There is massive literature about the notion of myth in German culture. See, for example, Manfred Frank, *Der kommende Gott* (Frankfurt am Main: Suhrkamp, 1995); Karl Heinz Bohrer, ed., *Mythos und Moderne: Begriff und Bild einer Rekonstruktion* (Frankfurt am Main: Suhrkamp, 1996); George S. Williamson, *The Longing for Myth in Germany: Religion and Aesthetic Culture from Romanticism to Nietzsche* (Chicago: University of Chicago Press, 2004), esp. 19–71; Bruce Lincoln, *Theorizing Myth: Narrative, Ideology, and Scholarship* (Chicago: University Of Chicago Press, 2000), 47–141.

11. See for example, Biale, *Counter-history*, 128–47; Moshe Idel, "Zur Funktion von Symbolen bei G. G. Scholem," in *Gershom Scholem: Literatur und Rhetorick*, ed. Stéphane Mosès and Sigrid Weigel (Cologne: Böhlau Verlag, 2000), 51–92.

12. See, for example, Hamacher, *Gershom Scholem und die allgemeine Religionsgeschichte*, esp. 170–94.

Jewish mysticism are to be found in his endeavors to rethink Jewish life from the sources of the German tradition, from the ideology of the youth movement, and, more specifically, from the discourse on myth so prevalent in the cultural context in which he grew up.

SCHOLEM'S TURN TO ZIONISM

Gerhard Scholem was an active member of a particular youth movement, in the direct sense of the word, only for very short periods of time. He did not have a taste for the singing, drinking, smoking, or hiking that were (and still are) so central to the youth movement experience. It was, he would later note, "the very kind of assimilationism [I] wanted no part in."[13] Nevertheless, he was a prominent member of the intellectual scene of the Zionist youth movements in Berlin in the years preceding the First World War and until 1918. In this period Scholem wrote prolifically in periodicals associated directly or indirectly with the youth movement about Zionist 'youth,' its problems, failings, and mistakes. When his views proved too radical to be printed elsewhere, Scholem had his essays published in an underground periodical, which he issued together with a few friends and which was printed at his father's workshop at night. Thus, even though he was not himself a member, his essays sparked heated debates among the members of the youth movements, and Scholem himself drew much of the fire.[14] As his correspondences and diaries show, Scholem was also personally acquainted with many active members of the Zionist movement and with a few of its leading figures, including Martin Buber, Siegfried Bernfeld, and Siegfried Lehmann.

Scholem's engagement with youth organizations was hardly unusual in the cultural environment of the time. Many young men and women who grew up in urban, middle-class Germany were attracted by the core ideas of the German youth movement, especially the Wandervogel.[15] Founded in 1901, the Wandervogel took a rebellious stance against mass society and its social institutions, which it deemed inorganic and inhumane. The movement aimed to facilitate

13. Scholem, *From Berlin to Jerusalem*, 58.

14. For more about the nature of Scholem's disputes with the Zionist youth movement, see Hannah Weiner, "Gershom Scholem and the Jung Juda Youth Group in Berlin, 1913–1918," *Studies in Zionism* 5 (1984): 29–42.

15. Ulrich Herrmann, "Wandervogel und Jugendbewegung im geistes- und kulturgeschichtlichen Kontext vor dem ersten Weltkrieg," in *"Mit uns zieht die neue Zeit...": Der Wandervogel in der deutschen Jugendbewegung*, ed. Ulrich Herrmann (Munich: Beltz Juventa, 2006).

the conditions for the emergence of a new kind of society by organizing such unorthodox activities as hiking and bathing in nature.[16] Many young Jewish men and women were drawn to the movement and its ideas. The "postassimilatory" generation of the German Jews felt similarly ill at ease with the rapid changes taking place in the social environment.[17] They too sought to assert themselves in a world that, they knew, belonged to old elites who essentially rejected Jews. The most influential Jewish youth movement in Germany, the Blau Weiß, was established in 1912, in part as a reaction to anti-Semitism in the German Wandervogel and in part in an attempt to develop and express Jewish particularity within the same neoromantic framework.[18] In most respects the Blau Weiß modeled itself on the Wandervogel. It too strove to lay the foundations for a new society through weekend hiking trips, organized discussion groups, and social action.[19]

Scholem first joined a youth movement at the ripe age of sixteen, but his involvement in the Zionist cause did not follow a direct path. As an aspiring young believer, who decided after his bar mitzvah to observe the Jewish code of law, the *halakha*, he first joined the youth group of the Jewish orthodox movement, Agudat Yisrael. In his memoir, he notes that as a young man he viewed favorably the programmatic statement of the movement, namely, to find "solutions to all problems of contemporary Judaism in the Spirit of the Torah."[20] It is easy to see why the young, liberally educated, and newly orthodox Jew found this formulation attractive. But, he further notes, he soon discovered that the movement's programmatic statement was more a diplomatic ploy than a statement of intent. For in fact, he claimed, the Agudat was guided less by the spirit of the Torah than by the code of Jewish law.[21] The strict demands of the *halakha* soon alienated the young Scholem. A few months after joining, the seventeen-year-old Scholem wrote the directorate of the group an officially worded letter proclaiming: "Your views about the essence of the Agudat do not coincide with the principles and the ideals to which I adhere, and which I had

16. For a general introduction to the history of the German youth movements, see Laqueur, *Young Germany*, xv–xx; Williams, *Turning to Nature*, 107–46. Herrmann, *"Mit uns zieht die neue Zeit . . . ,"* esp. 11–137.

17. See note 2 above.

18. See Chanoch Rinott, "Major Trends in Jewish Youth Movements in Germany," *Leo Baeck Institute Yearbook* 19 (1974): 77 –95.

19. See Jörg Hackeschmidt, *Von Kurt Blumenfeld zu Norbert Elias: Die Erfindung einer jüdischen Nation* (Hamburg: EVA Europäische Verlagsanstalt, 1997), 101–7.

20. Scholem, *From Berlin to Jerusalem*, 56.

21. Ibid.

hoped the Agudat would promote. Thereby . . . at the very least I feel obliged to forgo even my Platonic representation in the movement."[22]

This letter appears to convey that Scholem had decided to leave the Orthodox youth movement. And while his memoir supports this version, Scholem's diaries tell a slightly different story. In a short, undated entry, probably from May 1914, Scholem mentions that he was elected to the leadership of the group in January of that year but was subsequently accused of not abiding by Jewish law. "My career in the Agudah ended in May 1914," he wrote, "after a meeting of the executive, at which Herr Dr. Segal and Dr. Hofmann raised havoc by accusing me of not being true to the law [of the Jewish ritual]."[23] Given this turn of events, the formal language in the letter to the leadership of the group quoted above betrays an entirely different mood. The formality, it seems, was a product not of resigned confidence but rather of anger and frustration. Scholem had not, in fact, chosen to move on because Orthodoxy did not coincide with his views, but rather the opposite. He simply did not fit in. The Orthodox way of life was incompatible with the views and opinions of this liberal-minded, modern, aspiring young man, and it is for this reason that he was cast out.

This event had important implications for the life of the young Scholem. Like so many other young Jews, he became an Orthodox Jew after his bar mitzvah, which took place in a liberal synagogue. He mentions this fact in the very first entry in his diary. "My bar mitzvah took place on December 2, 1911. Since that day I have been an Orthodox Jew (I hate the Lindenstrasse [the liberal synagogue], where my bar mitzvah took place.)"[24] As can be gathered from this short note, the event of Scholem's bar mitzvah conjoins his hatred of liberal Judaism and his decision to observe the code of Jewish law, the *halakha*. Three years later, Scholem's clash with the Orthodox Jewish youth movement

22. Gershom Scholem, *Briefe I, 1914–1947*, ed. Itta Shedletzky (Munich: C. H. Beck, 1994), 2. I provide the translation myself when they do not already exist in the English edition of Scholem's letters, *Gershom Scholem: A Life in Letters, 1914–1982*, trans. and ed. Anthony David Skinner (Cambridge: Harvard University Press, 2002).

23. Gershom Scholem, *Lamentations of Youth: The Diaries of Gershom Scholem, 1913–1919*, trans. and ed. Anthony David Skinner (Cambridge: Harvard University Press, 2007), 26. This book is an edited volume of Scholem's diaries based on the two-volume German version, published by Jüdischer Verlag. I make use of Skinner's English translations when they are available; otherwise the translations are my own and I refer to the German edition.

24. This quote is from Scholem's first diary entry from early 1913. It is therefore uniquely telling, for in it Scholem introduces himself, thereby revealing who he believed himself to be. The very first lines read: "I am descended from Jews originally from Glogauer." Scholem, *Lamentations of Youth*, 22.

leadership gave rise to an entirely new set of realizations that went far beyond the youth movement itself. While he sought a solution to the Jewish condition in the spirit of the Torah, the Law was too unyielding for him, and he was expelled from the movement. This train of events thus forced him to reconcile himself to the tension of Jewish existence between modernity and the sacred law. "A month later [after resigning from the Orthodox youth movement]," he noted in his diary, "I left Orthodoxy. It was not an easy decision and it caused quite a stir."[25]

Neither liberal Judaism nor Jewish orthodoxy could therefore solve the problem that the young Scholem faced. The former offered an excessively lenient and insufficiently serious solution, while the latter was too stringent and dogmatic. This was the existential dilemma that Scholem confronted in June 1914, and he chose the only institutional alternative that remained, namely, the Zionist youth movement, created in the spirit of Martin Buber. By now Scholem was already fairly active in youth movement circles. But his decision to abandon orthodoxy ushered in a level of involvement with the movements that was more personal and more passionate than ever. Scholem, so it appears, was well aware of the significance of his decision to abandon the Orthodox movement and way of life. In the very last lines of the same diary entry he noted: "Full sail ahead toward Martin Buber. I've also become a socialist."[26]

THE IDEA OF ZION AND
THE PROLETARIAT OF YEARNING

In 1914 Scholem embarked on a new phase of his social engagement. He became active in Jung Juda, more a discussion group than a youth movement, which met regularly in a cafe at the Tiergarten railway station to discuss Zionism. As his diaries demonstrate, the young Scholem became preoccupied with his activity in the group, especially during the period before he was drafted into the army in 1917. Some of the members of the group became Scholem's lifelong companions, first in Berlin and later in Palestine and in Israel.[27] More important, it is in the context of the Jung Juda that Scholem first expressed his ideas in public, discussed them, worked on his first publications, and

25. Ibid., 26.

26. Ibid.

27. Scholem comments on the whereabouts of a few of the members in his memoir written more than sixty years after first encountering the members of the group in Berlin. See *From Berlin to Jerusalem*, 43.

defended his principles in the face of the prevailing beliefs. In other words, it is in this context that Gershom Scholem became politically active. In the most rudimentary sense, therefore, this was a formative period in the shaping of the future Zionist and Kabbalah scholar.

As the diaries show, the Jung Juda was something of a home for Scholem, but in many respects he was still an exile even among his closest friends. As an enthusiastic Zionist, he developed close ties to the members of the Jewish youth movement. Yet at the same time, probably under the powerful influence of his older brother Werner, he became a passionate opponent of World War I and was actively involved in the Social Democratic party. He even attended secret antiwar meetings together with his older brother, who was a dedicated Social Democrat just setting out on a tragic political career.[28]

Scholem's dual allegiance to both the Zionist and socialist ideologies placed him in an awkward situation. The Zionists suspected the socialist among them, and the socialists did not trust the Zionist in their midst. In a diary entry dated January 20, 1915, Scholem wrote: "Yesterday Jung Juda. Estrangement grows between me and the Jung Judeans, since my crossover to Rixdorf [the meeting point of the Social Democratic antiwar activists]. Plots are always felt in the air. We do not understand each other as we used to, and I am getting used to being silent again."[29] The conflict between Zionism and socialism was not merely an external matter, a question of alliances. Scholem believed in the Social Democratic cause, but he was at the same time a Zionist. This was an impossible position, as he was well aware. He could not have both the Jews and the proletariat spearheading the struggle for freedom. Ultimately, he chose Zionism because he believed in the primacy of Jewish existence and its abnormality. "For us," Scholem wrote in his diary, "class warfare retreats behind the national conflict."[30] It was for this reason that his primary

28. Gershom Scholem admired his older brother Werner for standing up to their father, who passionately opposed his sons' "anti-patriotism." But as Werner deepened his commitment to communism and Gershom embraced Zionism, the relations between the two cooled. Nevertheless, Gershom dedicated his memoir to his elder brother, who was murdered in Buchenwald in 1941 after being imprisoned for eight years. For more on the relationship between the brothers, see Mirjam Triendl-Zadoff, "Unter Brüdern—Gershom und Werner Scholem; von den Utopien der Jugend zum jüdischen Alltag zwischen den Kriegen," *Muenchener Beitraege zur juedischen Geschichte und Kultur* 2 (2007): 56–66; Mirjam Zadoff, *Der rote Hiob: Das Leben des Werner Scholem* (Munich: Carl Hanser Verlag, 2014), esp. 35–110.

29. Gershom Scholem, *Tagebücher: Halbbd. I 1917–1923*, ed. Herbert Kopp-Oberstebrink, Karlfried Gründer, and Friedrich Niewöhner (Frankfurt am Main: Jüdischer Verlag, 2000), 79.

30. Scholem, *Tagebücher I*, 93.

commitment was to the Zionist cause. As he elsewhere noted, "I am absolutely a Zionist and aspire, first and foremost, to national conciliation." Nevertheless, as the following sentence demonstrates, he continued to champion the socialist cause. "There are no contradictions with socialist principles. Our state or our community must from its inception be organized according to these principles, upon which we shall then be able to grow further, both spiritually and physically."[31] While the relation between Zionism and socialism seemed clear to Scholem, this linkage evidently raised some eyebrows among his colleagues and fellow activists. "It seems peculiar to me," he noted, "that among the Social Democrats I am attacked for being a Zionist and among the Zionists I am attacked for my socialist dispositions. Don't they know that I reject historical materialism? In any case, I struggle to restrain myself, because among the Zionists there is strong animosity towards [Karl] Liebknecht."[32]

An occasion to clarify his position between socialism and Zionism presented itself at a workshop organized by his friends, where Scholem planned to deliver a talk titled "On the Essence of Jung Juda." His preparatory notes and observations from this period bear an unmistakable trace of Nietzschean fury.[33] Both the content of his argument and his rhetoric are therefore of considerable interest. His writing has the ring of a young rebel's call to arms and obviously alludes to German national history:

> To my people [*An Mein Volk*],[34] says the voice of a messenger, woe unto those who have sucked up culture and education [*Bildung*] into their rankling hearts, who have introduced education to their nation, and who have brought ruin and death upon their brothers. Your God calls out that if you wish to die, you should continue on this path to the gates of perdition.
>
> . . .
>
> You are Orientals and not Europeans; you are Jews and humans, not Germans and degenerates, and your God's name is *Ha-shem* and not the belly. It

31. Scholem, *Tagebücher I*, 71.

32. Together with Rosa Luxemburg, Karl Liebknecht founded the Spartakist League and the Communist Party of Germany (KPD), for which he served as a member of parliament. He is famous also for his vocal opposition to World War I. Scholem, *Tagebücher I*, 93.

33. The publication of Scholem's diary has enabled a more careful scrutiny of his influences. For a more detailed discussion of, among other matters, Scholem's reading of Nietzsche, see Benjamin Lazier, "Writing the Judenzarathustra: Gershom Scholem's Response to Modernity, 1913–1917," *New German Critique* (2002): 33–65, esp. 37n.

34. By using this phrase "To my people" (An Mein Volk), Scholem alluded to the famous call to arms against Napoleon made by the Prussian king Frederick III in 1813.

is because of this that you should not wander onto their path. What for you is light is for them darkness, and what for you is holy is for them an abomination.[35]

The overarching thesis that Scholem expounded here was a revolutionary one. Zionism, he argued, was a revolt against the culture of exile. He denounced Germany and German culture just as he deplored the petrified Judaism of the past and the assimilated Jews of his present. He called upon the Zionist members of Jung Juda to turn Judaism inside out. "Our guiding principle is revolution, revolution everywhere! We don't want reform or reeducation but revolution or renewal. We seek to absorb the revolution into our innermost soul."[36] A few days later he noted: "Our Zionism is the doctrine of ramming ourselves headlong into a wall."[37]

In his notes, Scholem was quite clear about what he sought to rebel against; it was a rather long list. He vehemently opposed the idea of culture, *Bildung*, and decadence, all of which were synonymous in his view. He insisted on making a clean break with Europe in general and Germany in particular. He railed against the bourgeois idea of family and the parental home.[38] Scholem furthermore made it abundantly clear that Jung Juda should oppose Herzl's Jewish state by all means. "We as Jews know enough about the abominable idol state . . . we Jews are not a state-*Volk*."[39] Real Zionists must, furthermore, look forward, he wrote, rather than dwell on the past, like Herzl and his followers. In short, Scholem appeared to oppose virtually all the conventional tenets of bourgeois society as well as Zionism. Confronted with the world of exile, Scholem yearned for something different, namely, his own vision of 'Zion.'

Scholem's conception of 'Zion' was less lucid than his sketches of 'Exile.' Nevertheless it seems that this 'Zion' could be described as a pure negation of living in exile.[40] It signified a utopian desire for perfection. At one point Scholem noted: "I know that Zion is the absolute truth (the same cannot yet be said of the Land of Israel), I measure all things against it. My credo is that *Zion*

35. Scholem, *Lamentations of Youth*, 39–40.
36. Ibid., 47.
37. Ibid., 46.
38. Scholem, *Tagebücher I*, 83.
39. Ibid.
40. This argument should be understood in the context of Amnon Raz-Krakotzkin's influential critical discussions about Zionism and the concept of exile. See "Jewish Memory between Exile and History," *Jewish Quarterly Review* 97, no. 4 (2007): 530–43; "Exile within Sovereignty: Toward a Critique of the 'Negation of Exile' in Israeli Culture" (in Hebrew), *Theory and Criticism* 4 (1994): 23–55 and 5: 113–32.

is the measure of all things."[41] This position is further elaborated in several other reflections that Scholem recorded in his diaries during the same period. "We Zionists have but little to offer," Scholem noted to himself. "Our yearning is for the great, for unity, peace, and all things beautiful."[42] Zion was furthermore a place where there would be no conflict between the individual and society, for it would be based, so Scholem maintained, on socialist principles.[43] It is almost redundant to mention that Zion was a place meant for Jews, but to Scholem it was immensely important to stress this fact. 'Zion' was a new place for new people: "We are a new generation of the wandering Jew,"[44] Scholem declared. 'Zion,' then, was a fulfillment of all that Scholem yearned for. It followed that Zionists were, or should be, able to withstand history and realize this unbridled desire labeled 'Zionism': "We as Zionists are *pure* people and want nothing to do with the wickedness and the baseness of this universal slaughter [of the First World War] . . . the time can be called 'great' only when the commandment 'thou shalt not kill' is upheld . . . we will not be dazzled by the chatter of university professors, we, the agents of the *proletariat of yearning!*"[45]

As the diaries show, Scholem relentlessly propagated these ideas. He insisted that his fellow youth activists realize that as Zionists they were—or ought to be—whole, and that they should undergo an inner as well as an outer revolution. He demanded that they be entirely radical and follow their principles to the very end. He called on them to uproot themselves from the society in which they lived and the country in which they had grown up. He exhorted them not to heed the call of their parents, teachers, generals, community leaders, and, as we shall soon see, of the state itself. They were, he insisted, the "proletariat of yearning."

It is thus not hard to imagine that Scholem's interpretation of Zionism would run into difficulties with the Zionists themselves. And indeed all his enthusiasm seems to have come to naught. Scholem never delivered his talk about the essence of Jung Juda. In an entry dated January 23, 1915, Scholem mentions in passing a conversation with Erich Brauer, the organizer of this planned discussion meeting, who would become a lifelong friend: "I will soon be ostra-

---

41. Scholem, *Lamentations of Youth*, 143. Emphasis in the original.
42. Scholem, *Tagebücher I*, 65.
43. Ibid., 71.
44. Ibid., 81.
45. Ibid., 85. Emphasis in the original.

cized [*herausgeekelt*] from Jung Juda. I have considered the matter and will probably decline to deliver the lecture, as Brauer advised me."[46]

SCHOLEM'S POLEMIC AGAINST WORLD WAR I

As for many others of his generation in the youth movement and beyond it, the outbreak of World War I was a defining moment for Scholem.[47] Many years later Scholem would note that "the First World War was naturally the most important event of my youth. Today it is hard to imagine how profoundly everyone was affected by it."[48] And indeed, even a cursory glance at his diaries and letters from that time shows that if there was a single issue around which Scholem's loyalties were formed or shattered, it was the question posed by the hostilities and the war. This is hardly surprising. Scholem belonged to the social group that welcomed the decision to go to war most enthusiastically. Educated urban middle-class young men and women were among the most passionate supporters of the war,[49] and they were to bear much of its brunt. Scholem lost friends in the fighting, including one of his closest high school friends and companions, Edgar Blum. Hence, in being personally affected by the war, Scholem was hardly exceptional.

In most other aspects, however, Scholem stood out. Most important, the young Scholem steadfastly refused to join in the enthusiastic response to the war; the 'spirit of 1914,' which blew around him, did not sweep him off his

---

46. Ibid., 83.

47. See Wohl, *Generation of 1914*. Since the publication of this book there has been some debate about the concept of a generation. For an overview of the problem, see Ohad Parnes, Ulrike Vedder, and Stefan Willer, *Das Konzept der Generation: Eine Wissenschafts- und Kulturgeschichte* (Berlin: Suhrkamp Verlag, 2008). Nevertheless, Wohl's book retains, in this context, much of its original validity.

48. Scholem, *From Berlin to Jerusalem*, 32.

49. The widely accepted notion according to which young men and women submitted themselves gleefully to the war has undergone some revision over the last three decades. While the intellectual, religious, and political leaders of the time expressed their excitement at the 'August experience,' the general public seems to have been more skeptical. For a more nuanced account of the reception of the war by the general German public, see Jeffrey Verhey, *The Spirit of 1914: Militarism, Myth, and Mobilization in Germany* (Cambridge: Cambridge University Press, 2000), 12–114. Nevertheless, as we shall see, this enthusiastic outpouring of militarism made a deep impression on Scholem, largely because he belonged to the same middle-class, urban, politically involved elite that was gripped by enthusiasm in the summer of 1914.

feet.[50] He was even released from the army after feigning mental illness. Naturally, his antiwar views brought him into frequent conflict, with his father, at school, with the Zionist youth movements, and with its leaders. Scholem moreover disassociated himself from his onetime hero and spiritual mentor Martin Buber, because of the latter's initial enthusiastic support for the war. On a more personal level, it is clear that the war solidified Scholem's sense of being in exile, of feeling alienated from his environment and estranged from his friends.

The reality of war exacts a high price for principles. Denouncing the war would have been necessarily interpreted as asocial, antipatriotic, and defeatist. This position spelled at best social ostracism for the unyielding individual, and often led to imprisonment. Supporting the war, on the other hand, was an even more dangerous decision. A student or a member of a youth movement, like Scholem, was precisely of the right age to pay for his eagerness with his own life. The youth movements found themselves in the eye of the storm as its entire male leadership immediately enlisted in the army, its female members joined the Red Cross, and the younger members volunteered to support the war effort on the home front.[51] Scholem, however, would have none of this. In August of 1914, as many other young men and women of his generation celebrated the renewal of the national bond among them, he became a stranger. And in 1917, when others were groaning beneath the weight of the fighting in a seemingly endless war, Scholem headed to Switzerland to meet his friend and idol Walter Benjamin and to envision a new academia and a new philosophy.[52]

Scholem's opposition to the war was, however, far from simplistic and should be understood on two different plains. First, he opposed the war in the most general terms. Also under the influence of his older, communist brother Werner, Scholem believed that the war was the result of vain imperial aspirations. He did not do so often, but when he reflected on the war in his diaries, he expressed clear disdain for German militarism. One such reflection was recorded on the first day of August 1916, a holiday declared in celebration of the declaration of war two years earlier. "The day of Europe's funeral," the diary reads, "the German people will have to pay dearly for the crimes of its rulers, the miscalculations of its military, and the dirty tricks of its history and

50. For more on this issue see also, Verhey, *Spirit of 1914*, 1–11.

51. For more on the participation of the German youth movement in the war, see Laqueur, *Young Germany*, 87–99.

52. Gershom Scholem, *Walter Benjamin: The Story of a Friendship* (New York: New York Review Books, 2003), 57–59.

philosophy professors; oh, this abyss of wickedness!"[53] Comments decrying the war and in support of Karl Liebknecht's opposition to it appear sparsely in the diaries, but are usually couched in rather mild terms. Emotions, however, run high when the issue of the war appears as a Jewish political concern.

The general sense of camaraderie that swept over Germany in August 1914 did not leave the Jews untouched. This is a well-documented affair. "The intense and almost universal identification with the German cause in those initial days of the war," writes Peter Pulzer, "was born from the sense that the longed for moment had arrived when German Jews would finally be fully accepted as German citizens."[54] Many Jews volunteered to join the army and many fell in combat.[55] The Jewish youth movement, by and large, enthusiastically supported the war. The young vanguard of the Zionist movement, Stefan Vogt claims, "were convinced that the war and the enthusiasm it produced especially among the young bourgeoisie—to which they . . . belonged themselves—proved them correct in conceiving Zionism within strictly nationalist terms."[56] And their leaders were certainly infected by the general excitement, most notable among them Martin Buber.

The importance of Martin Buber to the Jewish consciousness of German-speaking lands in general and to the Zionist youth movement in particular cannot be exaggerated.[57] He was adored by the members of the youth movement,[58] including Gershom Scholem, who regarded him as the voice of their generation.[59] Buber's understanding of the outbreak of World War I is also well documented. He was elated by the opportunities that the war, in his view, had opened up for the Jews of Germany. Yet the war did not present itself to the publisher of the proudly titled journal *Der Jude* as an occasion on which Jews

53. Scholem, *Tagebücher I*, 345.

54. Peter Pulzer, "The First World War" in Michael A. Meyer , ed., *German-Jewish History in Modern Times*, vol 3: 293.

55. Peter Pulzer notes that "by the war's end ninety six thousand Jews had served in the Kaiser's armies, of whom twelve thousand died in action and thirty five thousand were decorated." Ibid.

56. Stefan Vogt, "The First World War, German Nationalism, and the Transformation of German Zionism," *Leo Baeck Institute Yearbook* 57, no. 1 (2012): 267–91.

57. Brenner, *The Renaissance of Jewish Culture in Weimar Germany*, 27–29.

58. Chaim Schatzker, "Martin Buber's Influence on the Jewish Youth Movement in Germany," *Leo Baeck Institute Yearbook*, 23 (1978): 151–72.

59. See, for example, Scholem's introductory remarks at the Jung Juda workshop on Buber on January 27, 1915. In Scholem, *Tagebücher I*, 111–12.

could finally prove themselves to be citizens of equal standing. He did not interpret the "civic truce" (*Burgerfrieden*) declared by Kaiser Wilhelm as the fulfillment of a long-awaited dream, as did so many other Jewish leaders.[60] To Buber
the truce was merely a means to an end, the means by which the Jewish nation
would finally be forged. Martin Buber's editorial essay in the inaugural volume
of *Der Jude* called upon the Jews to join the war effort. In battle, Buber believed,
the new Jewish community (*Gemeinschaft*) would be forged out of the host of
individuals that made up the Jewish people. Buber's argument was reinforced
by the rhetorical flair of the prophet. In the essay titled "Die Losung" (The Call)
Buber wrote:

> Manliness and trial, community and devotion—the call, which the nations in
> peace do not issue, is now a call for war. And with the others the Jews follow
> suit with passionate yearning, to share with their blood the experience and the
> suffering of Europe's fateful hour as a part, no, as parts of Europe.
>
> . . .
>
> They will learn to feel and to recognize their unity as Jews. They will deepen
> their experience of community [*Gemeinschaftserlebnis*] and will build their Ju-
> daism anew from this experience. They have observed the tatters of Judaism
> through blood and tears and they will be overcome by a longing to heal it.
>
> . . .
>
> The new unity of Judaism is represented in those Jews who, feeling re-
> sponsible for the fate of their community, were unsettled by this war's Jewish
> experience.[61]

Although Buber (b. 1878) was too old to join the ranks, he did not hesitate to
encourage his young friends and followers to join the fight themselves. In a
letter to a doubting member of the Bar Kochba circle in Prague, Hans Kohn,
Buber employed the famous words of the Gospel of John: "He that loveth his
life shall lose it."[62]

60. Meyer, *German-Jewish History in Modern Times*, 361–66.

61. The essay "Die Losung" appeared on the first page of the first volume of *Der Jude*, published in April 1916. Buber explicitly notes that the bulk of the essay was made public in a lecture
delivered in 1914. He writes, "Es sieht so aus, als ob es nur noch Juden, aufgeteilte Juden, und
kein Judentum gäbe . . . Und doch ist dem nicht so . . . Es sei mir gestattet, hier zu wiederholen,
was ich 1914 in einer Rede äusserte." The entire journal and many other German-Jewish historical publications can be found at http://www.compactmemory.de/

62. Martin Buber, *Briefwechsel aus sieben Jahrzehnten: 1897–1918* (Heidelberg : L. Schneider, 1972), 370.

It is impossible to know how many people were actually induced to enlist because of Buber's rhetoric. It is hard to imagine, however, that the call of the undisputed spiritual leader of the youth movement fell on deaf ears.[63] In any event, Buber's pro-war sentiment defined Scholem's cultural and political environment in the initial months of the war. And antiwar activity was in any case highly unorthodox. Scholem certainly felt ostracized because of his views on the war, and he paid dearly for them. His frustration with the Zionist youth movement and his personal sense of rejection are manifested in diary entries that display at times a highly emotional mixture of rage and sorrow.

While the war itself was of relatively little concern to Scholem, the Jewish reaction spurred him to fury and action. In February 1915, Scholem wrote, together with his brother Werner and a few friends from the Jung Juda, an open letter to the *Jüdische Rundschau*, the mouthpiece of the Zionist Association of Germany. The young men wished to protest an editorial column written by Heinrich Margulies, who argued for the war in the spirit of his mentor Martin Buber. "Then came the war," Margulies wrote. "And it suddenly took hold of the world and millions became what we always hoped. In the roar of the masses, we heard our own melody and suddenly we were surrounded by *community* [*Gemeinschaft*]. Man was awakened . . . Should we not also find strength in this: that we were no longer isolated, that everything by which we, the few, have been slandered now became the religious experience of millions?"[64]

Even as Buber mostly maintained a spiritual tone in his texts, Margulies arrived at an overtly political conclusion, concluding his essay with the words, "So it came to be that we were drafted into the war, *because* we were Zionists, not, however, despite the fact that we are Jews."[65] In his memoir Scholem

<hr />

63. There are many examples of 'grass roots' Jewish enthusiasm for the war. An anonymous essay by a 'Young Zionist' that was published in the *Jüdische Rundschau* in October 1914 reads "Unsere Zeit, von der viele glaubten, dass sie nicht fähig sei, gewaltige ideale Erregungen hervorzurufen, hat die einmütige wundervolle nationale Erhebung eines großen Kulturvolkes gezeitigt, das für seine Freiheit, für seine Ewigkeit kämpft. Diese, neue Epoche der Weltgeschichte muss auch die Erlösung des ältesten Kulturvolkes, das Jahrtausende lang unter unsagbaren physischen und seelischen Qualen geblutet hat, bringen." Anonym: Nationale Gedanken. Von einem jungen Zionisten, *Jüdische Rundschau*, October 16, 1914. See also Ulrich Sieg, *Jüdische Intellektuelle im ersten Weltkrieg: Kriegserfahrungen, weltanschauliche Debatten und kulturelle Neuentwürfe* (Berlin: Walter de Gruyter, 2008), 53–68.

64. Heinrich Margulies, "Der Krieg der Zurückbleibenden," *Jüdische Rundschau*, February 5, 1915, 46–47. Emphasis in the original.

65. Ibid. Emphasis in the original.

confessed that he had "hit the roof"[66] when reading Margulies's article. In the jointly signed letter to the *Jüdische Rundschau*, the brothers Scholem and their friends declared that they did not share the hope that the war would uncover "the secret of community" (*Geheimnis der Gemeinschaft*) and were not even certain that Germany's war coincided with Jewish interests. Their conclusions were formulated in the following statement: "We are not of the opinion that this war has unveiled 'the secret of community' or that it can even accomplish this. Furthermore, we doubt that Germany's issue, just like that of any other country in the world, is our issue. Whether our interests coincide with those of Germany is a thoroughly debatable question."[67]

This letter made a marked impact even as it failed to reach its destination and was never published by the *Jüdische Rundschau*. In fact, the letter was never even sent, because it found its way to the administration of Scholem's gymnasium, and he—"the ringleader"—was summoned to an inquiry that concluded in a decision to expel him for "antinational ideology."[68]

As David Biale already noted, Scholem's critique of Buber's and the youth movement's enthusiasm for the war went beyond the general questions of European politics.[69] It hinged, rather, on his understanding of Zionism. The war posed the following question: what is the relationship between Zionism and Europe? Scholem was infuriated by the suggestion that Zionism should grow to maturity in a European war. This contradicted everything that he considered Zionism should be. This would mean, first of all, that Jews essentially belonged in their countries of domicile, in which they enjoyed, to varying degrees, religious and civic freedoms. But more profoundly, supporting the war meant that Jews essentially belonged in exile and should, for that reason, participate fully in the imperial effort of the European nations. A true Zionist, so Scholem believed, could not adopt this position. Buber and the youth movement, he argued, had not drawn the conclusions from their own Zionist principles. How could the Zionist youth movement, Scholem asked, retain its most cherished ideals, namely, the belief in 'Zion' and homecoming, and yet at the same time join the European imperial war? How could the youth consider

66. Scholem, *From Berlin to Jerusalem*, 60.

67. Scholem, *Tagebücher I*, 90.

68. Scholem's diaries remain strangely silent about the whole affair. The most contemporary mention is to be found in a letter that Scholem wrote to Martin Buber on July 10, 1916. The quote is taken from there. See Scholem, *Gershom Scholem: A Life in Letters*, 29. See also Mirjam Zadoff, *Der rote Hiob*, 56–58.

69. Biale, *Counter-history*, 60–61.

FIGURE 2.1. "The Blue-White Glasses": Scholem's underground antiwar pamphlet, 1915. Courtesy of The National Library of Israel, Jerusalem.

itself radical and authentically Jewish and yet volunteer to serve the aristocratic generals of the German army? Those who heeded Buber's call to forge a Jewish community on the battlefields of central Europe either were misinformed, Scholem asserted, or had forgotten that they were homeward bound, that they were Zionists.

The very core of Scholem's belief dictated a radical break from Europe and European culture and from the exilic tradition that had governed Judaism for almost two millennia. This fact alone, as Klaus Samuel Davidowicz observed, constitutes a clear break from Buber's Zionist vision and even his political language.[70] Unlike Buber, Scholem called upon the youth to take up the cause of homecoming, the endeavor of Zionism. Thus, in his polemic against the war, the meaning of Scholem's Zionism and his idea of exile is gradually revealed amid its specific political and historical context.

Scholem's position on the war, on exile, and on Zion was further articulated in a series of handwritten papers that he prepared together with friends from Jung Juda, secretly printed at his father's print shop, and illegally distributed

70. Klaus Samuel Davidowicz, *Gershom Scholem und Martin Buber: Die Geschichte eines Missverständnisses* (Neukirchen-Vluyn: Neukirchener Verlag, 1995), 70.

among members of Jewish youth organizations.[71] In these pamphlets, titled *Die Blauweiße Brille*, Scholem attacked the Zionist youth movements for betraying their ideas and for forgetting what it meant to be a movement. While incidentally betraying a lack of wit, Scholem's dull sarcasm testifies to the intensity of his emotions. Scholem's contribution to the first pamphlet reads:

> *Youth-Movement*—a sweet word. One hears this: Jewish-youth-movement, etc., etc., etc. So one could by now imagine that it crackles there, it squalls there, there fireworks fly, there it is let loose, there the peddlers are driven out of the temple. Yes, sir! Cakes, my dear boy. But no Jewish Youth Movement
>
> . . .
>
> There you have your program, you stumbling barking-dogs: to Judaism, to Youth, to Movement (four walls echo Movvv . . . mee . . . nnt . . .)[72]

Scholem's critique was directed against the movement's tendency to serve as a location for social gatherings. He also castigated the decision to harness Zionism to the war. To Scholem this was tantamount to accepting exile as a fact. The war had, he argued, diverted the spirit of the nation from its original cause. "The struggle for Zion was exchanged for a homicidal struggle over the best pasture grounds."[73] Furthermore, he argued, Jewish youth was too important. Young men's lives should not be thoughtlessly laid to waste on the battlefields of foreign lands. As Scholem put it:

> We wish to draw the line of demarcation between Europe and Judea: "my thoughts are not your thoughts and your ways are not my way." We have insufficient people to voluntarily throw them into the pit for Moloch. No, we need people who have the courage of radicalism in thought and action, who are close to their nation [*Volk*], so that they do not subject themselves to every intoxicated flurry that erupts between London and Petersburg. We need people in whom the words "dogmatism" and "obsession" elicit only a smile.[74]

---

71. *Die Blauweiße Brille* was printed at night, without the permission of the print shop's owner, Scholem's father, who was furious about the antipatriotic stance taken by both his younger sons. The publication could not have been submitted to the censor for obvious reasons and was therefore illegal.

72. Scholem, *Tagebücher I*, 291.

73. Ibid., 297.

74. Ibid.

The demarcation line between Europe and Judea signifies, of course, the dichotomy between exile and home. In exile young men sacrifice their lives for the follies of other nations. Home, however, could be made real if these men would have the courage to think their principles through and act differently. In effect, Scholem expected the youth to emulate him, to take a step back from the clamor and take a stand against it. In essence, he wanted them to realize that they were living in exile and should thus refrain from taking up the cause of other nations.

This passionate appeal to the Jewish youth concluded by drawing a further distinction between exile and home. While exile was gloomy, being at home was a merry affair. "We *galut* [Diaspora] Jews have so much dejection in us," Scholem protested, "we cannot believe that we can redeem ourselves with this gloomy spirit, which is the fruit of banishment." Yet redemption was still possible. And the joy that accompanies a life of action was desperately called for: "And if we youngsters do not bring joy into our lives and in our actions . . . if we do not go forth and drive out the spirit of melancholy, which resides within the spirit of our people [*Volk*] and takes hold through the talk of the Old-New-Land [*Altneuland*], who will stand up and carry the banner of the future, the seven golden stars on a white field,[75] who will build Zion and create Jerusalem for all eternity?"[76]

Scholem thus drew the following distinction: on the one hand there was exile, gloominess, Europe, and the war, while on the other hand was joy, action, Zion, and youth. He did not refer here to any specific group of people, and evidently not to the young men and women of the Jewish movements. He talked about youth as they were meant to be: those who dedicated themselves to Zion. The youth, of course, did not heed Scholem's cry of warning.

THE IDEA OF MYTH IN GERMANY

By 1917 Scholem's polemic against the participation of Zionist youth movements in the war had run its course. A deep personal and emotional crisis ensued. Scholem naturally continued to combat the mainstream of Jewish youth activism. Most notably, in the final months of 1916, he engaged in a sharp

75. Theodor Herzl was probably the first to envision the flag for the Jewish state. In his book *The Jewish State* he suggested it should be composed of seven golden stars—to represent a seven-hour working day—on a white background. See *The Jewish State* (Rockville, MD: Wildside Press, 2008), 116.

76. Scholem, *Tagebücher I*, 298.

dispute with Siegfried Lehmann, the director of the Jüdisches Volksheim in Berlin, over the brand of Zionist ideology that was propagated there.[77] Yet while in his letters and articles Scholem expressed himself as poignantly and as bitterly as ever, his diaries betray a very different state of mind. In the spring of 1917, Scholem sank into despair. After over two years of intense activity and bitter disputes, Scholem now found himself lonely and directionless, uncomfortable in most of Berlin's Zionist circles, and estranged from the teaching of his one-time leader, Martin Buber.[78] He recorded his own self-doubt during this period in his diary: "Am I a Jew? No. A human being? No. An upstanding youth? No. What am I then? A nihilist who, spurned by God, goes behind God's back, because He's rejected him. All the piety in the world cannot wash clean the inner sins I've committed in the nineteen years of my life."[79]

Things took a further turn for the worse after Scholem's older brother, Werner, was finally discharged from the hospital after being treated there for a wound he sustained while fighting in Serbia. On the Kaiser's birthday, the 27th of January, he was arrested for participating in an antiwar rally in Berlin while wearing his uniform.[80] Werner's arrest upset the Scholem household, and Scholem's father, appalled by his son's disruptive behavior, unleashed his fury also on his youngest son, Gerhard. An intense quarrel ensued. On February 15, Gershom Scholem received a letter from his father ordering him to leave the house until he had reevaluated his loyalties and decisions: "I have decided to cut off all support for you. Bear in mind the following: you have until the first of March to leave my house, and you will be forbidden to enter it

77. The Jüdisches Volksheim, which was dedicated to helping young East European Jewish refugees who fled to Berlin during the war, was a locus for local Zionist enthusiasts. Visiting the Volksheim to attend a lecture by the director, Scholem was appalled at the ecstatic atmosphere and what he perceived to be a complete lack of knowledge about Jewish life and history. Scholem's letter to Lehmann can be found in Scholem, *Briefe I*, 43–52. For more on this dispute and others (in which the questions of the war were relatively marginal), see Scholem, *From Berlin to Jerusalem*, 76–80 and 88–90. For more about the Jüdisches Volksheim and Siegfried Lehmann, see for example Aschheim, *Brothers and Strangers*, 194–97; Brenner, *The Renaissance of Jewish Culture in Weimar Germany*, 204–5.

78. The falling out between Scholem and Martin Buber is an issue of some scholarly discussion including one monograph that explores many of the different facets. See Davidowicz, *Geschichte eines Missverständnisses*. But see also Weidner, *Gershom Scholem: Politisches, esoterisches und historiographisches Schreiben*, 85–88; Biale, *Counter-history*, 56–60.

79. Scholem, *Lamentations of Youth*, 173.

80. See Scholem, *From Berlin to Jerusalem*, 83–83.

again without my permission. On March first, I will transfer 100 marks to your account . . . Anything more than this you cannot expect of me . . . Whether I agree to finance your further studies after the war depends upon your future behavior."[81] This letter naturally placed Scholem in an entirely unfamiliar and difficult situation. He was now forced to move out and support himself.

The crisis at home, however, was merely a culmination of a much larger set of problems.[82] To fully appreciate Scholem's crisis, one needs to take into consideration the hopes and dreams that were now dashed. Scholem did not conceive of himself as a regular youth activist. His aspirations for himself were on a completely different scale. Indeed the protagonist of young Scholem's vision of Jewish renewal was, perhaps not surprisingly, Scholem himself. In his vision, however, he appears not as some charismatic pseudomilitary leader but in the guise of a scribe, a writer of myths.

This insight appears in its most powerful form in a diary entry dated May 1915. The text relates in Nietzschean terms the tale of a young man from an unassuming background who blazed the path of redemption for his people in their search for Zion. This young man was, of course, none other than Gershom Scholem himself, who had been roused by Martin Buber's "longing for unity and longing for beauty, longing for freedom and longing for reality," as well as by Buber's myth. Buber, Scholem noted there, "found in the nation—in the despised and pitied charitable cases of eastern Jews—beauty and reality, religiosity and unity. Out of the ruins of a century he has discovered Hassidism. He discovered how, through the youth, the bonds of Jewish mysticism and national myth join his people together. He recorded the myth not only as he found it. No, he did so as he found it in himself . . . the light of his longing casts a faint beauty on all the occurrences of myth."[83]

It was Buber's myth that provided Scholem with inspiration in his own search. And likewise, it was the search for knowledge that could redeem the soul of the nation and tie its people together. "And who is this dreamer whose name already marks him as the Awaited One? It is Scholem, the Perfect One. It was he who equipped himself for his work and began to powerfully forge together weapons of knowledge."[84] Shortly thereafter, in an additional diary entry, Scholem made an even more specific case for his mission: "I'll have to

81. See Scholem, *Gershom Scholem: A Life in Letters*, 41.
82. For more see Scholem, *From Berlin to Jerusalem*, 83–94. See also Biale, *Counter-history*, 26.
83. Scholem, *Lamentations of Youth*, 56–57.
84. Ibid.

compose the myth of the coming reality, a reality that arises out of our own needs like fog out of steamy water."[85]

The desire to write the myth of the Jewish people was not a modest one, for the concept of 'myth' bore considerable cultural weight in Scholem's intellectual and social milieu. Indeed, the fascination with myth and with mythological thinking was a salient theme within the German intellectual tradition.[86] David Biale also notes the interdependency between Scholem's concept of myth and those of other scholars, namely, Ernst Cassirer and Friedrich Delitzsch. In fact it is in this context that Biale calls Scholem "a child of the *Religionswissenschaft-Schule*."[87] This observation is correct, but it ignores the fact that this term plays an even much larger and much older role in the German cultural discourse.

There are many reasons to see Scholem as part of German culture,[88] and yet it would seem that it is within the context of "myth" that Scholem's work bears the most overt debt to the German intellectual tradition. The centrality of this idea is beyond dispute. Thomas Mann even suggested that the fascination with myth defined the German spirit over and against other cultural traditions: "Between the social instinct of the French work and the mythical primitive poetic spirit of the German . . . the intricate old question of 'what is German' perhaps finds its answer."[89] Be that as it may, Scholem's debt to the German discourse on myth is manifestly obvious not only in his academic studies but also in his diaries, in which he frequently cited and discussed well-known as well as more obscure texts on mythology. To be sure, in his own work Scholem added a further unique facet to the existing body of knowledge. Nevertheless, there was a general consensus about its conceptual premise. To Scholem, as to the German romantics, Bible scholars, philologists, and Protestant reformers of the nineteenth and early twentieth century, as well as to thinkers like Nietzsche and Schelling and musicians like Wagner, mythology was a stepping stone on the path to social, religious, and political rejuvenation.[90]

85. Ibid., 64.

86. For a historical account of the German fascination with myth and the history of its reception in the eighteenth and nineteenth centuries, see Williamson, *Longing for Myth in Germany*.

87. Biale, *Counter-history*, 142.

88. See, for example, George L. Mosse, "Gershom Scholem as a German Jew," *Modern Judaism* 10, no. 2 (May 1, 1990): 117–33; Noam Zadoff, *From Berlin to Jerusalem and Back*; Jay Howard Geller, "From Berlin and Jerusalem: On the Germanness of Gershom Scholem," *Journal of Religious History* 35, no. 2 (2011): 211–32.

89. Williamson, *Longing for Myth in Germany*, 1.

90. See above, note 10.

One of the earliest and most concise formulations of the idea of 'myth' is to be found in a short text known as the "Oldest Systematic Program of German Idealism." This obscure fragment was composed in around 1793 by Hegel and discovered many years later by Franz Rosenzweig.[91] The closing lines of the fragment read:

[M]ythology must become philosophical and the people reasonable, and philosophy must become mythological in order to make philosophy sensual. Then external unity will reign among us. Never again a contemptuous glance, never the blind trembling of the people before its wise men and priests. Only then does equal development of all powers await us, of the individual as well as of all the individuals. No power will be suppressed any longer, then general freedom and equality of spirits will reign—a higher spirit sent from heaven must establish this religion among us, it will be the last work of the human race.[92]

This text is considered to contain the kernel of the romantic conception of myth, and it indeed introduces many of the elements that would subsequently appear time after time as thinkers sought to imagine a new mythology during the following 150 years.[93] For our purpose here it is important to note only that this text criticizes the state for being a mechanical and inhumane entity and calls upon 'myth' to deliver humanity from evil by fusing philosophy and myth.

It is not coincidence that the ideas expressed in the "Oldest Systematic Program" come remarkably close to Scholem's conception of Jewish mysticism. Biale points out that Scholem's notion of Jewish mysticism was situated at the joint between myth and philosophy: "myth and philosophy" he argues, "were fused by mysticism in order to save Jewish monotheism from its own internal problems."[94] And the resemblance between Scholem's conceptualization of Jewish mysticism and the early romantic formulation is likewise transparent. Scholem took this conception from a living tradition. Indeed, he did not need

91. For more about the authorship and the discovery of this fragment, see Christoph Jamme and Helmut Schneider, eds., *Mythologie der Vernunft: Hegels "Ältestes Systemprogramm des deutschen Idealismus"* (Frankfurt am Main: Suhrkamp, 1984), 21–78.

92. "The Oldest Systematic Program of German Idealism," as cited in Ernst Behler, ed., *Fichte, Jacobi, Schelling: Philosophy of German Idealism* (New York: Continuum, 1987), 162–63.

93. See Frank, *Der kommende Gott*, 153–161.

94. Biale, *Counter-history*, 128. Scholem's interpretation of the role of myth in Judaism was later criticized by Yehuda Liebes. See *Studies in Jewish Myth and Jewish Messianism* (Albany: SUNY Press, 1993), esp. 1- 64.

to be influenced directly by the "Oldest Systematic Program" of the young Hegel because this understanding of myth was pervasive in the German cultural environment in which Scholem operated.

As Scholem's diaries clearly show, he was familiar with virtually the entire gamut of German romanticism and idealism, as well as with later neoromantic, academic, and theological writings on myth. It is likewise clear that the young Gershom Scholem was deeply inspired by German romanticism; he even considered himself a 'romantic.'[95] In his later work he acknowledges his intellectual debt to figures such as Georg Friedrich Creuzer and Franz Joseph Molitor, who are nowadays largely forgotten but had a considerable influence on the formation of the study of religion and philology in German universities.[96] As Elisabeth Hamacher argues, Scholem partook in an ongoing debate about myth and monotheism in German academia during the Weimar period.[97] It therefore does not seem surprising or frustrating that Scholem never bothers to fully account for his use of this term. It was a known and self-evident element of the scholarly discourse and therefore required little explanation.[98]

95. Scholem's debt to the German romantic and idealist school has been acknowledged by most commentators. See, for example, Nils Roemer, "Breaching the 'Walls of Captivity': Gershom Scholem's Studies of Jewish Mysticism," *Germanic Review: Literature, Culture, Theory* 72 (1997): 23–41. Daniel Weidner discusses in detail Scholem's adoption of the language theory of the early romantics. His work shows conclusively that Scholem was immersed in early romantic thought during the years of the First World War, especially in the context of his collaborations with Walter Benjamin. See Weidner, *Gershom Scholem: Politisches, esoterisches und historiographisches Schreiben*, 197–211. It is appropriate to note here a short yet touching entry in Scholem's diary: "Es ist nicht meine Linie: Aristoteles, Leibniz, Goethe, ich gehe ganz andere Wege, auf denen das Wort Klassizismus nicht vorkommt. Ich kann Goethe nicht lesen, ohne ich über irgendetwas in ihm, was ich selber nicht ausdrücken kann, zu ärgern. Aber ich kann Novalis, Vischer oder Cervantes lesen, und seine Saiten tönen die Melodien meiner Tage. Trivial gesagt: ich gehöre zur Romantik hin." Scholem, *Tagebücher I*, 157.

96. On Scholem's relation to these figures see also Hamacher, *Gershom Scholem und die allgemeine Religionsgeschichte*, 170–90. On Creuzer see also Williamson, *Longing for Myth in Germany*, 121–79. On Molitor see Katharina Koch, *Franz Joseph Molitor und die jüdische Tradition: Studien zu den kabbalistischen Quellen der 'Philosophie der Geschichte'* (Berlin: Walter de Gruyter, 2006), esp. 69–70. On Scholem and Molitor see Idel, "Zur Funktion von Symbolen bei G. G. Scholem."

97. Hamacher, *Gershom Scholem und die allgemeine Religionsgeschichte*, 177.

98. Elisabeth Hamacher writes for example: "Scholem talked about myth or mythological thinking so often, but only rarely did he discuss what he means by these terms." Ibid., 171 (my translation).

Nevertheless, even if the exact source of Scholem's notion about myth cannot be ascertained, the conclusion is inescapable. Without the idea of myth as a source for social and spiritual renewal, which Scholem found in the German intellectual tradition and which appears already in the "Oldest Systematic Program," his work on the Kabbalah would have been unimaginable.[99]

The suggestion regarding the source of Scholem's conception of the Kabbalah holds not merely for his later work as a Kabbalah scholar. The relation between myth, political rejuvenation, and mysticism is already evident in Scholem's early writings, almost a decade before he embarked on his first philological study of the Kabbalah. In December 1914, Scholem reflected upon the greatness of the Bible. "People have forgotten how to read the Bible . . . the way they treat this book is silly and perverse," Scholem contended. "I would love to teach people to read the Bible for its own sake and not for the sake of dogma."[100] But how, we may ask, does one read the Bible for its own sake, ignoring the tradition that defines, explains, and gives meaning to the sacred text?

This question touches upon a fundamental issue in the history of philology. How does one read holy texts as a philologist, without, that is, believing them to be holy, to have been handed down from the deity, or to embody a special truth? One widely accepted answer to this question, at least from the mid-eighteenth century onward, was to read the holy text as a myth.[101] And this is precisely what Scholem sought to do. "To my mind," he noted in the same entry, "the biblical stories are the mightiest of myths, the like of which no other nation has ever created." Scholem here reconnects to the Jewish tradition through an existing philological discourse on the Bible within the German intellectual interpretation of myth. "What does the book of Genesis teach us?" Scholem asks. "It reveals the greatest discovery a human can make, which is the divinity of daily life . . . These tales recount not monumental things but

---

99. This conclusion is supported by, for example, the works of the preeminent scholar of the Kabbalah, Moshe Idel. See "Zur Funktion von Symbolen bei G. G. Scholem." In this article, Idel convincingly demonstrates the relation between Scholem's conception of myth and of the idea of the symbol to an older, German tradition of interpretation of these concepts. See also Idel, *Old Worlds*, 111–13; Bram Mertens, *Dark Images, Secret Hints: Benjamin, Scholem, Molitor and the Jewish Tradition* (Bern: Peter Lang, 2007).

100. Scholem, *Lamentations of Youth*, 44.

101. Williamson, Longing *for Myth in Germany*, 151–79. On myth as a cornerstone of secular culture, see also Talal Asad, *Formations of the Secular: Christianity, Islam, Modernity* (Stanford: Stanford University Press, 2003), 21–66.

completely normal everyday life with a few festive interruptions . . . they present common life as being truly divine and ideal. Beauty is uncovered amid endless repetition."[102]

The young Gershom Scholem was drawn by myth. He was taken by the biblical myth and the myth of Hasidism newly introduced by Martin Buber, understood in the spirit of the German idealist and romantic traditions.[103] He too believed that these myths had the power to rejuvenate a spiritually exhausted nation after two millennia in exile, and to introduce a powerful aesthetic synthesis into its bloodstream. Scholem himself, however, was destined to write another myth altogether, namely, the myth of exile. In November 1914 Scholem called in his diaries upon a new Moses to salvage the lost herd of Israel from destruction. "*The myth of Exile!*" he writes. "Exile will have to become for us a myth."[104]

The aspiration to create the myth of exile unites all the elements in the young Scholem's story. Scholem's myth of exile would combine his political yearning to create 'Zion,' his longing for knowledge, and his search for social unity with his adoption of the German discourse on myth. It would turn exile in both its senses—a national condition as well as a personal existential problem—into a source of political power of a unique kind. As noted above, Scholem did not call for a Jewish state but rather yearned for the transformation of exilic culture into a source from which social harmony, spiritual renewal, and political autonomy might spring. This would be the purpose of the myth of exile: to overcome the contradictions of human (exilic) conditions and to contain, *ex negativo*, the notion of Zion in its most profound form. And it was this myth that Scholem sought to recreate.

To Scholem's chagrin, no one seemed to be interested. The youth movement chose the war rather than national rejuvenation, and its members preferred experience to myth. As a result, Scholem sank into depression. His psychological crisis of 1917 reached its climax and resolved itself by July that year, when Scholem was drafted into the army. As we shall see next, Scholem's adventures in the military brought him brief relief but ultimately led him to confront his greatest and most transformative disappointment yet.

102. Scholem, *Lamentations of Youth*, 44.

103. For more on Buber's concept of myth in this intellectual context, see Biale, *Counterhistory*, 43–47.

104. Scholem, *Lamentations of Youth*, 43. Emphasis in the original.

A STORY OF A FRIENDSHIP

Despite the many difficulties he had endured in the years 1914–17, the last year of the war took Scholem further away from home than ever. It was in Switzerland in 1918 that Scholem considered committing suicide more intensely than at any time before. And it was there that he penned his farewell letter to the Jewish youth movement. In it, he declared that he had now completely abandoned all his previous hopes for it. He vowed to forgo any further criticism he might have and never again to comment on the internal intricacies of Jewish youth. There was simply no longer any point in trying to help, he declared. Scholem's farewell letter is thus immensely instructive because in it he seeks again to define what he thought 'Zion' was and how it should be achieved. Yet, the intensity of his farewell letter and the disappointment it expresses cannot be understood without taking into account the context in which the letter was written. Upon his release from military service, Scholem traveled to Switzerland in order to be with his friend and idol Walter Benjamin. Never before had Scholem felt so hopeful about another's ability to understand him and the theoretical complexities he faced in attempting to restore a Jewish home. When Walter Benjamin appeared to be a lesser man than he had thought him, Scholem was devastated and mentally broken.

Scholem was hardly fit for military service. Not only did he strenuously object to the war, he was also an opinionated intellectual and a nonconformist who was more often than not in conflict with peers and superiors. It is difficult to envisage him wearing a uniform, and even harder to imagine him fighting a war. Nevertheless as an able and healthy young man, Scholem was drafted in July 1917 and served for a short yet personally intense period. Soon after he was recruited he was hospitalized in the mental ward of the military hospital in Allenstein, and after less than three months in uniform he was declared unfit and sent home. What actually took place during the period that Scholem spent in Allenstein remains unclear. In his letters he refrained from commenting about the events. He knew that someone was reading his letters. In his autobiographical writings he simply seems unwilling to discuss the topic.[105]

Something, however, can still be gleaned from Scholem's writings. The

105. In his memoir, Scholem simply states: "My military period was short and stormy, and I do not wish to discuss it here. I rebelled against everything that went on there, and after a little more than two months I was discharged as a 'psychopath' under the category 'temporarily unfit for duty.'" *From Berlin to Jerusalem*, 95.

radical youth activist who had, it seems, the sensitivities of a petit bourgeois was disgusted by the obscenities common to barracks everywhere. In a letter from his military base Scholem wrote: "Here in the military I've had to learn in the most terrifying fashion what sexual impurity does to people. We are simply doomed if we strive to attain the kind of 'national fitness' that turns these Germans, my fellow recruits, into a 'healthy' *Volk*."[106]

To gain release from active duty Scholem feigned insanity. He was initially transferred to a military hospital and then released after over a month of observation. This must have been experienced by Scholem as a triumph against both the army and his own father, who had expelled him. At home, Scholem related proudly, his father awaited his return after offering "peace without annexation."[107]

The little information Scholem revealed about his experiences in the military appears somewhat contradictory. On the one hand, he insisted, both in his letters and subsequent to the event, that he was healthier than any of the doctors. In a letter to his friend Aharon Heller, Scholem affirmed in a short paragraph written in Hebrew that all was in fact well. "You've probably guessed that I was never really sick; it was a colossal fabrication."[108] On the other hand, he obviously constituted a rare phenomenon in the military. He needed to exaggerate his actual mental disposition only slightly in order to be found unfit. In a letter to Werner Kraft he acknowledges: "I view my release as a victory earned through spiritual exertions that have cost me dearly. I can easily comfort myself with the well-known fact that psychiatrists do not need much research zeal to pronounce someone crazy. Anyway, from the standpoint of the war I *am* crazy. Had the doctors read my previous letter to you . . . they would have enough material to declare me unfit for service."[109]

When interviewed many years later Scholem further confessed: "I acted without knowing what I was acting. I acted myself only with a certain exaggeration."[110] Whether or not Scholem experienced an actual mental breakdown is unclear. Nevertheless, this experience was without doubt stressful. Feigning

106. Scholem, *Gershom Scholem: A Life in Letters*, 48.

107. Scholem, *Briefe I*, 95.

108. Scholem, *Gershom Scholem: A Life in Letters*, 59.

109. Ibid., 57. Emphasis in the original.

110. See Scholem's interview with Muki Zur, in Gershom Scholem, "With Gershom Sholem: Muki Zur Speaks with Gershom Scholem," in *Devarim be-go: pirke morashah u-tehiyah (Explications and Implications: Writings on Jewish Heritage and Renaissance*, vol. 1) (in Hebrew) (Tel Aviv: Am Oved, 1975), 24.

insanity, he would note, was the most intense experience in his life.[111] Scholem's father, it would appear, did not think his son's illness was feigned or merely ephemeral. And his concern may have been justified.

Less than a year later, the released soldier was seeking a new path for himself. In April 1918, Scholem received the long-awaited permanent discharge from the military and with it a travel permit. His plan was to leave Germany and join Walter and Dora Benjamin in Bern. On that day Scholem was beside himself with joy. His personal diary records a playful spirit, which is extremely uncommon:

> Last night I could barely sleep due to my excitement. I was aroused to the core by anticipation of the morrow. I rose early and went to the district doctor. And I received the certificate, as I could have only imagined in my wildest dreams! During the next hour I saw the heavens open; all my inner desires seemed fulfilled . . . I mustn't write Walter till it's certain . . . No, it would be better to surprise them, when I ring the bell, Dora answers, and I say "Good day, madam, my dear lady!" Oh, how I'd like to sleep till this moment arrives.[112]

By traveling to Bern, Scholem hoped to recreate and rejuvenate himself in a new place with an older and deeply influential friend. In fact Walter Benjamin was more than a friend to Gershom Scholem. "He stands," Scholem wrote of Benjamin in his diary "entirely beyond 'relationships.' He and he alone stands at the center of my life."[113] And in the very same entry he notes, "For some time now, the truly established harmony mutually ordering our lives has been the anchor regulating my life."[114] Yet these hopes were soon to be dashed. After the brief initial excitement, Walter Benjamin and his wife Dora proved to be thoroughly disappointing, as Scholem's expectations of an epic new spiritual bond turned into a soap-opera-like drama of insult and pain.[115]

In retrospect, this outcome is hardly surprising. Scholem was a young, single man, recently discharged from the army following a feigned but nevertheless exhausting mental experience, who was seeking to realize himself, once

111. Ibid.

112. Scholem, *Lamentations of Youth*, 225. The translation is emended.

113. Ibid., 210.

114. Ibid.

115. See also Gershom Gerhard Scholem, *Walter Benjamin: The Story of a Friendship*, 52–85. It is striking to read, in this context, the correspondence between Scholem and Dora Benjamin, which masquerades as a correspondence between "uncle Gerhard" and the few-month's-old Stefan (Dora and Walter's son). Ibid., 68–75.

and for all, through spiritual affinity with his older friend and his wife, whom he greatly admired. Walter and Dora Benjamin, on the other hand, were caring for their first (and only) child, who was only several weeks old when Scholem arrived in Bern. Rearing a newborn child presents difficulties that can tear loving partners apart. And indeed the tensions between the couple appear in the background of Scholem's diary entries.[116] A three-way ecstatic (even if platonic) relationship might have been too much to bear. Walter Benjamin was, moreover, engaged in the initial stage of writing his dissertation on German romanticism, hoping for a stable career in German academia. Scholem, on the other hand, was seeking something grander, and his contempt for "university professors" is sometimes palpable in his diaries. It is therefore safe to assume that Benjamin and Scholem conceived their relationship in a rather different manner.

As high as Scholem's expectations had been, so deep was his subsequent downfall. Following the discord with Walter and Dora Benjamin, Scholem sank into despair and suicidal thoughts. "O God," he wrote, "I cannot stand this!"

My life converges on suicide. This is the naked truth that's been circulating in my brain like a millstone for four weeks now. Never have I considered death—death by my own hands—with such intense immediacy as in these four weeks. I do so day in and night out. And Walter and Dora, instead of helping me, only make things worse. Through some sort of dreadful imponderable they are literally driving me to my grave. There are moments—God and the two of them forgive me for this—in which I consider them to be perfectly ignoble . . . this is killing me.[117]

Yet Scholem survived this episode and went on to better things. In a letter to Escha Burchhardt, whom he would later marry, he indicates that although things were rather difficult, he already knew that all was not quite lost: "I can here burrow into myself. I can work, think, take walks, or cry, just as I please . . . now I know . . . that I left my childhood behind when I left Germany . . . I can only wait humbly and see what will come of all this commotion. I'll become hard as granite—which is the only way to avoid being consumed by flames."[118]

116. See, for example, the diary entry dated November 5, 1918. See Scholem, *Lamentations of Youth*, 272.

117. Scholem, *Lamentations of Youth*, 240.

118. Scholem, *Gershom Scholem: A Life in Letters*, 76.

People who knew Scholem personally would probably concur: Scholem did indeed become as hard as granite.

Throughout his sojourn in Bern, Scholem hardly wrote about current events, and for this reason it is difficult to assess to what degree he was aware of the fact that the war was then finally drawing to a close. After the war ended, Scholem returned to Germany. He eventually joined Escha Burchhardt in Munich, where he began his first rigorous study of the Kabbalah.[119] In November 1923 Scholem and Burchhardt left Germany and immigrated to Palestine, where the two were married. But in the summer of 1918 this future was still unimaginable. At that moment, it would have been absurd to imagine that it would be Scholem, rather than Benjamin, who would embark on an enormously successful scholarly career, or that it would be Benjamin, rather than Scholem, who would take his own life and die in obscurity in a little village far from home.

Nothing testifies more vividly to Scholem's desperate state during those months in Switzerland than his "farewell" letter to the youth movement. Indeed it was in Switzerland and in proximity to Walter Benjamin that Scholem bid his dreams and the youth movement farewell in a polemical open letter to the editor of *Jerubbaal*, Siegfried Bernfeld.[120] Scholem's explanations for taking his leave of the youth movement might appear somewhat obscure, yet the caustic, damning, and hostile tone of his critique of the movement is unmistakable. Furthermore, this letter contains what is perhaps the young Scholem's most mature discussion of exile and Zionism and seems to be the culmination of all his previous phases and development.

At the core of Scholem's polemic against the youth movement was the question of the location of Jewish action. For Scholem this was a rhetorical question. The only possible locus of action for Zionist youth could, he claimed, be Zion. Any pretension to "work" for Zion or to act on its behalf from the outside

119. It was not until the spring of 1919 that Scholem finally decided where and what to study. For more on his decision to study in Munich, see David A. Rees, "Ein Dichter, ein Mädchen und die jüdische Speisegesetze. Gershom Scholems Entscheidung für München und die Kabbala," *Münchener Beiträge zur juedischen Geschichte und Kultur* 2 (2007): 19–29.

120. Siegfried Bernfeld had a remarkable life: an ardent follower of Gustav Wynekens's ideas, a member of the Jewish youth movement in Vienna with close contacts to Martin Buber and later to Freud's psychoanalytical circle, Bernfeld was a major figure in the Jewish youth movements. In 1934 he moved to San Francisco, where he became one of the founding members of the local psychoanalytic society. For more on Bernfeld's involvement in the Jewish youth movement and his journal *Jerubbaal*, see Willi Hoffer, "Siegfried Bernfeld and 'Jerubbaal,'" *Leo Baeck Institute Yearbook* 10 (1965): 150–67.

was, Scholem believed, a blatant misconception of the basic principles that should motivate the youth. "Zion, the source of nationhood, is the common, indeed in an uncanny sense the identical solitude of all the Jews . . . as long as this center is not restored to radiant brightness, the order of our soul, which honesty bids us to acknowledge, must be anarchic. In *Galut* [exile] there can be no Jewish community valid before God. And if community among human beings is indeed the highest that can be demanded, what would be the sense of Zionism if it could be realized in *Galut?*"[121]

While in exile, Scholem argued in his letter, the youth should restrict itself to anarchy and resistance, lamentation, belief, silence, and solitude. Scholem's choice of words here was of course anything but accidental. His discussion of solitude and silence was a direct polemic against the Buberian vocabulary of the youth movement. Scholem demanded silence rather than chatter, lamentation rather than experience, solitude rather than movement, belief rather than escapism, self-perfection rather than idle clamor. These were the authentic values to which the youth should commit itself in order to justify its self-perception as Zionist. Scholem makes this point clearly: "A life, however, that is related to these basic principles can rightly be called youthful. Zion is the object of this life."[122]

Notably, Scholem's demands of the youth movement were not ecstatic, messianic, or apocalyptic. He did not wish them to transcend time or overcome politics. Scholem's insistence on solitude, silence, and lamentation might be a reference to his own spiritual condition. Be this as it may, it suggests the dire need to discover the conditions for taking up Jewish politics, and to do so before engaging in frantic involvement in history. These conditions must provide the possibility for Jews to assert their role in history without reverting to either the bourgeois politics of the state or the tyrannical lure of apocalypse and destruction. Scholem vehemently opposed both these solutions, which were all too familiar to him. Rather, he sternly believed that the Jewish youth could succeed where the Europeans had failed. This was his original idea and hope.

Yet by 1918 Scholem had concluded that this political solution would not be achieved by the youth movement, and he decided to break away from it. The movement, he argued, was totally immersed in chatter and in foolish attempts to gain "experiences," as Martin Buber would have instructed them. By doing so, Scholem contended, they were taking a disastrous path into history,

121. Gershom Scholem, "Farewell," *On Jews and Judaism in Crisis* (New York: Schocken, 1987), 55.

122. Ibid, 60.

which was beyond repair. And he, in response, was forced to bid the movement an unhappy farewell. Thus Scholem finally placed himself where he had probably already belonged for some time: on the outside, alone, and in exile.

This sense of loneliness is reflected in what is, as Anthony David Skinner suggested,[123] Scholem's saddest diary entry of all. In this entry, Scholem seems to realize that he had failed to live up to his expectations of himself; no one understood what he was doing. His yearning to write and his ideas about the national myth of rejuvenation, the myth of exile, had come to nothing. "Today I still can't write," he notes; "I am a composer of symbolic literature [i.e., mythology], comprehensible only to myself. If I could write like the philologists— and if I were truly *permitted* to write thus—I could create a forbidden library out of the few things I hope to know someday."[124]

At this moment he was of course unable to imagine it, but later in life, as an adult, Scholem would indeed write a library. Possibly, it was not quite what he had initially had in mind. Nevertheless, it would bring together his imagination of the Jewish past and future, exile and homecoming, myth and renewal. And it is this library that will command our attention next.

123. See Scholem, *Lamentations of Youth*, 232.
124. Ibid., 287.

CHAPTER 3

Messianism as Symbol: The Lurianic School and the Emergence of a Mystical-Political Society

One is tempted to interpret this withdrawal of God into his own Being in terms of Exile.

GERSHOM SCHOLEM, *Major Trends in Jewish Mysticism*, 1941

An immaculate and unmovable God, one that is essentially a "logically flawless theological formula," does not satisfy the human thirst for the transcendent.[1] This was Gershom Scholem's deepest historical and philosophical working assumption. Humans, Scholem claimed, need a God that is present in their lives, His transcendent qualities notwithstanding. And this need, he believed, was the fundamental impetus for the existence of Jewish mysticism. It is also the reason why he believed that Jewish mysticism is contrived of myths. According to Scholem, the Kabbalah was an attempt to accommodate this basic human metaphysical desire by envisioning an intricate God who appeared in the world in a multitude of forms and exhibited the dynamism of cause and effect. In short, the Jewish mystical tradition essentially comprised a collection of symbolic mythologies as they had evolved in the history of the purest monotheistic religion, in an attempt to satisfy the need for a tangible God.[2] Yet strangely, when Scholem approached what he himself described as an abundant and complex mythological corpus, he extracted from it only one tale of

1. See Gershom Scholem, "Kabbalah and Myth," in *On the Kabbalah and Its Symbolism*, trans. Ralph Manheim (New York: Schocken, 1965), 87.

2. Moshe Idel traces Scholem's concept of 'symbol' back to the German romantic tradition. See Idel, "Zur Funktion von Symbolen bei G. G. Scholem." On Scholem's concept of myth, see also Biale, *Counter-history*, 51–70.

creation, which he recounted as a myth replete with primordial beings, forces, and effects. This was the myth of exile according to the sixteenth-century Kabbalist from Safed, Rabbi Isaac Luria (the Ari). This is a striking fact, one that raises questions about Scholem's use of the term myth to describe the Kabbalah.

From a literary perspective Scholem's work on the Lurianic myth constitutes his greatest achievement. It is as if his description of his mentor's work became relevant also to himself: "Out of the ruins of a century," Scholem wrote of Martin Buber, "he has discovered Hasidism. He discovered how, through the youth, the bonds of Jewish mysticism and national myth join his people together."[3] Now, from a vast collection of manuscripts and books, the mature historian Gershom Scholem salvaged a new spiritual and political myth, the Jewish myth of exile. And he drew from it two powerful symbols—the concept of *tsimtsum* and the idea of *tikkun*, which weaved the disparate elements of modern Jewish national rejuvenation into a seamless tale of creation. These symbols were presented not merely as a trophy of the past but also as a treasure for future-oriented thinking.

The objective of this chapter is to carefully examine Scholem's one myth, namely, the myth of exile according to Luria. As we shall see, Scholem's unfolding of the Lurianic myth brings to the fore many of the concerns that Scholem expressed as a young activist in Berlin. Scholem's retelling of the myth fuses the political and the spiritual, the Jewish and the universal, and the personal and the social and places the result within a concrete historical context. Put differently, Scholem's youthful concerns are to be found in his discussion of the sixteenth-century Jewish occult. Scholem's analysis of the Lurianic Kabbalah turns our discussion in an entirely new direction, however. The previous chapter narrated the key-life experiences and beliefs that Scholem held as a young activist in Berlin around the years of World War I. It reached its culmination around the end of the war, shortly before he decided to move to Munich and to take up the academic study of the Kabbalah. This chapter, conversely, discusses Scholem's historiographical account of the Lurianic myth, which he composed years later; between 1938 and early 1941. This leap requires explanation.

The overarching argument presented in this book is that Scholem's biography is weaved into his historiography. I furthermore argue that these stories are the reason for Scholem's presence so far beyond the narrow confines of

3. Scholem, *Lamentations of Youth*, 56–57.

the academic discipline he help found. My argument, in other words, is that Scholem brought his social, political, and spiritual concerns into his study of the Kabbalah. This, I now argue, is nowhere more apparent than in his study of the myth of exile. As we have seen in the previous chapter, both the problem of life in exile and the promises of 'myth' played a central role in the thinking and political activism of the young Gershom Scholem. The seventeen-year-old Scholem unambiguously expressed the desire that myth would dissolve the contradictions of life in exile. "*The myth of Exile!* Exile will have to become for us a myth," he wrote in his diary.[4] Here I will argue that Scholem's study of the Lurianic myth of exile brings his mature work full circle by fulfilling his fanciful youthful aspirations. We have also seen that Scholem's use of the term 'myth' is very much within the perimeters of an existing discussion. Here I will show that Scholem understood myth as an attempt to fuse the contradictory tendencies of experience by coalescing them into symbols, thereby facilitating the triumph of the human spirit over the mundane.

According to Scholem, the historical appearance of the Lurianic myth of exile in the mid-sixteenth century was a transformative moment in Jewish history and religion.[5] This is because, for most its history, the Kabbalah had belonged to the highest echelons of the Jewish spiritual elite. Only the initiated and most ardent students could gain access to its secret. Scholem discusses the history of the ideas of the Kabbalah, presenting them as a highly complex intellectual endeavor, in the first six lectures of his monumental book *Major Trends in Jewish Mysticism*. However, Scholem claims, in the very first lines of the seventh lecture of *Major Trends*, the social role of mystical thinking changed in the sixteenth century as a result of the Spanish expulsion of 1492, which transformed both the Kabbalah and the Jewish people. From a multifaceted symbolic speculation and highly complex system, the Kabbalah grew into an accessible ideology. And the Jewish people transformed by absorbing

4. Ibid., 43. For more on this topic see the discussion in the second chapter.
5. Scholem was by no means the first to suggest this historical narrative. In a basic form it already exists in the fifth and seventh chapters of the tenth volume of Heinrich Grätz's monumental work *The History of the Jews*, first published in 1868. It seems to me more than likely that the canonical stature this work achieved may explain the wide reception the historical thesis (about the development of the Kabbalah in the wake of the Spanish expulsion, its wide reception in the Jewish public, and its role in the Sabbatean conflagration) enjoyed among Jewish scholars. This thesis can be also found in, for example, Yitzhak R. Baer, *Galut* (New York: Schocken, 1947); Martin Buber, *The Tales of Rabbi Nachman*, trans. Maurice Friedman (New York: Humanity Books, 2011), 3–18.

the principle of Kabbalistic thinking into its daily religious practices and social conceptions, in fact, into the first Jewish ideology in modern history.

Scholem thus tacitly argues that this Jewish ideology was unique in the annals of nations, and particularly in the history of the Jewish people. It was based
on the Lurianic Kabbalah, and was older, more daring, and more consensual
than almost any other national ideology in modern times. It was daring because
it projected an ideal society not merely in political terms but rather in terms of
spirituality, freedom, and commonalty. It was older than any other Jewish ideology not only because it appeared in the sixteenth century but because it was
deeply rooted in a secret Jewish tradition hundreds of years old. As it seeped
into the daily practice of Jews, it was, according to Scholem, accepted across
the board, by Jews wherever they might be. It was the last doctrine in Jewish
history to unite the entire nation through a given set of beliefs and a shared
sense of destiny. And finally, this ideology was uniquely Jewish because, ostensibly, it had grown organically within the innermost recesses of the Jewish
religious tradition. Ostensibly at least, it needed nothing and borrowed nothing
from other political and social traditions. As we shall see next, however, this
ideology bears the distinct signs of the German youth movement at the turn
of the twentieth century. And it is for this reason that the story of Scholem's
involvement in the youth movements, narrated to this point, must now shift into
the realm of the Jewish occult.

Thus, beyond unpacking this crucial yet somewhat overlooked aspect of
his historiography, an analysis of Scholem's Lurianic Kabbalah hopes to offer
some resolution to a much-debated question in the scholarship. As noted, the
question whether Scholem was a theologian, mystic, or a Kabbalist is often and
widely debated in the literature. I argue conversely that much of this debate is
premised on an anachronism. It is true that the Kabbalist that is represented in
Scholem's writing turns out to be curiously similar to an anarchist and a philologist, like Scholem himself. But this does not necessarily mean that Scholem
was similar to those he wrote about. Rather, I suggest, it might mean that he
constructed the textual materials in accordance with his own sensitivities, assumptions, and concerns. Like others, Scholem too sought and found in his
textual evidence those elements that interested him most and accentuated the
ideas that best fitted his already existing conceptual apparatus. In other words,
I argue that more than he had a Lurianic ideology, Scholem in fact organized
the Lurianic myth according to his understanding of myth and his political
beliefs.

Of course, Scholem did not write the myth of exile as a young man in Berlin
but only much later. Nevertheless, the similarity between Scholem's notion of

the myth of exile and his own reworking of the problem of exile years earlier cannot be coincidental. Therefore, despite the gap in time, these two elements of Scholem's life and work must be understood in tandem. It seems indeed likely that when Scholem was faced with the question of exile and the promise of redemption, he reached down to his own experience and found there the most immediate vision of exile, myth, and redemption that was available to him. Despite the time that had elapsed between his engagement with the Zionist youth movement and his study of the Lurianic myth, I would argue that the vision of exile we find in both cases draws from the notion he himself had developed in Berlin during World War I.

THE FELLOWSHIP OF THE LION

In order to better understand Scholem's reworking of the Kabbalistic sources into a myth of exile, it is helpful to contrast his interpretation of the Lurianic sources to that accepted by contemporary research. My aim here, it should be clear, is not to criticize Scholem for what may be construed as inaccurate or incomplete reading. Rather, I wish to emphasize the kind of work Scholem has undertaken in reformulating the Lurianic sources. As we shall see, this work includes, at the very least, extensive editorial effort.

As scholars have often noticed, the first challenge facing anyone who attempts to capture the authentic figure of Rabbi Isaac Luria and the content of his teachings is to remove the distorting layers of hagiography and pseudoepigraphy that conceal his historical nature.[6] The distortion of the image of the Ari (Lion), acronym for the Ashkenazi (or Divine) Rabbi Isaac (*ha-Eloki Rabbi Yitzhak*), stems largely from the dramatic discrepancy between his prominent role in the history of the Kabbalah and the meager heritage that can be attributed directly to him. The bulk of his written legacy comprises half a dozen short Sabbath poems, which are laden with complex Kabbalistic intertextual references and secret allusions.[7] Therefore the great majority of our knowledge about the content of his teaching as well as his person depends upon the works of his immediate followers and their students. The second challenge in portraying the content of Luria's teachings is to prioritize the

6. For a useful summary of the genealogy of Luria's teaching, see Lawrence Fine, *Physician of the Soul, Healer of the Cosmos: Isaac Luria and His Kabbalistic Fellowship* (Stanford: Stanford University Press, 2003), 1–3, 16–17, 124–26.

7. See Yehuda Liebes, "Hymns for the Sabbath Meals Composed by the Holy Ari" (in Hebrew), *Molad* 23 (1972): 540–55.

plethora of manuscripts and books written by his students and their students.[8] Scholars must contend here with contradictory reports about Luria's teachings, hyperbolic tales about his person, and rivalries among his followers.[9] It is thus unsurprising that until relatively recently, the Lurianic Kabbalah has received relatively little scholarly attention.[10]

Some facts have been well established. It is known that Luria grew up in Egypt and was recognized as an exceptional Talmudic scholar. At a certain point he secluded himself almost entirely and devoted himself to the study of Kabbalistic texts, most notably the Book of Splendor (Sefer ha-Zohar). At the age of thirty-six he left Egypt in order to partake in the revival of Jewish life that had commenced in the Galilean city of Safed under the conditions generated by the new Ottoman rule. Luria was active as a spiritual leader for less than three years, from his arrival in Safed in 1570 up to his death in August 1572 at the age of thirty-eight. Despite his young age and his premature death, he left a decisive imprint on Jewish spiritual thought. The spiritual revival of Safed of the sixteenth century is nowadays virtually synonymous with the name of Isaac Luria, even though he was only one among a group of productive and influential thinkers.

According to recent studies, Luria and his associates believed that they embodied biblical and other legendary figures who represented facets of the divine being. The connection between Luria's fellowship and the divine was established through a complex system of esoteric and symbolic allusions as

8. For a survey of the sources on Lurianic Kabbalah and their history, see also Gerold Necker, *Einführung in die Lurianische Kabbala* (Frankfurt am Main: Verlag der Weltreligionen, 2008), 77.

9. See Ronit Meroz, "Faithful Transmission Versus Innovation: Luria and His Disciples," in *Gershom Scholem's Major Trends in Jewish Mysticism 50 Years After: Proceedings of the Sixth International Conference on the History of Jewish Mysticism*, ed. Joseph Dan and Peter Schaefer (Berlin: Mohr Siebeck, 1993), 257–74. The debate about the relationship between Luria and Rabbi Israel Sarug is a case in point. Gershom Scholem argued that Sarug was not a direct student of Luria's and that his imaginative teachings were therefore largely of his own making. Later scholars disagree. See also Ronit Meroz, "Israel Sarug, A Disciple of the Ari: Reconsidered" (in Hebrew), *Da'at* (1992): 41–50. The discrepancies between Meroz's and Scholem's accounts of Israel Sarug exemplify the nature of the transformation in Kabbalah scholarship over its first fifty years.

10. Important studies were published earlier, most notably Isaiah Tishby's *The Doctrine of Evil and the "Kelippah" in Lurianic Kabbalism*, 1941. Studies on the Lurianic Kabbalah in Hebrew, English, and German appeared only in the twenty-first century. See the works of Yosef Avivi (2008, Hebrew), Lawrence Fine (2003, English), and Gerold Necker (2008, German).

well as through metempsychosis. Embodying divine elements, as Luria and his fellows did, meant that they could exercise their power over them. Luria developed highly complex rituals designed to facilitate the powers of his group to harmonize the various divine elements that were deemed to be out of joint.[11] Luria's objective was therefore to form a completely harmonious group around him and by doing so harmonizing the world's divine formation and thus instigating the redemption of the world.[12]

Contemporary scholars furthermore argue that the Lurianic myth of creation constituted but one element of Luria's complex undertaking. The myth meant to elucidate his own role in the universe as well as those of his fellows. These scholars agree that the myth also served to explain the meaning and the procedure of his complex rituals. For this reason, they suggest that even though Isaac Luria made innovative use of the Kabbalistic mythological trope, his myth of creation does not represent the core of his achievement or his worldview, nor is it the reason for his wide reception. In a seminal paper written in 1992, Yehuda Liebes comments:

> In recent years, I have come to the conclusion that it is necessary to fundamentally change the approach based on the unconscious assumption according to which the essence of the Lurianic Kabbalah lies in the theurgist-theological domain [his myth] and not in the personal. The Ari and his fellowship are not only the teachers of the Lurianic Kabbalah and its students; they are the principal subject of this teaching. Of course, the significance of the Lurianic Kabbalah as a theory about the structure of the universe is beyond doubt, but this aspect is subordinate to the personal meaning of the teaching and is derived from it.[13]

The unnamed scholar to whom Liebes refers, who unconsciously assumed that the Lurianic Kabbalah was first and foremost of a theoretical nature, is, naturally, Gershom Scholem. To Scholem, Luria was not a member of an observable society but rather the inventor of the greatest myth of its kind. But before discussing Scholem's version of Luria's Kabbalah in further detail, it is necessary to note the broader implication of Liebes's comment in particu-

---

11. Fine, *Physician of the Soul*, 187–300.

12. Fine, *Physician of the Soul*, 300–361; Yehuda Liebes, "Two Young Roes of a Doe: The Secret Sermon of Isaac Luria before his Death" (in Hebrew), *Mehqarei Yerushalayim* 10 (1992): 67–119.

13. Liebes, "Two Young Roes," 68.

lar, and of the conclusions of other contemporary scholars concerning the interpretation of the Lurianic Kabbalah.

In a recent comprehensive study of the Lurianic Kabbalah, Lawrence Fine characterizes the sources of the Lurianic myth with the following words: "While we tend to think of creation myths in terms of a single, coherent narrative that can be told as one does a simple story, Luria's mythological teachings have not come down to us in this way. Instead, we discover a seemingly endless series of inordinately complex notions, presented in often fragmentary and conflicting versions by multiple authors and editors."[14] Similar remarks were made by other scholars as well.[15] In his comprehensive study of the Lurianic Kabbalah, Scholem, on the other hand, does not discuss the predicaments generated by the diffuse character of his textual sources or by the lack of any definitive version of Luria's thought. He altogether avoids mentioning that his version of the myth cannot be traced to any single source or document. And he fails to acknowledge the extent, nature, or significance of the editorial choices he must have undertaken in order to create it. Scholem's study of the Lurianic myth is, therefore, more than a mere example of the literary creativity assumed by every historian. Indeed, considering the scarcity and vagueness of the writings left by the Ari, they could hardly have served as the coherent foundation for a new mystical paradigm. Scholem's discrete myth appears therefore to be a creative synthesis of different complementary and even somewhat questionable sources.[16]

The dissenting conclusions of recent studies of the Lurianic Kabbalah point likewise to other weaknesses in Scholem's scholarship, beyond the lack of transparency. Scholem's centerpiece, the integration of Lurianic Kabbalah into the foundation of Jewish history, hinges on a heuristic and a historical observation. According to Scholem, the Kabbalah was universally accepted in the sixteenth century because it offered a tangible solution to the conundrum of exile that appeared with great urgency in the wake of the Spanish expulsion.

14. Fine, *Physician of the Soul*, 124.

15. See for example, Necker, *Einführung in die Lurianische Kabbala*, 30–52.

16. This is of course not to suggest that Scholem was unaware of the philological problems and challenges he faced. In his more minute philological studies, he addresses such problems as those discussed above. However, he never revised his more general understanding of Lurianic Kabbalah, and it would indeed seem that these more careful studies did not affect his overall view. As a result, the essential problems in the approach to the Lurianic Kabbalah are familiar only to the expert audience, that is, to those who engage in Scholem's narrower philological studies. These studies were republished in Gershom Scholem, *Lurianic Kabbalah: Collected Studies*.

While this observation rings true, Scholem does not support it with material evidence, and it has been squarely rejected by later scholarship.[17] Scholem's study is the result of a novel historiography, a synthesis of history and mythology that seeks—as we shall soon see—to produce a concise representation of the complex development of Jewish modernity. But its outcome is debatable. These difficulties will be discussed in greater detail below. It must be clear, however, that they do not, in any way, diminish the allure of Scholem's writings, but rather have the opposite effect.

THE MYTH OF EXILE: THE CONCEPT OF *TSIMTSUM* AND THE DOCTRINE OF *TIKKUN*

To Gershom Scholem, the essence and peak of Luria's accomplishment was the myth of exile. The myth of exile is in fact a creation myth. It starts, therefore, at the very beginning. In the beginning there was *tsimtsum*, which Scholem terms "one of the most amazing and far-reaching conceptions ever put forward in the history of Kabbalism."[18] *Tsimtsum* literally means 'concentration' or 'contraction,' but in this context it is better translated as 'withdrawal' or 'retreat,' and it represents the first dramatic moment of creation. At the moment of *tsimtsum*, God, who is infinite and encompasses everything, retreated from himself and into himself in order to create space for the creation. Flying in the face of intuition, in other words, the first act in the history of the universe was not one of emanation but on the contrary, an act of receding spirituality, of passing into exile. *Tsimtsum* was, according to Scholem, one of the greatest inventions in the history of the Kabbalah, a deep and complex symbol of exile.

From a philosophical point of view, the greatness of Luria's *tsimtsum* stems from its bold position toward what is one of the most fundamental problems of monotheism. Succinctly put, the idea of the singular and all-encompassing God appears to contradict the possibility of creation. According to Scholem, Luria provided the most dramatic, most imaginative, and probably the most influential answer to the following questions: "How can there be a world if God is everywhere? If God is 'all in all' how can there be things which are not God? How can God create the world out of nothing if there is no nothing?"[19]

17. See, for example, Moshe Idel, "'One from a Town, Two from a Clan': The Diffusion of Lurianic Kabbalah and Sabbateanism: A Re-examination" (in Hebrew), *Jewish History* 7, no. 2 (Fall 1993): 79–104.

18. Scholem, *Major Trends,* 260.

19. Ibid., 261.

FIGURE 3.1. Scholem next to the entrance to a burial cave somewhere in the hills around Jerusalem, 1928. Courtesy of The National Library of Israel, Jerusalem.

The greatness of Luria's answer lies in its indirect nature. Luria never properly solved these questions but chose, rather, to create a myth. This is a mystical tale laden with profound and suggestive symbols, which mysteriously mitigates the contradictions inherent in the idea of creation contained in monotheistic religion. Yet the notion of *tsimtsum* functioned as a double-edged sword. While it created the conditions for creation, it likewise opened a gaping wound in the being of the universe.

Tsimtsum was the first act of creation, and, as Scholem underscores, it also introduced the first, most absolute and terrible form of evil into the universe. "One is tempted to interpret this withdrawal of God into his own Being in terms of Exile, of banishing himself from his totality into profound seclusion. Regarded this way, the idea of *Tsimtsum* is the deepest symbol of exile that could be thought of. . . *Tsimtsum* could come to be considered as an Exile [of the Divine Being] into Himself. The first act of all is not an act of revelation but of limitation."[20] This is a highly significant assertion. Exile, the most concrete form of evil, found its place already within the very first moment of creation. "In the final resort," Scholem argues, "the root of all evil is already latent in the act of *Tsimtsum*."[21]

Once the contraction of the *tsimtsum* had taken place and the seeds of evil were planted in the universe with the exile of God, it was time for the first act of creation. Creation, in a positive sense, began with a ray of divine light that emanated from infinity [*or ein sof*] inward, into the primordial space of the *tsimtsum*. The first being in the history of the world was primordial man [*adam kadmon*]. This man may be understood as a formal and fundamental organization of the divine light emanating in the shape of an archetypal human being. The light emanated from the pores of the face of this primordial man, from his eyes and ears and from his mouth and nose, and was thus further separated and further alienated. This was therefore the very first act of differentiation in the story of creation. The world now consisted not of one concentrated beam in the empty void of *tsimtsum*, but rather of many differentiated lights, each embodying a slightly different aspect of the divinity. Yet this was only a very basic form of separation. The lights had to be set apart and arranged even further in order to enable the creation of more beings.

The next phase of differentiation instigated the tragic climax of the Lurianic myth. Special vessels (*kelim*) were created in the primordial space. They were designed to capture and contain the content of the light that poured from the divine source itself. The primordial light was still so powerful and so confused, according to Scholem's unfolding of the myth, that had it not somehow been contained, creation could not have come about. In other words, discrete things, regular mundane objects, could not have appeared as long as everything was infused with the light of infinity. The vessels were thus created in order to contain the light and create order. Yet as the light poured into them, the vessels broke, proving too fragile to withstand the immense pressure of the divine light. This momentous event is known as "the breaking of the vessels" (*shvirat ha'kelim*). In the wake of this breaking most of the light quickly withdrew to its infinite source. But a few particles were caught in the fragments of

20. Ibid.
21. Ibid., 263.

the vessels, and, together with the fragments, they fell into the lowest part of creation, namely, into materiality.

The world was thus once again put out of joint. The next step in the process of creation brings us to more familiar territory. Adam, the first man, was created in order to remedy the deficiency of the world. The creation of the first man had, therefore, a distinct and concrete end: to free the sparks of divine light from material creation, send them home, and thereby reverse the direction of creation. Had he not fallen into sin, Adam could, together with the rest of creation, have enjoyed an endless day of rest and harmony, a never-ending Sabbath. When Adam ate the fruit of the tree of knowledge, the entire cosmos erupted once more, and spirituality sank deeper into materiality, into evil, into the world. As a result, a few sparks of divine light fell onto the earth. While only a finite number of sparks fell thus, their presence on earth was sufficient to endow creation with religious meaning.

This, then, was the existential condition that was entrusted to mankind. The world of crude materiality which humans inhabit was endowed with a limited, almost quantifiable,[22] amount of divine presence; a few sparks of divine light trapped in the shells of materiality. It is incumbent upon humanity to redeem the world and the godhead by reuniting the sparks that have fallen with the light of the upper worlds. Once all the sparks have been released from their material prison and dispatched to heaven, the divine being will be able to resume its original wholeness. It is not entirely clear from Scholem's analysis what this actually entails, since he mentions two possible scenarios. When all the sparks are sent back to their source, either the world will collapse back into its original form, into the final and total being of God, or it will continue to exist without a flaw, since divine abundance would now finally flow freely between God and creation. One way or another, the basic idea is pretty clear. Once all the sparks are freed from the material shells, all the tensions and contradictions that have characterized the existence of man and the universe will be finally and conclusively resolved, and the world will be at peace, at home.

Scholem employed the term *tikkun* (literally "repair") to indicate the struggle to release the sparks from their captivity.[23] According to Scholem, *tikkun*

---

22. Speculations about the exact number of fallen sparks is of course rife. Scholem refers to a source that claims there are 634 fallen sparks, one for each commandment of the Jewish code of law, the Halakah.

23. The term *tikkun olam* (repair of the world) has a far longer and more complex history than Scholem leads his reader to assume. It appears, for example, already in the Mishnah, in Tractate Gittin 4:2.

olam, or the repair of the world, is carried out, first and foremost, by following the decrees of Jewish law. Through the Lurianic Kabbalah, the act of washing one's hands and reciting the appropriate blessing thereafter attains a new meaning. This action ostensibly constitutes yet another ritual in the endless chain that makes up Jewish life. Yet the doctrine of *tikkun* dramatically expands the meaning of the fulfillment of such mundane chores. The notion of *tikkun* transforms this action into an event that is part of the process of the restitution of the world. Reciting a blessing becomes an attempt to free a divine spark from the material soil and return it to its source. The meaning of sin is likewise enhanced. Committing a sin might now be interpreted as pushing a spark deeper into the shells.

Tikkun thus bestows upon man the power to channel the inner energy of creation and to meddle with the mechanism of the cosmos. "The doctrine of *Tikkun*," Scholem maintains, "raised every Jew to the rank of a protagonist in the great process of restitution."[24] The doctrine thus exerted considerable pressure on every individual, who saw himself as a responsible part of creation. This is obvious: redemption itself was at stake and every act might hinder or hasten the end. "The true worshiper," Scholem writes, "exercises a tremendous power over the inner worlds, just as he bears a correspondingly great responsibility for the fulfillment of the messianic task."[25] According to Scholem's analysis, *tikkun* emerges as something more than a religious concept. It is in fact a doctrine and, as we shall see, constitutes the foundation for an ideology. *Tikkun* occurs not on some mythical plain but in the actual world, and it is implemented not by mythical forces but by human beings.

In his descriptions of the Lurianic Kabbalah, Scholem construed the historical project of *tikkun* as the direct continuation of the mythological tale, but the relation between the myth of exile and the doctrine of *tikkun* warrants careful consideration. Formally, the Lurianic myth ends with a series of momentous complications. As a result of the series of ruptures—the breaking of the vessels and the sin of the first man—that which was once perfectly whole is now shattered. The elevated worlds of spirituality are incomplete and have become detached from the lower worlds of materiality, in which the divine is present only to a limited degree. This is where the myth, as myth, ends, even if the tale is far from complete. The *tikkun* offers every Jew a chance to play an active role in the drama of the universe. The final chapter in the story of the world, from the creation of man to the reintegration of the cosmos, is therefore

24. Scholem, *Major Trends*, 284.
25. Ibid., 276.

yet to be told. Better still, the script for this latter part of the story is yet to be written. In this sense, therefore, God and all of creation are waiting to see how the myth unfolds. They are anticipating, so to speak, the completion of the story of creation, undertaken by the Jews in world history. Thus, with the transition from the breaking of the vessels to the idea of repair, Scholem's account of the Lurianic tale undergoes a fundamental transformation, which he never explicitly discussed. The myth that originated in the realm of the divine transforms into a tale of human action, and the story of extraterrestrial exile turns into contemplation of the living experience of exile in the actual world. In other words, at the moment of transition from the world of *tsimtsum* to the world of *tikkun*, the myth transforms into its dialectical opposite, into history.

This unstated transition from myth to history hinges upon another more fundamental transition: the shifting of responsibility from the divine to the human. This is Scholem's deepest, most consequential argument in his interpretation of the Lurianic myth. The notion of *tikkun* effectively absolves God of responsibility toward the universe and places it on the shoulders of human beings. The state of the universe, according to Scholem, is in the hands of mankind. Put differently, the myth of exile places responsibility for overcoming exile (in its concrete as well as its otherworldly sense) in the hands of a host of individuals, who must now jointly take concrete action in order to reverse the order of creation and overcome the most terrible and deeply rooted form of evil—being in exile.

In the Jewish context, such transference of responsibility is a tantalizing idea. For generations, Jews had ostensibly waited for God to redeem them. Now, the myth informs a completely different notion. In fact, so we learn, it is up to the Jews to act in order to find a home for themselves in this world and for God in His. This idea, Scholem insists, transformed the Jewish people, and its implications should be clearly spelled out. It effectively forces the Jews to abandon their submissive stance toward history, to which they have ostensibly clung ever since the destruction of the Temple in Jerusalem, and to adopt a proactive, political approach that spurs them to action. In other words, the Kabbalah has turned the Jews into a nation in the modern sense. Jews suddenly came to regard themselves as active participants in the formation of world history, engaged, as a collective, in a task of the utmost importance. Thus, Scholem could argue, the Lurianic doctrine had transcended the realm of mythology, becoming a social, political, and spiritual event in the history of the Jewish people. And it is this development that enabled him to argue persuasively that the Lurianic Kabbalah had triggered the creation of modern Judaism.

Scholem hardly marked this momentous transition from the elevated world of myth to the world of human action and history. Instead, he portrays the historical plane and the human protagonist as a natural continuation of heavenly occurrences, since both were part of the Lurianic Kabbalah. Not surprisingly perhaps, the passages in the text in which Scholem blends these otherwise rather distinct spheres of existence probably constitute the most dramatic and moving sections in his rather dry, historical textual work. In these passages, the onetime political activist seems to emerge from the scholarly figure. Scholem's succinct summary of the Lurianic myth delivered at the Eranos conference in 1949 serves as a telling example:[26]

[E]very man, and especially every Jew, participates in the process of the *Tikkun*. This enables us to understand why in Kabbalistic myth the Messiah becomes a mere symbol . . . For it is not the act of the Messiah as executer of the *Tikkun* . . . that brings redemption, but your action and mine. Thus, for all its setbacks, the history of mankind in its exile is looked upon as a steady progress . . . as the logical consequence of a process in which we are all participants. To Luria, the coming of the Messiah means no more than a signature under a document that we ourselves write.[27]

Scholem, furthermore, did not conceal the political implications of the *Kabbalistic* myth, as he envisioned it. He expressed them rather clearly in his closing remarks on the same occasion: "[I]f, as it has been said, all *fulfilled* time is mythical, then surely we may say this: what greater opportunity has the Jewish people ever had than in the horror of defeat, in the struggle and victory of these last years, in its utopian withdrawal into its own history, to fulfill its encounter with its own genius, its true and 'perfect nature'?"[28]

A SOCIETY OF EXILES AND THE IDEOLOGY OF *TIKKUN*

The Lurianic Kabbalah was not merely a theory that could endow certain actions with meaning but, according to Scholem, an idea that in fact propelled people to action and changed history. The doctrine of *tikkun*, he claims, served as the basis for Jewish religious practice and Jewish social organization

26. For more on Scholem's work in the context of the Eranos conferences, see Wasserstrom, *Religion after Religion*.
27. Gershom Scholem, "Kabbalah and Myth," in *On the Kabbalah and Its Symbolism*, 117.
28. Ibid.

beginning in the late sixteenth century in all Jewish communities, everywhere Jews can be found. This argument is fundamental to Scholem's historical analysis. As is discussed in greater detail below, the broad and unusually enthusiastic reception of the Lurianic Kabbalah played an essential role in Scholem's historical analysis. It explained the rise of the Sabbatean movement as well as the ensuing streams in modern Judaism that emerged in response to the Sabbatean debacle. In short, Scholem could not have described Jewish history as he did without assuming that *tikkun* had come to define Jewish existence within historical reality.

And yet the evidence that Scholem provides in support of this general observation is scant. In fact, Scholem never quite describes the society that ostensibly operated under the premise of *tikkun*. As a philologist, he perhaps had little or no access to material that could support such a description. It may also be argued that such a general claim is rather difficult to corroborate. And in fact the suggestion that every Jew throughout the Diaspora, from Sana'a to Amsterdam, accepted and was motivated by the principles of Lurianic Kabbalah seems at least somewhat unlikely.

However, even if the image of the society of the *tikkun* tells us only a little about early modern Jewish culture, it provides a valuable insight into Scholem's social vision. Indeed, Scholem's attempt to imagine how a society built on the premise of *tikkun* may operate yields fascinating results. The following discussion entails, therefore, an attempt to take the principles of the *tikkun* to their practical conclusions. In other words, it seeks to describe the kind of Jewish community that is based on devotion to this principle. In this community both the behavior of the individual members of the collective and the group ethics were to be determined in accordance with *tikkun* and the aspiration to reverse the order of exile through action.

According to Scholem's description, the *tikkun* functions as a uniquely Jewish intellectual doctrine that determines its adherents' entire worldview and social activity. It is therefore fitting that Scholem should attribute to the Lurianic Kabbalah the charged term 'ideology.' In his book on Sabbatai Zevi published in 1957 he notes, "the inner world which the Kabbalists discovered in their symbolic forms [originally] did not have a function primarily in terms of a social ideology of any kind. But once Kabbalism came to perform a social function it did so by providing an *ideology* for popular religion."[29] Luria's Kabbalah can be

29. Gershom Scholem, *Sabbatai Sevi* (Princeton: Princeton University Press, 1976), 23. Emphasis added.

cast as an ideology because it defines the condition of the Jews—all of them—as 'being in Exile.' But 'exile' should be understood here as a worldview, or a prism through which one devises and explains one's past, present, and the means by which one could revolutionize one's existential position in the world. Exile was, therefore, to be understood not at face value as a historical event, but as a phenomenon that urges one to action.

The single most important element in this ideology was, according to Scholem, the idea of *tikkun* or repair. As we have seen, this notion essentially linked everyday actions with the restitution of the world, thereby transforming every act and every religious ritual into an ethical standard of behavior, under the assumption that strict adherence to the rules of *tikkun* should ultimately lead to the complete resolution of the cosmological and worldly drama. As Scholem noted, "This new doctrine of God and the universe corresponds to the new moral idea of humanity which it propagates: the ideal of the ascetic whose aim is the messianic reformation, the extinction of the world's blemish, the restitution of all things God—the man of spiritual action who through the Tikkun breaks the exile, the *historical exile* of the community of Israel *and* the *inner exile* in which all creation groans."[30]

According to the principles of *tikkun*, every single act could be the last one and every single moment could be crucial to the process of restitution, and therefore no act could be unimportant or insignificant. This, as noted above, "raised *every* Jew to the rank of a protagonist in the great process of restitution."[31] But this naturally also meant that in order to harness oneself to the mission, one need not be outstanding in any sense. It required one to be aware of the inner meanings of one's action and to devote oneself to it, but nothing more.

The Lurianic Kabbalah thus transcends most religious schemes by endowing even the simplest act of piety with extraordinarily special meaning. The Jewish code of law, the *halakha*, is an obvious case in point. Every act in one's daily life—from one's moment of waking, through one's familial and business interactions, procreating, eating, and up to the moment one surrenders to sleep—is subject to the edicts of the law. This way every act—from the most glorious act of piety to the most inconspicuous dietary prohibition—attains significance in the ultimate mission to repair the world. While this doctrine, or rather ideology, does not render great acts of piety meaningless, it places the emphasis on mundane acts and on regular people. In fact, since every man, woman,

30. Scholem, *Major Trends*, 286. Emphasis added.
31. Ibid., 284. My emphasis.

or child has certain halakhic and moral obligations, they are each granted direct access to the *tikkun* and assume responsibility for it. This agency entrusted to individuals is so radical that the equality derived from it is absolute. Each and every action might free up a spark; any person may reverse the movement of time at any moment. According to this worldview, then, money and political power are meaningless when compared with the potential vested in simple people through their mundane actions.

Somewhat paradoxically, the almost anarchic impulse of *tikkun* becomes a basis for social organization. According to many modern religious doctrines, the decision to participate in the morning prayer or to adhere to dietary restrictions is relegated to the private sphere. Under the premise of *tikkun*, however, good deeds as well as transgressions assume dramatic import. If every action of every Jew might hinder or hasten the end, it follows that every action of every Jew becomes the responsibility of all those who have a common goal and therefore share the same fate. *Tikkun* thus introduced a new form of socialization. It enforced solidarity and mutual responsibility, thereby creating the conditions for a shared social body. In effect, Scholem's depiction of the doctrine of *tikkun* entails a social body that comprises spiritual actors who work in concert for a better future and that organizes itself around the concepts of agency, mutual responsibility, and equality. Thus the group of people that commonly understood itself as 'being in exile' became a cohesive and ideological whole, that is, a community.[32]

Scholem emphasizes the egalitarian social vision of the Lurianic Kabbalah in his discussion of the role of the Messiah. According to his interpretation of the Lurianic Kabbalah, the Messiah was merely a symbol for the world of restitution. "The world of the *Tikkun*," Scholem argues, "is the world of messianic action."[33] In other words, the Messiah is not conceived here as an extraordinary leader who galvanizes his people. In the context of the *tikkun*, in which each and every Jew plays a small messianic role, the Messiah symbolizes the coordinated effort to redeem the world. This emphatically nontraditional conception of the role of the Messiah is further expressed by a subtle

32. Here I refer to Tönnies's definition of community (*Gemeinschaft*) which he developed in his seminal work. See Ferdinand Tönnies, *Gemeinschaft und Gesellschaft* (Leipzig: Fues, 1887), esp. 9–41. It may also be noted that this notion of *Gemeinschaft* was enthusiastically adopted by the German youth movement in the years before World War I. See for example Ulrike Pilarczyk, "Gemeinschaft. Jüdische Jugendfotographie 1924 bis 1938," in *Deutsch-Jüdische Jugendliche im "Zeitalter der Jugend*, ed. Yotam Hotam (Göttingen: Vandenhoeck & Ruprecht, 2009), 75–93.

33. Scholem, *Major Trends*, 274.

yet important stylistic gesture. In his discussion of the Messiah in the Lurianic Kabbalah, Scholem suddenly shifts from the ubiquitous third person form to the first person plural: "In a sense therefore we are not only masters of our own identity, and in the last resort are ourselves responsible for the continuation of the *Galut*, but we also fulfill a mission which reaches far beyond that."[34] In other words, the Messiah has no concrete role in the system of the *tikkun*, and it is rather up to "us," as Scholem notes in no uncertain terms, to redeem the world.

Seen through the prism of Lurianic ideology, not only the contemporary social order but also the past and the future were duly arranged and explained. The future of the Jewish people was conceived as a redeemed or messianic future. When a sufficient number of Jews have fulfilled their mission and released all the sparks from their material prison, the world of exile will come to an end. This was the promise of the Lurianic Kabbalah and the motivation for engaging in the practice of *tikkun*. Past events were likewise fitted into the Lurianic scheme, most importantly the Spanish expulsion. Through the Lurianic looking glass, Scholem suggests, the Alhambra decree, which forced all the Jews out of the Iberian Peninsula in 1492, appeared as yet another mundane expression of a deeper reality. In fact, as we shall see below, the Spanish catastrophe instigated the creation of the Lurianic myth, which imparted to this otherwise inexplicable tragedy a new meaning. In short, the entire gamut of experience, the present social condition, the past, and the imagined future were made meaningful by placing them into the Lurianic scheme, which thus took shape as an ideology in the exact sense of the word.[35]

It is not entirely clear whether, and if so to what extent, Scholem believed that such an ideologically driven society had actually existed in Jewish history. The notion that an egalitarian, spiritual, committed, and cohesive society once existed seems somewhat unlikely. The idea that Jews throughout the Diaspora adopted this ideology without reservation seems even less plausible. Nevertheless, the ideology of *tikkun* played a decisive role in Scholem's historical account. The dissemination of the Lurianic Kabbalah, Scholem argues, sowed the seeds of Sabbatai Zevi's messianic misadventure by generating an unbearable social tension. "The spread of Lurianic Kabbalism with the doctrine of *Tikkun* . . . ," Scholem states in *Major Trends*, "could not but lead to an explosive

34. Ibid.
35. Compare Susan Silbey, "Ideology," *The Cambridge Dictionary of Sociology*, ed. Bryan S. Turner (Cambridge: Cambridge University Press, 2006), 279–80.

manifestation of all those forces to which it owed its rise and success."[36] And as
will be elaborated in chapter 5, Scholem understood Jewish modernity as a reaction to the Sabbatean debacle. Scholem perceived Frankism, the Haskalah,
liberalism, Hasidism, and ultimately even Zionism to constitute responses to
and a continuation of the Jewish theory of action that originated in the Lurianic Kabbalah. Implicitly, therefore, Scholem does indeed claim that the society of the *tikkun* existed and that the ideas about the curtailment of exile were
indeed applied as actions in the world. In other words, long before Zionism
was even imagined, the Jewish people had formed a cohesive entity compris-
ing free and equal individuals dedicated to the spiritual task of redeeming this
world and bringing exile to an end. This was Scholem's thesis.

FROM KABBALAH TO JEWISH MODERNISM

Scholem's assertion that the Lurianic Kabbalah became an engine for social
change by evolving as a cohesive ideology for Jews in the Diaspora is important
for several different reasons. It allows him, first and foremost, to explain the rise
of the Sabbatean movement. But at the same time this claim introduces a subtle
but important shift in Scholem's work. With this suggestion the very subject
matter of the book *Major Trends in Jewish Mysticism* is tacitly transformed. In
its entirety, the book traces the evolution of the mystical idea throughout Jewish history. Following a phenomenological analysis of the idea of Jewish mysticism in the first lecture, Scholem proceeds to address the mystical idea in the
period prior to the destruction of the Second Temple in Jerusalem. He then
follows the development of the mystical tradition (leaving at least one notable
gap)[37] up to what he believed was the decline of mysticism in Judaism with the
advent of the Enlightenment and liberalism in Central Europe in the eighteenth century. In other words, Scholem traces the entire history of the mystical
idea in Judaism from an original prerabbinical era to the decline of religiosity
in the modern age. However, while his account of Jewish mysticism from the
second century BC to the sixteenth century AD focuses on the mystical idea,
its variations and its developments, his discussion in the subsequent and final
two chapters moves on to the social and political events in Jewish history. In

36. Scholem, *Major Trends*, 287.
37. Most notably, in *Major Trends* Scholem does not discuss the emergence of Kabbalism
in the twelfth century with the book *Bahir*. See Gershom Scholem, *Ursprung und Anfänge der
Kabbala* (Berlin: Walter de Gruyter, 2001).

other words, with the discussion of the Lurianic Kabbalah in the seventh lecture of *Major Trends*, the book changes course from addressing the history of the mystical idea to portraying the social history of the Jewish people as it was shaped by mystical ideas.

This fundamental shift in Scholem's discussion is based on a historical observation. According to Scholem, the Spanish expulsion of 1492 wrought radical social and ideological changes in Jewish life and thought. Having believed throughout the Middle Ages that they could live a perfectly fulfilled life in exile, Jews were now shaken by the catastrophe. The sudden expulsion of the most sophisticated, productive, and well-integrated Jewish community in the Diaspora forced them to face the existential conundrum of life in exile. What was the meaning and sense of an entire history of banishment and exile? Why were the chosen people subjected to it? And ultimately, what could be done to curtail the period of life in exile? According to Scholem, the Kabbalists in general, and above all the Kabbalist of Safed, Rabbi Isaac Luria, were the first to offer tangible and suggestive answers to these questions. And this was the reason, Scholem claims, for the immediate and widespread dissemination of the Kabbalah.

The Spanish expulsion thus informs a dual transformation. On the one hand, Scholem maintains, the Kabbalah underwent radical change, and on the other hand the Jewish people underwent a deep transformation. Historically, the Kabbalah had always consisted of mysterious ideas, convoluted mythological schemes, and esoteric symbols. It was confined and restricted because its secrets were deemed dangerous. However, as a result of the expulsion and with the emergence of the Lurianic myth, the Kabbalah became a doctrine for the masses. As Scholem puts it in the first lines of the seventh chapter of his *Major Trends*, "After the exodus from Spain, Kabbalism underwent a complete transformation. A catastrophe of this dimension, which uprooted one of the main branches of the Jewish people, could hardly take place without affecting every sphere of human life and feeling. In the great material and spiritual upheaval of that crisis, Kabbalism established its claim to the spiritual domination of Judaism. This fact became immediately obvious in its transformation from an esoteric into a popular doctrine."[38] Consequently, by incorporating this mystic ideology into its religious imagination, the Jewish people changed. In Scholem's words, "Kabbalism triumphed because it provided a valid answer to the great problems of the time. To a generation to which the facts of exile and the precariousness of existence in it had become a most pressing and cruel

38. Scholem, *Major Trends*, 244.

problem, Kabbalism could give an answer unparalleled in breadth and in depth of vision. The Kabbalistic answer illuminated the significance of exile and redemption and accounted for the unique historical situation of Israel within the wider, in fact cosmic context of creation itself."[39]

With this dual argument, Scholem effectively fuses the Kabbalah and the national narrative of the Jewish people. It is, to be sure, a rather entangled historical observation. On the one hand, Scholem claims, the mystical idea of Judaism, which was always esoteric and elitist, transformed in order to address the conundrum created by the historical upheaval in Spain. On the other hand, Jews of every walk of life enthusiastically received the Kabbalah because it offered an answer to a pressing question in an hour of need. Thus both the Kabbalah and the Jewish people were transformed in the wake of the renewed sense of exile and, so to speak, found each other. As a result, the religious consciousness of the Jewish nation transformed as it incorporated the mystical ideas into its mainstream thought and practice and disseminated them beyond the walls of the cloisters to become a thing of the people.

This observation is pivotal to Scholem's assumption about the history of the Jewish people. Once the mystical idea was incorporated into mainstream religious practice, he implies, the history of mysticism became a history of the Jewish people. Ostensibly, the ideological developments of the Kabbalah now began to affect an entire nation, its practices, and eventually also its history. Therefore, the developments in the mystical teachings informed the events in the people's social history. At the same time, since the Kabbalists now deemed national history a worthy object of mystical meditation, the social history of the Jewish people was being recorded in the manuscripts of the Kabbalah. In short, as a result of Spanish expulsion the Kabbalah became a driving force in Jewish history, which was now described in Kabbalistic terms and expressed in mythological symbols. If this is indeed the case, then it follows that the history of Jewish mysticism and the social history of the Jews had fused into one and the same thing. It furthermore follows that the expert on Jewish mysticism is afforded a unique view of Jewish history.

This complex argument has been criticized by a younger generation of Kabbalah scholars as well as by social historians. Contemporary scholars of the Kabbalah tend to reject the contention that the Kabbalah transformed as a result of the Spanish expulsion.[40] And contemporary social historians argue

39. Scholem, *Sabbatai Sevi*, 20.

40. See, for example, Idel, "One from a Town"; Moshe Idel, "Subversive Katalysatoren: Gnosis und Messianismus in Gershom Scholems Verständnis der jüdischen Mystik," in

against the notion that the Kabbalah came to play such a decisive role in shaping the ideological streams of the Jewish people.[41] These critiques, however, should not alter the focus of our discussion here. Without ever making this point explicitly, Scholem portrays the Kabbalah as a fundamental aspect of Jewish society. Indeed, in his monumental achievement *Major Trends in Jewish Mysticism*, Scholem successfully describes how the historical trajectory of an entire people was dramatically and unexpectedly shaped by the visions of mystics and myths.

Considering the immense importance of his historical observation about the effects of the Spanish expulsion for Scholem's historical paradigm, it is striking to note how scarce the material evidence that he offers in its support is. Scholem provides practically no evidence to substantiate his claim that the Kabbalah had indeed become so widespread and influential. This is not altogether surprising. Scholem was not, after all, a social historian but a philologist, and the manuscripts he studied could have recorded such social changes only indirectly. It is therefore understandable that he could offer no real proof that the Jewish people had indeed understood the Lurianic myth as an inner explanation of the Spanish catastrophe, or that the Kabbalists had indeed ventured into the secret realm in order to confront the conundrum of the Spanish upheaval, rather than for other reasons.

Some noticed the problematic character of this historical assertion immediately. Joseph Weiss, one of Scholem closest students, wrote the following lines in a diary entry from 1943. "Two weeks ago I bothered Scholem after class . . . with questions about the relation between the Ari's Kabbalah and the travails of the Spanish expulsion. He assumes that the exile that became the central issue in the gnostic speculation of the Lurianic Kabbalah has a direct causal relation to the historical events. That is to say, the transformation of the mystical thought to gnosis—is the result of external reasons . . . I disputed him and mentioned H. Jonas . . . Eventually he dismissed me with nothing."[42]

Gershom Scholem, *Zwischen den Disziplinen*, ed. Peter Schaefer and Gary Smith (Frankfurt am Main: Suhrkamp, 1995), 80–121; Moshe Idel, "On Mobility, Individuals, and Groups: Prolegomenon for a Sociological Approach to Sixteenth-Century Kabbalah," *Kabbalah: Journal for the Study of Jewish Mystical Texts* 3 (1998): 145–73.

41. See, for example, Jacob Barnai, *The Sabbatean Movement—The Social Perspective* (in Hebrew) (Jerusalem: Shazar, 2000); Shmuel Feiner, *The Origins of Jewish Secularization in Eighteenth-Century Europe*, trans. Chana Naor (Philadelphia: University of Pennsylvania Press, 2010), 64–83.

42. Quoted from Noam Zadoff, *Gershom Scholem and Joseph Weiss: Correspondence*, 12.

Still, most commentators have not seen the problem, and this fact alone calls for some attention. Indeed, the reason Scholem's argument seems plausible has to do with the role of the Spanish Golden Age in the Jewish imagination of his time. The plausibility of the answer uncovers the deeper layers of Scholem's historical narrative. For, in fact, Scholem's historiography is tacitly based on the 'Sephardic mystique.' As Ismar Schorsch argues, Jewish Spanish or *Sephardic* culture served in the nineteenth-century German Jewish imagination as a symbol of everything a Jewish community could become. It was the gold standard for Jewish emancipation because it was deemed to be both more Jewish and more open to the non-Jewish environment.[43] Obviously, this image was aligned with the new self-perception of the Jews in modern Central Europe. Ismar Schorsch notes, "The full-blown cultural critique of the *Haskalah* (German Jewry's ephemeral Hebraic version of the European Enlightenment) drew much of its validation, if not inspiration, directly from Spain. The advocacy of secular education, the curbing of *Talmudic* exclusivity and the resumption of studies in Hebrew grammar, biblical exegesis, and Jewish philosophy, and the search for historical exemplars led to a quick rediscovery of Spanish models and achievements."[44]

By the turn of the twentieth century the idea of Sephardic culture was already clearly manifested in myriad aspects of Jewish life in Germany. As Schorsch shows, it was a motivating factor in synagogue architecture (known as 'Moorish style'),[45] prayer books (which exhibited an overwhelming bias not only toward Sephardic liturgy but also to Sephardic pronunciation of Hebrew), Hebrew literature (which imitated the Sephardic poetic example), and scholarship (which depicted medieval Spanish Jewry not only as culturally diverse but as harbingers of Greek philosophy in Christian Europe). In short, the image of the Golden Age of Sephardic Jewry was a fixture in German Jewish

43. See Ismar Schorsch, "The Myth of Sephardic Supremacy," *Leo Baeck Institute Yearbook* 34 (1989): 47–66.

44. Ibid., 49.

45. The assertion that the design of nineteenth-century synagogues was influenced by "Sephardic" bias was challenged by Ivan Davidson Kalmar. See "Moorish Style: Orientalism, the Jews, and Synagogue Architecture," *Jewish Social Studies* 7 (2001): 68–100. Kalmar, however, notes that "references to medieval Sephardic synagogues appear only in the last decades of the nineteenth century, when the Moorish-style synagogue was possibly past its heyday. Even then, we shall see, references to Muslim Spain and its Jews are embedded in broader references to the Orient (i.e., the world of Islam) as a whole." This indicates that for the time period relevant to this study, the connection between synagogue architecture and the "Sephardic" tradition is nevertheless valid.

self-consciousness, and therefore a living symbol for Scholem and his most immediate audience. To them *Sepharad* served as a model of cultural receptiveness, sophistication, and excellence that they could only attempt to imitate.

Scholem draws upon this complex network of associations in his argument about the proliferation of the Kabbalah in the wake of the expulsion. According to him, the reception of the Lurianic Kabbalah was as wide and as deep as the shock of the expulsion. This conclusion seems to follow directly from the premise. The greater Sepharad was, the more terrible was its fall, and the more demanding were the questions that must have surfaced in the aftermath of the catastrophe. If, therefore, the Lurianic Kabbalah offered, as Scholem indeed argues, the only tangible solution to these penetrating questions, it must follow that the Kabbalah had spread to every location at which these questions were asked. Since Jewish Spain ostensibly played such a significant role in its time, its collapse reverberated throughout the Jewish world and was followed closely by the Lurianic Kabbalah, offering answers. This constitutes Scholem's explanation of the dissemination of the Kabbalah in the wake of the Spanish expulsion. And it was a claim that required, in Scholem's own context, no further proof. It is structured as an analytical argument: since Sepharad was a fixture, its downfall called for a radical explanation. Similarly, the contention that the spiritual elite sought deeper explanations for the trauma and that the popular mind desired these explanations needed no scholarly references. These claims appear to be self-evident conclusions drawn from the obvious mystique built upon the splendor of this community and the tragedy of its fall. In fact, this conclusion might very well have been based on more recent historical experience. During the second half of the twentieth century the cruel destruction of arguably some of the most prosperous and well-integrated communities in Jewish history again called for an urgent explanation.

Scholem's argument about the proliferation of the Kabbalah in the wake of the Spanish upheaval should thus be read as more than a reference to an existing dogma about the Golden Age in Spain. It is likewise a polemic against the traditional role of *Sephardic* culture in the contemporary imagination, conducted by shifting the focus of discussion from the grandeur of the Spanish Jewish "Golden Age" to its inexplicable downfall. Eventually, Scholem tacitly argues, exile was a fundamental experience even for the most prosperous and well-integrated community in Jewish history. Even the greatest community in Jewish history, in other words, could not escape the paradigmatic Jewish fate of exile. For this reason, exile had to be understood as more than a mere historical or political problem. The condition of exile was also, or perhaps primarily, an existential problem. And, indeed, in his discussion of exile Scholem never mentions the loss of life, property, income, and social stature that the Spanish exiles certainly endured. Rather, to him the problem of exile was first and foremost one of general, philosophical, theological, and existential proportions. Scholem notes, "The exiles from Spain must have held an intense belief in the fiendish realities of exile, a belief that was bound to destroy the illusion that it was possible to live peacefully under the Holy Law in exile. It presented itself in a vigorous insistence upon the fragmentary character of Jewish existence . . . Life was conceived as Existence in Exile and in self-contradiction, and the suffering of Exile was linked up to the central Kabbalistic doctrines about God and man."[46] With this observation Scholem expands his assertion about the Kabbalah and the Spanish expulsion to its fullest proportions. If exile was not merely a problem that affected one's political power or one's economic stability, if it was indeed an existential problem, then it necessarily confronted not only the Jews banished from Spain in 1942, but also Scholem's own German Jewish community, and in fact every Jewish community that failed to choose Zion as the solution to its continued existence in exile.

Scholem did not discuss this general aspect. In his works he addresses only the Spanish exiles of the fifteenth century, who were forced to come to terms with their sudden loss. Yet this loss, Scholem's argument implies, is shared by those who, four centuries later, adopted the Sephardic past as a model and a guide for their own cultural aspirations. How could the worst of fates have befallen the most cultivated, well-integrated, and successful Jewish community of all? Scholem's analysis is purely historical. In the sixteenth century, he maintains, the solution to the problem of exile was found in the mystical myth of Rabbi Isaac Luria. Furthermore, integration of the Kabbalistic myth of exile into everyday life had significant historical ramifications, including, as we shall see in the following chapters, the rise of the Sabbatean movement and the splintering of Jewish consciousness that ensued.

To his contemporary readership Scholem thus offered no more than provocations. But these provocations exist within a certain intellectual atmosphere. Indeed, Scholem's tacit calls to reevaluate the memory of Sepharad partakes in a larger scholarly discussion and thus continues and answers the work of others, most notably that of his colleague from the Hebrew University Yitzhak Fritz Baer. Scholem effectively argues that the quintessential legacy of Sepharad was to be found not in its cultural receptiveness or poetic sophistication, but in the

46. Scholem, *Major Trends*, 249.

manner in which it faced up to the problem of exile. The real lesson of the Sephardic "Golden Age," it follows, is that even for the most cultivated and well-integrated society in Jewish memory it was exile rather than wealth and culture that defined Jewish existence. Baer makes this point explicitly in a book originally published in 1936,[47] which David Myers rightly describes as "decidedly lugubrious."[48] According to Baer, the downfall of Sepharad was prepared from within. "Whenever Jewish communities developed to any considerable extent," Baer writes, "they fell sick to the diseases characteristic of the . . . *ancien régime* . . . Rich families separated themselves from the community; in Spain and Italy especially, they gave their children to non-religious education and followed a worldly course of life."[49] Baer's argument about Spanish indifference to the problem of exile and the need for redemption is echoed in Scholem's analysis of the Kabbalah of the same period. "The mystical meditations of the Kabbalists [before the expulsion] on theogony and cosmogony thus produced non-Messianic and individualistic modes of salvation."[50] In other words, medieval Kabbalah, the center for which was in Spain, was, according to Scholem, theoretical and decidedly apolitical. As such it was uninterested in the problem of Exile and ill prepared for the tragedy that lay ahead.

With this lesson in hand Scholem proceeds to excavate the Jewish mystical past and the social history of the Jews. His study of the mystical tradition thus constituted a further provocation. In the forgotten and misunderstood realm of mystical thinking Scholem found the Lurianic Kabbalah, which, he believed, embodied a social, political, historical, and spiritual idea about confronting exile. Just as Yitzhak Baer construed Judah Ha-Levi and Don Isaac Abarvanel as the "Heroes of Galut,"[51] so too Scholem construed Rabbi Isaac Luria, the lion, as a champion. The Ari could not have offered a solution to the problem in any simple sense, but rather, as we shall see next, he created an entirely new way of

47. Yitzhak Baer, *Galut* (Berlin: Schocken Verlag, 1936).

48. Myers, *Re-inventing the Jewish Past*, 120.

49. Yitzhak Baer, *Galut* (New York: Schocken Books, 1947), 47. This book was originally published in 1936. See note 47.

50. Scholem, *Major Trends*, 245.

51. Myers, *Re-inventing the Jewish Past*, 121. In his discussion of Yitzhak Baer's book *Galut*, Myers argues that "Baer joins a long line of premodern Jewish thinkers whose response to the catastrophe has been to assert the inviolability of the bond between the Jewish people and their God." I accept Myers's observation but argue conversely that one has to reverse the order of things. Rather than seeing Baer as a continuation of an already existing tradition, it is necessary to keep in mind the possibility that Baer was the one who constructed Judah Ha-Levi and Don Isaac Abarvanel as his predecessors.

thinking, one that was direct and forthright even though it originated from the complex symbolic literature of the Kabbalah.

JEWISH MYTH, JEWISH POLITICS

The power and allure of Scholem's Myth of Exile stem, it would seem, from its successful recreation of a myth, in the German romantic sense of the term. As we have seen, the myth of exile is located at the juncture of politics, society, and religion, merging these otherwise conflicting elements almost seamlessly into one other. It touches upon all these issues, and while it resolves none, it mysteriously manages to overcome them. With this work, therefore, Scholem fulfilled his youthful ambition to become an excavator of the past, an agent of symbols, and a narrator of myths. More precisely, with his unfolding of the Lurianic myth Scholem became a captivating, evocative, and convincing author. The facts of the historical matter are therefore of secondary importance here. The point is that Scholem's interpretation of the Lurianic Kabbalah suggests a broad lesson about Jewish life, its revival and history. While Scholem never explicitly made such a claim or divulged what this lesson may be, the gist is rather clear. With this tale, Scholem tacitly asserts that the tensions between the spiritual and the social realms and between the national and private worlds had once, in the past, been resolved and had effectively disappeared. Moreover, the myth of exile, in Scholem's narration, proves that these various contradictory elements of the human experience can be reconciled through symbols that possess the power to synthesize these opposites into a new whole.

The myth of exile goes directly to the heart of the young Gershom Scholem's political concern, silently rekindling the activism of his youth. As we have seen in chapter 2 above, Scholem had personally faced many tensions in his attempts to formulate his positions on political and internal struggles. He strove to overcome these tensions through his engagement with the Zionist youth movements, which purported to pave the way for a new, harmonious social arrangement. During the early years of his activism Scholem conceived of 'Zion' as something that belonged exclusively to the youth and that was thus untouched by the problems of politics, society and justice. Yet this outlook was not easily explained and quite impossible to realize. Probably for this reason it also gained little traction among his Zionist friends and fellow activists. This difficulty, as we have also seen, effectively impeded Scholem's personal aspirations. He yearned to recreate a myth for his own people, assuming, in the tradition of German romanticism, that it alone could overcome the tensions of spiritual nationalism. Yet he experienced nothing but disappointment. "Today

I still can't write," Scholem noted in his diary; "I am a composer of symbolic literature comprehensible only to myself."[52] Eventually he chose an academic discipline, first mathematics and then philology. This choice created yet another irresolvable problem. The myth must ameliorate the contradictions of experience and serve as a catalyst for personal and national spiritual rejuvenation. Philology, on the other hand, was bound by the facts of the past. There was no middle ground, and yet Scholem seemed to have found something of a solution:[53]

Scholem's society of *tikkun* is as close as he ever came to explaining what 'Zion' and 'Zionist Youth' might really look like. As mentioned previously, the young Scholem advocated rejuvenation of the Jewish spirit. In order to achieve this, he called upon Jews to isolate the new Zion from European (and especially German) influence. While Scholem's advocacy may have stirred some emotions, it was largely overlooked by the active forces of history and the mainstream Zionist movement. His political activity in Palestine, discussed in the next chapter, would prove to be even more marginal and, as far as it was heeded at all, more polarizing. These developments, however, could have been foreseen. Scholem sought to persuade his peers to adopt ideas that were somewhat outlandish. Through Zionism he hoped to provide a solution to the social ills of modern Europe by building an open yet cohesive, free yet Jewish society. But this vision left many questions unanswered. How was it possible to create a deeply spiritual yet fully functioning Jewish collective? Upon which principles would its activity, organization, hierarchy, and historical consciousness be established? How would it define its goals and generate solidarity among its members?

Scholem never quite addresses these problems in his youthful political writing, but in his reading of the Lurianic Kabbalah he appears to be offering some indirect answers. This is not to suggest that Scholem advocated a return to the Kabbalah in any practical sense. The Kabbalah, he believed, was a thing of the past. By the twentieth century it had lost its hold on political, social, or even religious reality.[54] But it could still serve as a historical example. Scholem tacitly argues here that Jewish history had already dealt with the issue of the feasibility of Jewish ideology. He claims that Judaism had successfully provided conceptual tools whereby Jews could deliberate on their actions in the world, their

52. Scholem, *Lamentations of Youth*, 287.

53. It is in this context that Andreas Kilcher's remarks about Scholem's philology have distinct resonance. See Kilcher, "Philology as Kabbalah."

54. Huss, "Ask No Questions."

social condition, and their past. According to Scholem, the historical precedent already existed. The Jews qua Jews had in the past forged a spiritual and cohesive community whose members had acted in concert to resolve their existential state of exile. This was, furthermore, a project in which all Jews were equally engaged and for which they were mutually responsible. Effectively, therefore, Scholem argues that the Lurianic Kabbalah precipitated the emergence of the body politic of the Jewish people, which, furthermore, derived its ideological principles from its own spiritual tradition. The historical record therefore showed that Jews had not needed to adopt foreign ideologies in the past. It appeared, therefore, to follow that they had no need to do so in the present.

Furthermore, this Jewish body politic, which had apparently come into being in the sixteenth century in the wake of the Lurianic Kabbalah and the Spanish banishment, had its own distinctive history. The ideology of Lurianic exile represented only the first phase in a convoluted historical path. As we shall see in subsequent chapters, the new Jewish ideology planted the seed of (messianic) hope in the heart of the nation. This developed, according to Scholem, into the Sabbatean messianic movement, which in turn ultimately brought about terrible disappointment on the plane of history. The Lurianic Kabbalah facilitated the creation of the Sabbatean movement, which in turn transformed into (among others things) the Hasidic movement, the Jewish enlightenment (Haskalah), and eventually also into Liberal Judaism. This was the history of the modern Jewish nation, according to Scholem. Thus, while purporting to be merely a study of a forgotten tradition, Scholem's historical work appears to be at the same time a fully fledged account of the emergence of modern Jewish political history. Without the mystical tradition, Scholem in effect claims, one cannot understand the pivotal historical moments and the fundamental social movements that define Jewish modernity. More important, without understanding this past, it is impossible to confront the future problems of Jewish politics, nationhood, and spirituality.

The significance that Scholem attributes to the Kabbalah also endows with special meaning his polemics against scholars who, he believed, had insufficiently appreciated the Kabbalah in their studies. In an article in the annual literary supplement of the daily newspaper *Ha'aretz*, which was published in 1944, Scholem went as far as blaming them for filling rows of graves with the dead Jewish past.[55] At that moment, such accusations could not have been merely metaphorical. Indeed, more than by any other group of thinkers,

55. Gershom Scholem, "Thoughts on the School of Jewish Studies," in *Devarim be-go*, 385–404.

Scholem was outraged by the members of the Wissenschaft des Judentums, who, he repeatedly claimed, were blinded by their European liberal tendencies and had as a result neglected the study of the Kabbalah. For this reason, Scholem never seemed to tire of chastising this previous generation of scholars for misunderstanding the Kabbalah. And the discussion of the Lurianic Kabbalah, which was also published in the 1940s, seems to give the debate about the Wissenschaft des Judentums deeper meaning.

Although Scholem never makes this point explicitly, the spiritual and political poignancy that he attributes to the Kabbalah may explain the anger he felt toward those who had forgotten it. The Jewish mystical myth informed a Jewish historical experience that found within itself the resources to imagine its own ideological and political revival. Ignoring the importance of the Kabbalah, it follows, repressed the possibility of a historic national and spiritual revival of the Jewish people in the present day. This interpretation becomes all the more powerful if one imagines Scholem's rendition of the Lurianic myth of exile in light of contemporary events. The tragedy of banishment and persecution, the spiritual crisis that envelopes an entire nation, regardless of their current location, and the question of hope and of God's presence, which Scholem describes in his reworking of Luria's myth of exile, must have seemed all too familiar to Scholem's 1940s audience. Again, Scholem did not believe that the Kabbalah constituted a viable principle for contemporaneous Judaism. But he offered it as an essential resource for the renewal of its spirit on the strength of its own distinct past, unhindered by the European experience.

It is thus somewhat ironic that Scholem's work, including these very arguments, is so closely bound up with the German culture in which he grew up and with which he was so intimately familiar. As shown in chapter 2, Scholem speculated about the importance of myth as a focal point for spiritual and national rejuvenation in the spirit of the German romantic tradition, long before he ever studied the Kabbalah. It was also shown that Scholem advocated the creation of a Jewish political-spiritual community in the spirit of the German youth movement long before he took a specific interest in the history of the Kabbalah.

Scholem's discovery of the historic import of the Kabbalah constitutes a direct continuation of his ambitions as a young political activist in the Zionist circles of Berlin before and during World War I. Already then he dreamt of becoming a scribe, writing the Jewish myth for the renewal of his nation. Already then he sought to write the myth of exile. As a young activist, Scholem was for the most part unsuccessful. No one seemed to seriously consider what appeared to be outlandish, extreme, and unattainable ideas. Yet as a historian, Scholem had a significant impact. His myths are read to this day; his history is considered canonical. It would thus appear that when a mature and acclaimed historian speaks to an educated audience, his words sound different, even if he speaks with the voice of a young rebel.

CHAPTER 4

When a Dream Comes True:
Zionist Politics in Palestine, 1923–1931

By God, this is not what we wanted.

[Bei Gott, es war ja nicht dieses das was wir wollten.]

GERSHOM SCHOLEM, "Zionism Will Survive," 1924

Strangely, being in exile entails an almost equal measure of despair and hope. Living in a foreign land, among strangers who speak a foreign language, invariably induces a deep sense of disorientation. Exile is therefore often a stressful and frustrating experience that touches upon the very foundation of one's identity, sense of self, and existence. On the other hand, the knowledge that exile is by nature a transitory phase endows the experience with a certain meaning, a sense of direction and hope. In exile, strength stems from the conviction that one day everything will assume its correct place, the world will be at peace, and its original wholeness will be restored. Thus, the suffering of exile is dialectically coupled with the unadulterated hope and belief that eventually everything that is wrong "here" will be repaired "there" and will remain that way forever. Thus, contrary to what we may imagine, a person in exile may feel vibrant, enthusiastic, and full of life. For it is precisely the imperfect reality of exile that fuels the hope of homecoming and turns it into so desirable a notion. The experience of exile, in fact, transforms homecoming into an urgent need and thus also into a concrete possibility. And it is therefore no coincidence that, as Arnold Eisen noted, "Paradise . . . has never preoccupied the Jewish imagination as much as exile."[1]

The coupling of exile and hope was discussed in different contexts and in some detail in chapters 2 and 3. In both cases, the consciousness of exile facilitated the emergence of a revolutionary spirit. In chapter 2, we saw how the young Gershom Scholem dreamed of being at home in Zion while living

1. Eisen, *Galut*, xi.

in Germany. Zionism and the idea of Zion structured his life and gave him a sense of purpose. These elements played such a central role in his life that he was willing to disavow those closest to him, following fundamental disagreement about the essence of the vision. He even completely rejected the Zionist youth movement after a long and arduous struggle to win its approval for what he believed to be a more authentic program. As we have seen, Scholem also rejected his onetime spiritual father, Martin Buber. Nevertheless, he never ceased to believe in the cause.

In exile, the young Scholem saw himself as a member of the revolutionary vanguard: a Zionist, a reformer, and someone who was willing, as he described himself, to "run, head first, into the wall."[2] Scholem assigned himself the role of recorder of the ancient myth of his people, which he would rediscover in order to bring about its spiritual renewal. He would introduce "Zion" to his fellow Zionists. Therefore, although the young Gershom Scholem experienced extremely difficult times and was acutely aware of the material difficulties associated with living in Palestine and of the spiritual and political aberrations of the Zionist movement, he never ceased to hope that "there" things would be better than they were "here." Judging by his posthumously published personal diaries, it indeed appears that his belief in a set of ideals subsumed under the title "Zion" sustained Gershom Scholem as long as he lived in exile. Ultimately, it was also this idea of Zion that motivated him to leave Germany once and for all in the autumn of 1923 and settle in Jerusalem.

As we saw in chapter 3, the Lurianic myth of exile replaced the grim reality of living in exile with excitement, action, and a vision of a better future. This is rather remarkable given that the myth begins with the greatest and deepest form of evil imaginable, namely, the exile of God. It is at once the source of all evil in the world and a representation of the exile experienced by Jews in the world. Nevertheless, through the idea of *tikkun*, the restitution of the world became a possibility. More accurately, through this idea, the power to redeem the world and overcome historic exile was invested in humans. Through their mundane, daily actions, ordinary Jews could turn back time and bring both human and divine exile to an end. This theology had been developed and later received, according to Scholem, as a religious response to the Spanish expulsion of 1492, which Jews perceived as a catastrophe of inordinate proportions in a history of exile and banishment. In the aftermath of the Spanish expulsion, Scholem maintained, the Kabbalah had spread far and wide and had effectively welded the Jewish people into a community of action that shared a common goal and a common hope: to

2. Scholem, *Lamentations of Youth*, 48.

bring exile to an end. The myth thus transforms the horrific events of Jewish history and the purest form of evil into an engine for hope and action.

In both cases, being in exile dialectically corresponds to harboring a deep belief in a better future. However, in the rare event that hopes materialize and dreams come true, nothing remains to divert one's attention from reality. And reality tends to be imperfect, at best partial, temporary, and insufficient. In more direct words, the reality of a fulfilled dream is often a matter of bitter disappointment. In reality, the actual event of homecoming can hardly fulfill the promise it entailed while it was still only a vague and necessarily incomplete idea. Things never quite turn out the way they were dreamt up in the darkness of exile. This was true of Scholem's personal experience in Zion. In September 1923, Scholem finally committed himself to the cause. Having completed his doctoral degree in Munich, he packed his books[3] and headed east, to Palestine. There, he encountered a reality that was radically different from that which he had desired and hoped for. Worse still, this reality proved more powerful than any dream or expectation. And thus Scholem's homecoming, the fulfillment of his Zionist expectation and the realization of his most intimate dream, proved to be something of a nightmare.

The crisis of Scholem's immigration to Palestine, I argue, serves as the most relevant context whereby we may understand his best-known and most influential scholarly project. For it was in Jerusalem during the late 1920s and 1930s that Scholem embarked on his seminal work: writing the history of the Sabbatean messianic movement. In essence, the Sabbatean movement had, according to Scholem, crystallized the revolutionary excitement of the Lurianic myth into a concrete historical and political movement. And here too, the historical experience of messianic hope ended bitterly. Thus, both Scholem's personal experience and the underlying theme of his work on the Sabbatean movement share a common leitmotif, which can be summed up in one word: disappointment. Disappointment serves as the theme of both this and the following chapter. These chapters deal with the crisis that Scholem experienced following his immigration to Palestine, and the crisis of Judaism in the wake of its messianic experience generated by Sabbatai Zevi.

It is important, however, to stress that Scholem's disappointment upon failing to realize his longstanding dream was neither total nor irrevocable. His

---

3. In a letter to Salman Schocken dated September 8, 1923, Scholem notes: "Unexpected circumstances, hopes, and plans have all contributed to the decision to expedite my trip . . . I've even managed to talk my entire personal library into joining me in solidarity. It's already swimming towards Hamburg." Scholem, *Gershom Scholem: A Life in Letters*, 123.

considerable frustration notwithstanding, Scholem never lost faith in the driving forces of the original revolution. He never ceased to believe in the Zionist cause, namely, in the idea that Jews have the right and the duty to rejuvenate their spiritual existence and renew their presence in the Land of Israel. And his fascination with the sources of the Sabbatean messianic movement remained undimmed. Therefore, Scholem's retrospective analysis of messianism and of Zionism produced rather complex results. On the one hand, his enthusiasm for the revolutionary impetus is unmistakable. He regarded and wrote about men of action and revolutionary forces with a certain romantic pathos. And yet Scholem is cagily critical of these visionary, enthusiastic, and revolutionary ideas. His misgivings, it seems, stem from his familiarity with the destructive forces that lodge themselves within belief in a revolutionary historical transformation. Many commentators have misunderstood Scholem's position toward revolutionary messianism. They maintain that Scholem believed the messianic idea to have had an entirely positive effect on Jewish history, facilitating the creation of a historical political agency for the Jews.[4] In fact, however, Scholem appears to be both drawn by and wary of the historic attempts to realize the myth of exile and to lead the people of Israel back to their home, be this in a spiritual or a physical manner, or in both senses in parallel.

Thus, in retrospect, it appears as if Scholem dressed up his revolutionary soul in the suit and tie of a German university professor; while inwardly he remained a raging prophet of the revolution, his external appearance was that of an even-tempered historian who has seen everything. This fact too may have confused scholars. While this view might not be entirely false, the moderation of the romantic spirit should be understood in relation to real, unresolved, perhaps even irresolvable, historical circumstances. After all, Scholem's approach toward messianic and revolutionary phenomena was shaped not only by his political activism and romantic inclination, but also by the experience of having realized his dream and then having to face its imperfections. The following chapter, therefore, will be devoted to this very experience.

HOMECOMING: THE DREAM OF ZION
AND THE REALITY OF PALESTINE

Scholem decided to realize his long-cherished dream and migrate to Palestine at an ominous moment. Both Germany and Palestine were experiencing

---

4. These are discussed in more detail in chapter 4 below.

a drastic economic downturn in the early 1920s. Germany underwent legendary hyperinflation as a result of its war debt. In her frequent letters to her son in Palestine, Scholem's mother, Betty, told of her hardship: "Note that this letter cost 15 million in cash; it will be 30 million from the day after tomorrow."[5] And in another letter she noted, "Just be glad that you've escaped this witches' cauldron."[6] Yet circumstances in Palestine were better only to a degree. There, too, the effects of the postwar recession were clearly evident. To make matters worse, fundraising, which sustained the Zionist project in Palestine, slowed down considerably. The economic crisis in Palestine rapidly developed, according to Anita Shapira, into a crisis of self-confidence among the Zionist leadership and within the project itself: "In the 1920s nobody was certain that this interesting project—Jewish colonization in Palestine—would, indeed, survive."[7]

In Germany, the mouthpiece of the German Zionist Association, the weekly newspaper *Jüdische Rundschau*, conveyed the economic impasse on its front page. Under the menacing title "What Next?" the editorial stated: "The autumn months are approaching and the perturbing question is on the lips of many Zionists: is last year's scenario about to repeat itself? Will the Zionist movement pass the endurance test, something that even the president of the organization [Chaim Weizmann] doubts?"[8] And directly alongside the editorial, in the center of the page, the paper's headline announced: "1 Goldmark = 110 Million." These headlines appeared on the front page of the issue of October 5, 1923, that is, only days after Gershom Scholem finally arrived in Mandatory Palestine.

The Scholem family was well off. Gershom's father, Arthur Scholem, owned a print shop and had made a fortune printing forms for the German army during World War I. During the economic crisis he obtained another lucrative contract from the German government, to print money. Nevertheless, both father and son were too proud to overcome their differences and reach out for help. In his memoir, Scholem recalls that when he informed his father about his impending emigration, his father responded by remarking: "My son, I assume you realize that you cannot expect any financial support for your

5. Scholem, *Gershom Scholem: A Life in Letters*, 124.

6. Ibid., 125.

7. Anita Shapira, *Land and Power: The Zionist Resort to Force, 1881–1948* (Stanford: Stanford University Press, 1999), 131.

8. *Jüdische Rundschau*, October 5, 1923.

undertaking from me."[9] Arthur Scholem was disappointed to hear that his twenty-six-year-old son, who had just received his Ph.D. in Semitic culture from Munich University, had turned down a research position (*Habilstelle*) at Berlin University in order to travel to Palestine.

In Palestine, on the other hand, Scholem had no real prospect of employment. He left Germany with nothing but a handful of contacts and the hope that his German state certification in mathematics would enable him to obtain a teaching position at the Hebrew Gymnasium in Tel Aviv.[10] Nevertheless, Scholem had the good fortune to find employment within a very short period of time. After some institutional finagling and with the help of Samuel Hugo Bergman, he secured a halftime position as a librarian at the newly founded national library in Jerusalem. Like most Zionist enterprises of the time, the library was infused with a sense of historical import. In a letter written in July 1924 to his dissertation advisor Fritz Hommel in Munich, Scholem wrote: "I am the director of the Hebrew division in the Jewish National and University library, which itself serves to prepare the way for a great undertaking that will be closely connected with the rebuilding of the holy land by Jewish hands."[11]

Economically secure, Scholem turned to domestic matters. Only two months after arriving in Jerusalem, he married his first wife, Escha, whom he had known already in Germany.[12] Only a year and a half thereafter he took up a halftime position teaching Kabbalah at the newly founded Institute for Jewish Studies, the seed institute that would later develop into the Hebrew University in Jerusalem.[13]

9. Scholem, *From Berlin to Jerusalem*, 160.

10. "Upon my return to Berlin [from Munich in 1922] I reported for my *Staatsexam* in mathematics . . . I also bought the Hebrew mathematics textbooks which were being used in the Gymnasium in Tel Aviv in order to familiarize myself with the mathematical terminology I would need to know as a teacher in Eretz Yisrael." Scholem, *From Berlin to Jerusalem*, 142.

11. Scholem, *Gershom Scholem: A Life in Letters*, 135.

12. After leaving Switzerland and parting ways with Benjamin, Scholem contemplated what and where to study. His decision to study Semitics in Munich was influenced, to a large degree, by Escha Burchhardt, who wished to live in Munich where she could find kosher food, which was unavailable in smaller university towns. Rees, "Ein Dichter, ein Maedchen und die juedische Speisegesetze. Gershom Scholems Entscheidung fuer Muenchen und die Kabbala."

13. See Scholem, *From Berlin to Jerusalem*, 163–74; Shaul Katz, "Gershom Scholem and His Early Work at the Hebrew University," in *The Chronicles of the Hebrew University—Roots and Beginnings* (in Hebrew), ed. Shaul Katz and Michael Head (Jerusalem: Magnes Press, 1998).

And so by April 1925 Scholem's new life was well under way. He was married and employed. Most important, Scholem now lived in Jerusalem. It would thus indeed seem that Scholem's Zionist odyssey had reached its happy conclusion. This impression was reinforced by Scholem himself, who ended his memoir, published in 1977, at the point when he had become a young and promising professor in a new institution, nestled between the hills of the city of Zion. The title of the memoir, *From Berlin to Jerusalem*, serves only to stress the point further. It perfectly conveys Scholem's self-fashioning, as he relates a coming-of-age tale, describing the protagonist's progression from his unfulfilled state of exile to his self-fulfillment in Zion. According to Scholem, therefore, the story of his life that had begun in Berlin in 1897 ended in 1925 in Jerusalem. Everything that took place after that, the memoir seems to suggest, was in comparison merely a series of benign nonevents and trivialities, and therefore not worth telling. This self-portrait is indeed convincing and was accepted by scholars almost across the board.[14] Yet this narrative was, in fact, selectively crafted to create a certain impression, which is, as is always the case, incomplete.

To judge from his personal writings, letters, and publications from the years 1923–33, Scholem's life reached nothing near the fulfillment that the term Jerusalem (or indeed 'Zion') came to represent. Rather than bringing an end to Scholem's difficulties after many years of yearning, the reality of life in Palestine became a source of newfound anxiety. The Zionism that Scholem encountered in Palestine was nothing like that he had envisaged while still in Germany. His immediate impression was that Palestine was a catastrophe in the making. During the first decade after his arrival to Jerusalem, the dream he had once entertained, which had sustained him in exile, the dream of Zion, was dashed by the reality of Jerusalem. And as a result, Scholem discovered that being truly at home in the real world was in fact an unattainable desire.

THE POLITICS OF PALESTINE AND BRITH SHALOM

Shortly after arriving in Palestine, Scholem sensed that the political situation in the country was critical. It was not so much the economic downturn that worried him as the direction that the Zionist project in Palestine had taken on the ground. In Palestine, Zionism was taking an entirely foreign path to that which

14. On this matter see my own discussion in "Reading Gershom Scholem in Context: Salomon Maimon's and Gershom Scholem's German Jewish Discourse on Jewish Mysticism," *New German Critique* 41, no. 1 121 (December 2014): 33–54.

Scholem had hoped for as a young, enthusiastic activist in the Zionist circles in Berlin. As we have seen in chapter 2 above, before immigrating to Palestine, Scholem had tried to convince his fellow Zionists that the Jewish youth should learn the lessons of Europe's ideological experiments. Zionism could not be liberal in the vein of the Jewish liberal movement in Europe. Such a solution would spell the end of the dream of *Jewish* renewal. Yet neither could Zionism be nationalistic or imperialistic. World War I or, as Scholem viewed it, "the war of imperialism" bore undeniable evidence of the dangers, injustices, and follies of nationalistic chauvinism and colonial aspirations. In answer to these grave historical lessons, Scholem called for the creation of Zion. According to this vision, Zion would resemble an organic community rather than a state and would be primarily a spiritual center rather than a land of farming and industry, a place for reflection rather than the breeding ground for a new, robust Jew. Zionism, Scholem advocated, should tread a central path between what he deemed to be liberal self-denial and his perception of national chauvinism.

While Scholem's version of the Zionist national awakening might seem somewhat naive, it was hardly unusual within its historical context. As discussed, among the members of the youth movement in Germany during the late 1910s these ideas had gained more than a little traction. As we have seen, the vision of a new, harmonious society, made up of enthusiastic young men and women who had the energy to discard the mantle of an institutionally organized mass society, was a fairly common one. The Zionist youth movement drew heavily on its German counterpart, which in turn based its ideology on readings from the German romantic tradition and Nietzsche, among others. Serving as the basis for a critique of the German state and for advocacy of a new and more harmonious society, these sources were intimately familiar to the young Gershom Scholem, who counted himself among the "romantics." As we have seen, Scholem did not invent the vision of a harmonious society but tailored it to his specific social context and his personal views. And he debated his vision with those who despite their many differences were, in fact, like-minded people, most of whom were members of the Zionist youth movement in Germany.

Yet in Palestine of the 1920s, these ideas, while inspiring, appeared outlandish. The concerns of the Zionist establishment in Palestine after World War I were entirely different from those of the Zionist youth circles in Berlin prior to and during the war. After the war, the Jewish Zionist settlement in Palestine, the Yishuv, was occupied primarily with its standing among the Jewish communities outside Palestine and with its relationship with the ruling power, Britain.[15] It was almost universally recognized that the fate of the Zionist project in Palestine depended, first and foremost, upon these relations. Without the support of Britain and of international Jewry, the attempt to rebuild Jewish life in Palestine was doomed to fail. These relations, in other words, it was generally understood, would ultimately define the character the Zionist project in Palestine.[16] The concerns of the Yishuv were therefore dramatically incompatible with those of the young Gershom Scholem. To Scholem, Zionist preoccupation with the colonial powers on the one hand, and with Jewish communities abroad on the other, seemed misguided. It contributed nothing to the realization of what Scholem perceived to be the true goal of the Zionist movement, namely, the creation of a harmonious Jewish society in the land of Zion. In fact, Scholem believed that these diplomatic efforts were reducing the likelihood of ever realizing such a society.

In response to the political reality in Palestine, Scholem commenced a period of hectic political engagement of the most direct kind. He joined the radical coterie of Brith Shalom and alongside individuals such as Samuel Hugo Bergman and Hans Kohn formed one of the most active and ideologically driven factions within the organization.[17] Brith Shalom (lit., Covenant of Peace) was founded by Arthur Ruppin in 1925 in order to create the ideological basis for and undertake preliminary research designed to promote future Arab-Jewish cooperation in Palestine. The assumption that motivated the Brith Shalom organization was that the national Jewish movement could not fulfill its goals without taking into consideration the existence of another people living on the same land, sharing its resources, and likewise aspiring to self-determination. The solution that Brith Shalom proposed was to create a binational Jewish-Arab state in Palestine, possibly under the auspices of the British Mandate.[18] Brith Shalom stood out in the political and social context of the emerging Yishuv. Unlike most Zionist organizations, it comprised almost exclusively German-speaking intellectuals of Central European descent who chose to

15. See Tom Segev, *One Palestine, Complete: Jews and Arabs under the British Mandate* (New York: Henry Holt, 2001); Shapira, *Land and Power*, esp. 84–218.

16. For an almost real-time account of the creation of the Yishuv with respect to these two concerns, see Hannah Arendt, "Jewish History, Revised," in *The Jewish Writings* (New York: Schocken, 2008), 303–11.

17. See Ratsabi, *Between Zionism and Judaism.*

18. For more on the early phase of Brith Shalom, see Aharon Kedar, "Brith Shalom: The Early Period (1925–1928)," in *Studies in the History of Zionism* (in Hebrew), ed. Bauer Yehuda, Moshe Davis, and Israel Kollat (Jerusalem, 1976), 224–85. See too Ratsabi, *Between Zionism and Judaism*, pt. 2.

live in Jerusalem.[19] And unlike most Zionists, they believed that the relationship between the Jews and the Arabs would play a decisive role in the realization of the Zionist project in Palestine. As we shall shortly see, most members of the Yishuv predictably interpreted Brith Shalom's activity as eccentric at best and treasonous at worst.

Scholem's first action as a member of Brith Shalom was to address the so-called "Jewish Legion debate." Indeed, it was in this context that he wrote what he would later call "my first political statement,"[20] which he published together with a handful of other intellectuals.[21] The statement appeared in the Berlin newspaper *Jüdische Rundschau*[22] on April 23, 1926, under the unassuming title "Clarification" (*Erklärung*). In it Scholem and his Zionist associates stated: "We, the undersigned, consider it our duty, in the context of the propaganda for a Jewish Legion, to clarify the following: We view with regret that governments and peoples [*Völker*] still prefer to entrust their security to the force of guns rather than to the creation of just and friendly relationships, and that the masses attach more importance to armaments than to cultural and economic development . . . We reject all propaganda calling for the creation of a Jewish legion, for any reason, even the most pressing one."[23]

The truth of the matter was that the leaders of the Yishuv were less concerned with creating a Jewish legion than with securing Jewish representation

19. As Dimitry Shumsky shows, many of the members of Brith Shalom indeed spoke German, but their worldview was crucially molded in the multicultural environment of Prague. *Between Prague and Jerusalem: The Idea of a Binational State in Palestine* (in Hebrew) (Jerusalem: Leo Baeck Institute, 2010).

20. In a letter to Ernst Simon dated May 12, 1926, Scholem takes responsibility for composing the letter. "Contrary to your assumption, not only did I sign the letter against the legion (which generated a flood of slander against us all, true to the dictum: "who asked you?"), but I am the one who more or less composed it." See Scholem, *Gershom Scholem: A Life in Letters*, 154–55.

21. The "clarification" was reprinted in Scholem, "My First Political Statement," in *'Od davar: pirke morashah u-tehiyah 2* (*Explications and Implications: Writings on Jewish Heritage and Renaissance*, vol. 2) (Tel Aviv: Am Oved, 1989) (in Hebrew), 61–62. The editors of this volume mention that on the newspaper clipping of this publication Scholem wrote "my first political statement." The editors thus chose this as the title for the text, whose original title was merely "Erklärung," that is, "clarification."

22. The choice to publish this statement in Germany indicates who the members of Brith Shalom considered to be their most direct and natural audience. See also Michael Nagel, "Jüdische Rundschau," in *Enzyklopädie jüdischer Geschichte und Kultur*, vol. 3, ed. Dan Diner (Stuttgart: Metzler, 2012), 253–55.

23. Scholem et al., "Erklärung," *Jüdische Rundschau*, April 23, 1926.

in the newly formed Mandatory police. In 1926, ostensibly for economic reasons,[24] the British High Commissioner to Palestine disbanded the paramilitary police created four years earlier (when the legal mandate replaced Britain's military occupation of Palestine), in order to create the Trans-Jordanian Police Force. During the course of this reorganization, however, the ethnic composition of the police force was transformed. The High Commissioner eliminated all the posts of Jewish policemen in the Mandatory police, thereby creating a predominantly Arab police force. This apparently administrative alteration was perceived by Zionist circles as a frontal assault. Long before the conflict between Arabs and Jews became violent, the Yishuv, having a good measure of confidence in British rule, did not fear that Arab policemen would fail to protect Jewish property or lives, as one might suspect today. Rather, the Zionist inhabitants of Palestine were outraged by the symbolic significance of the decision. The Jewish population, they argued, had the right to equal representation in the government's institutions. Moreover, it was widely assumed that by giving precedence to Arabs at the expense of Jews in the new Mandatory police, the British government was signaling that the Arabs were the more legitimate citizens of Palestine. To most members of the emerging Jewish community in Palestine that was still fighting for recognition, this was clearly unacceptable.[25]

To the members of Brith Shalom's "radical coterie," on the other hand, the issue at stake was quite different. In fact, the very notion that Zionism could draw its legitimacy from representation in the armed forces seemed to them absurd. Zionism, their message conveyed, should establish its legitimacy not by sharing the power of colonial authority but rather by sharing its ideals of peace, tolerance, and humanity as well as by making an economic contribution along with the local Arab population. In other words, the only means by which Zionism could fulfill its promise was by eschewing power and promoting understanding between the nations living in Palestine, and by furthering their mutual interests. Ultimately, they believed, only peace would allow Jews to devote themselves to the creation of Zion, as a spiritual, free, yet Jewish society. It was thus only peace that could maintain the long-term interests of the Zionist movement. Needless to say, this clarification by the members of Brith Shalom, while obviously courageous, made very little impact.

24. This argument was presented in an official press release in *Davar*, April 18, 1926.

25. See, for example, the opinion column by Y. Shuchmann, "The Draft Ends" (in Hebrew), *Davar*, May 28, 1926.

More than two years later, Scholem published his second political statement, this time on his own. This statement appeared on November 20, 1928, again in Berlin's *Jüdische Rundschau*. The title of this statement was "Has Communication with the Arabs Broken Down?"[26] In it, Scholem commented on the heated debate following an incident at the Jews' most sacred site on the holiest day of the Jewish calendar. In the early morning hours of the Day of Atonement (Yom Kippur), on September 24, 1928, a British police detail arrived at the Wailing Wall in Jerusalem with orders to dismantle a screen (*mechitza*) that separated the worshiping men from the women. Placing the wooden frame and the cloth partition next to the Wailing Wall violated the Ottoman status quo that prohibited erecting any lasting structures on the site. The Muslim leadership complained, and the policemen, headed by the Mandatory Chief of Police Douglas Daf himself, arrived on the scene after the order to remove the screen, issued on the previous day, was ignored. They forcibly dismantled the cloth screen and its wooden frame, violently beating worshipers who protested at their actions. As a result, a few elderly women were injured.[27]

The events at the Wailing Wall created a furor among Jewish communities all over the world, among the local Arab population, and in British government circles. The Jews protested particularly at the beating of elderly men and women on the Day of Atonement next to the Western Wall. The police, they claimed, had exhibited an alarming insensitivity in employing force on this special day at such a special site against obviously harmless elderly people who had gathered to fulfill a religious duty. The Arabs were incensed by the Jewish attempt to alter the status quo next to al-Ḥaram al-Šarīf. This was not, they believed, a naive action. And the British, for their part, claimed that they were merely fulfilling their duty to keep the peace by enforcing the law.

The issue at stake was, of course, far broader than police brutality, the cloth screen, or the status quo. The Wailing Wall events, as they were known at the time, raised one of the most volatile questions in the region to this very day: who is the legitimate sovereign of the Mountain, even the name of which cannot be agreed upon? In the months following the events, Jews from around the world openly proclaimed their entitlement to the Temple Mount and protested at the British conceit in attempting to control it by force. Even the Zionist leadership, which was not especially religious, rallied in response to the

26. Gershom Scholem, "Ist die Verständigung mit den Arabern gescheitert?," *Jüdische Rundschau*, November 20, 1928.

27. The episode is described with characteristic verve by Segev in *One Palestine, Complete*, 295–97.

events. They insisted that the reemergence of Jewish life in the region should, at the very least, ensure Jewish religious freedom in Palestine. Hayim Nahman Bialik, Israel's national poet and a key figure in the Yishuv, declared at an urgently convened meeting of the Zionist General Council in Tel Aviv that "the [British] government disguises its intentions with the false pretense of 'law' in order to stop us from reclaiming that place."[28] An outspoken critic of Jewish religiosity and an avowed Zionist, Bialik did not, on this occasion, shy away from overtly messianic vocabulary, which is lost in the English transition. In his speech, he called for *ge'ulat ha-makom*, which may be translated literally as "reclaiming the place," that is, the Temple Mount. Yet every Hebrew speaker in the audience and among the readers of the newspaper report was perfectly aware that the term he used expressed also divine redemption. The word *ge'ula* means redemption, and *ha-makom* serves as one of the names of God in the Jewish tradition and is an overt reference to His seat on the Temple Mount.[29] Bialik, in other words, argued that in their actions at the Wailing Wall the British had invoked technicalities in order to hinder the Zionist effort to attain complete redemption, understood here in the most direct religious sense.

In response to the worldwide Jewish public outcry, the Arab leadership raised the alarm, claiming that the Jews were poised to take control of the revered Noble Sanctuary, the location from which the Prophet Muhammad had ascended to heaven. The tension between Jews and Arabs with regard to the Wailing Wall that surfaced in September 1928 escalated slowly and finally erupted.[30] In August 1929 riots broke out throughout the land. Most severely, the old Jewish communities in Hebron and Safed were attacked; men, women, and children were killed and their properties ransacked. In total, 116 Arabs and 133 Jews were killed during the riots, which to this day signify a turning point in the relations between Arabs and Jews in the region.[31]

28. Editorial, "After the Events in Jerusalem" (in Hebrew), *Davar*, September 26, 1928.

29. For more on the term *makom* or 'space' in Jewish literature, see Amir Eshel, "Cosmopolitanism and Searching for the Sacred Space in Jewish Literature," *Jewish Social Studies* 9, no. 3 (Spring/Summer 2003): 121–38.

30. Most of the relatively little scholarship on these events seems to portray the events leading up to the riots as done here. In his recent book, Hillel Cohen seeks, for the first time, to broaden the perspective. He does not quite dispute the importance of the events of Yom Kippur 1928 but places them in a larger and more intricate context. See *Year Zero of the Arab-Israeli Conflict, 1929*, trans. Haim Watzman (Waltham, MA: Brandeis University Press, 2015).

31. The riots of 1929 are commonly described as a watershed in the history of the Jewish-Arab conflict and of the Zionist movement. See Hillel Cohen, *Year Zero of the Arab-Israeli*

Scholem's letter to the *Jüdische Rundschau*, published a month and a half after the events at the Wailing Wall and less than ten months before the violent riots swept the country, was, first and foremost, an attempt to stave off the polemical attacks against Brith Shalom. The British should not, indeed, have acted so brutally, Scholem conceded. It was also true that the Arab protests against the screen were far from innocent, he admitted. Nevertheless, he emphasized, the process of reaching an understanding with the Arabs would be long and arduous, something that no one, not even Brith Shalom, had ever denied. Furthermore, he claimed, the emotional outcry of Jews from around the world could only be understood by the Arabs as the preliminary stage of a Jewish offensive designed to reclaim the Temple Mount. "One need only imagine the feeling of a simple and harmless landlord, from whom ten square meters of his front yard is to be appropriated, in order to appreciate what is to be expected from religious fanatics and nationalist Arabs, at the prospect of losing only the edge of the holy Arab Temple to the Jews."[32]

According to Scholem, the Arab response to the events should be perfectly understandable to anyone with even a limited imagination. Therefore, the attempt to interpret the Arab response as proof of their reluctance to deal peacefully with the Jews was misinformed, as was the criticism leveled at Brith Shalom. The fact of the matter was, Scholem claimed, that both sides of the conflict commonly employed barely veiled threats and inflammatory rhetoric. Therefore, it was now imperative to rein in the fanatics on both sides, to commit to negotiations, and to find a lasting agreement as soon as possible, before further violence caused yet more suffering.

All the hopes for a better, more harmonious life in Zion notwithstanding, the truth of the matter was that Scholem had relatively little in common with most members of the Yishuv.[33] In fact, it would seem that he felt less at home

---

Conflict, 1929; Benny Morris, *Righteous Victims: A History of the Zionist-Arab Conflict, 1881–2001* (New York: Knopf, 1999), 111–20. Anita Shapira discusses the effect of the riots on Zionists in Palestine in *Land and Power*, 173–206. Tom Segev discusses the events in Hebron; see *One Palestine, Complete*, 314–28.

32. Scholem, "Ist die Verständigung mit den Arabern gescheitert?"

33. The conclusion that Scholem's political views had little in common with those held by most people in the Yishuv derives not only from the meager influence he exerted as a member of Brith Shalom, or from the association's limited membership, but also from the general reaction toward Brith Shalom, which was branded at best as an elitist group of German intellectuals and at worse as a band of traitors. These reactions clearly emerge from Scholem's apologetic justifications, in which he feels impelled to demonstrate not only that Brith Shalom was a Zionist

with them than he had done back in Germany. And it also seems that he was painfully aware of this fact. Be that as it may, it is clear that for most members of the Yishuv, Brith Shalom's endeavors and views were outright foolish, if not in fact treasonous. Even among German Zionists, and even at the liberal-minded *Jüdische Rundschau*, Scholem's ideas were viewed with overt suspicion. Clear evidence of this is provided by the unusual note that appeared next to Scholem's remarks about the Wailing Wall events. Immediately below the provocative title "Has Communication with the Arabs Broken Down?," the editors state: "The author deems it important to state that he alone bears responsibility for the following remarks. It naturally follows from this that these remarks do not convey the opinion of the editorial board."[34]

Brith Shalom's position on the Jewish-Arab conflict was so marginal that most of Scholem's public statements were apologetic in essence, constituting attempts to ward off polemical attacks against its members and their ideas. These attacks reached their peak in the months following the 1929 riots.[35] One letter to the editor of the newspaper *Davar*, written by a Dr. A. Rosenthal, likened the members of Brith Shalom to patients in a mental asylum. The members of Brith Shalom, Rosenthal suggested, were so afraid of confrontation with the Arabs that they were willing to surrender everything, including the Zionist ideal itself. "This resembles the textbook case," Rosenthal wrote, "that describes a patient so mortally afraid of death that he takes his own life to free himself of the anxiety."[36] This view of Brith Shalom apparently represented the prevalent attitude in the Yishuv. Their sincerity and courage notwithstanding, many thought Brith Shalom's ideology was at best simply absurd.[37]

---

movement but also that its members were clinically sane. See Gershom Scholem, "Echad Ha'am and Us," in *'Od davar*, 72–73.

34. "Der Autor legt Wert auf die Feststellung , daß für die nachfolgenden Ausführungen nur er persönlich die Verantwortung trägt. Damit ist natürlich auch bereits gesagt, daß hier nicht eine Stellungnahme der Redaktion vorliegt.—Red." Scholem, "Ist die Verständigung mit den Arabern Gescheitert?"

35. Some examples of the polemics directed against Brith Shalom were diligently collected and appear in the appendix of Adi Gordon, *Brith Shalom and Binational Zionism* (Jerusalem: Karmel, 2008), 287–322.

36. A. Rosenthal, "Psychosis of Fear" (in Hebrew), *Davar*, November 14, 1929.

37. For more on the relation of the Yishuv to Brith Shalom, including the editor of the influential newspaper *Davar*, see Ratsabi, *Between Zionism and Judaism*, 137–47. Even though the members of Brith Shalom were barred from publishing their opinions in *Davar*, a reply to Rosenthal's letter was published on November 24, 1929. See also Gordon, *Brith Shalom and Binational Zionism*, 307–8.

WINNING THE WRONG BATTLE

Scholem's comments on current affairs prove that his political, historical, and emotional landscape underwent a deep transformation following his immigration to Mandatory Palestine. From his new point of view in Jerusalem, Scholem recognized that the problems facing the Zionist project were of a radically different magnitude and nature from those he had perceived while still in Germany. Together with the other members of Brith Shalom, Scholem advocated a binational—Jewish-Arab—democratic society under the auspices of the British Mandate in Palestine.[38] The political arguments in favor of such a solution have been expounded since the 1920s and remain under discussion to this day. What makes Scholem's political writings noteworthy is, therefore, not so much what he said as how he went about saying it. Indeed, Scholem's style and rhetoric signify the depth of the changes in his political activism. In his private notes as well as in public, he freely admitted that the battle for the soul of Zionism, which had seemed so clearly defined in exile, had reached a dead end in Zion, and that the dream for a better home entertained in Berlin might have already been dashed in Jerusalem.

Scholem's political comments, published mostly in Brith Shalom's own journal *She'ifotenu* (Our Aspirations), are remarkable for their strictly matter-of-fact approach that largely circumvents moral, spiritual, or historical argumentation. He could have based his argument on humanity's innate goodness, irrespective of creed or origin, or have drawn the moral lesson of the Jewish past, or maintained that the true nature of the Zionist endeavor dictated a different, more peaceful response. Yet this was not how Scholem chose to approach the issues at hand. Rather, he appealed to the common sense of his readers, reflecting on what even any "landlord" would be able to grasp. This is a remarkable turnaround in view of his earlier diatribes. Scholem's lofty visions of a harmonious "Zion," expressed in his early polemics in the context of the German youth movement, now made way for a pragmatic voice desperately calling for a negotiated political solution.

The fact that Scholem modified his style of argument so dramatically reflects a change in attitude since his arrival in Palestine and a new appreciation of the situation. This change is naturally also indicative of the time that had elapsed since his days as a young and enthusiastic member of the Zionist youth movement. Yet Scholem's mature, more considered and fact-oriented

---

38. For more, see Gershom Scholem, "About the Problem of the Parliament," in *'Od davar*, 63–67; Gershom Scholem, "The Final Goal," in ibid., 68–71.

FIGURE 4.1. Scholem in Berlin, 1920. Courtesy of The National Library of Israel, Jerusalem.

arguments cannot be attributed to age alone. In his political statements Scholem was clearly appealing to the common sense of the widest possible audience. This did not seem to work. Furthermore, the public in Palestine in the late 1920s was infinitely more diverse than the membership of the Zionist youth movements in Berlin during the 1910s. Indeed, Scholem's later political comments disclose that, their many differences notwithstanding, the debates that took place in the Zionist youth movement in Berlin had been held among like-minded people inspired by similar ideas, who entertained similar hopes. True, Scholem had expressed unorthodox views already in Berlin, but his articles had been published in highly respected journals and had stirred the emotions of many members of the youth movement. In Palestine, on the other hand, Zionism was driven by a far broader set of concerns and was being undertaken by people from far more diverse origins and backgrounds.

In the circumstances that evolved in Palestine, Scholem's brand of Zionism was merely one among many other kinds. He was painfully aware of this fact. In a letter to Werner Kraft, written about a year after Scholem's immigration, he wrote: "You can't possibly imagine the sorts of worlds that bump into each other in this place. For thinking minds, it's an open invitation to go overboard . . . You can get away with all kinds of remarks about the new Palestine (if I make myself clear) . . . and how could it be otherwise, given this un-imaginable collision between various types of creativity released from the four corners of Heaven and Earth?"[39]

Scholem responded to the transformation he had undergone during the first few years after his immigration to Palestine in a series of private, mostly unpublished notes and letters.[40] In these texts, Scholem openly confessed to his deep disillusionment at the way that Zionism realized itself on the ground, in Zion. Indeed, the most salient emotions that emerge from these typed docu-ments are anger and frustration. "This is not what we desired," Scholem notes again and again. And while he generally failed to elaborate on the reasons for his frustrations in these texts, it is here that he began to reflect on central is-sues that would pervade both his private and his public writings for the years to come.

Perhaps the most revealing document is dated to "End [of] 1924." This detail is scribbled in Scholem's handwriting on the upper corner of the typed page. If the date is correct then Scholem must have written this note about a year after he arrived in Jerusalem from Berlin. This document discloses, prob-ably better than any other available source, Scholem's reaction to the reality in Palestine. The title of the text is ominous: "Zionism Will Survive Its Catastro-phe." The text itself is reminiscent of Scholem's earlier writings. It is lofty and unequivocally critical. In it, Scholem discusses the decline of the idea of Zion.

> The hour is upon us in which hearts must decide whether Zionism, the pur-pose of which is the preparation for the eternal, should capitulate in the face of the Zionism of the Jewish state, which is the catastrophe. By God, this is not what we wanted. We inwardly believed in the fullness of the heart, and now this meager and cold petty bourgeois that brings together a *halutz* [pioneer] and a [Joseph] Klausner . . . is killing us. And why? *Because the drying language of our heart was desiccated* . . . We came and thought to plunge into the midst of an ocean, not on the outside, but in the intensity of growing life. Instead, we wade in the mire of idle chatter. Metaphysically, we have lost on the field of battle that which Zionism won in the world.[41]

39. Scholem, *Gershom Scholem: A Life in Letters*, 137.

40. These notes were mentioned and quoted also in Weidner, *Gershom Scholem: Politisches, esoterisches und historiographisches Schreiben*, 104–9.

41. Arc 4° 1599/277–1 Nr. 52, Gershom Scholem's personal archive, Archive of the National Library of Israel, Jerusalem.

The text discloses how Scholem reacted to what he saw around him. He appears to have realized that his erstwhile dream was now fading away. He could have reformulated his earlier vision or adopted a more charitable interpretation of the situation in Palestine. But he chose neither of these paths. Instead, he accused the Zionists of being too petty-minded, too mundane, and incapable of finding a language ambitious enough to express the magnitude of the moment. And he confessed, at least to himself, that reality had fallen short of his vision. Scholem had visualized Zion as a place of intense spiritual life and admitted that what he found was a quagmire.

Similar ideas couched in a more bitter tone are to be found in a letter Scholem wrote to his friend Ernst Simon, still living in Germany, in September 1925, exactly two years after arriving to Palestine. The letter reveals that like many recent immigrants, Scholem found himself stranded in a life completely different from that he had sought. It indicates that like many other new immigrants, Scholem laid the blame for his disappointment on someone else.

> No one should foster the illusion that what is happening here and will occur in the future (after the open retreat from everything to do with human *tikkun* [betterment]) has the slightest thing in common, in *substantia et essentia*, with Zionism, in whose name your faithful servant is here. In the battle between the building of Palestine *coûte que coûte* and Zionism, the latter is hopelessly outgunned . . . I consider it God's just punishment for the misuse of the *halutz* (pioneer) that the most conniving sharks and the seven streams of hell now pour in upon us from Lodz.[42]

Like most immigrants, Scholem too was obliged to adapt to his new life circumstances. He modified his political concerns and the language that he used in his public statements, and, most important, he developed new insights regarding the meaning of the historical hour. Scholem believed that the Zionist movement in Palestine was facing a critical crisis, if not a catastrophe. The roots of the crisis were to be found in the recent history of the Zionist movement and the political decisions it had taken. Again and again, Scholem argued

---

42. Scholem, *Gershom Scholem: A Life in Letters*, 143–44 The city of Lodz in Poland was a central location for Jewish life in Eastern Europe as about one third of the city—the third largest city in Poland—was Jewish. In this context, Scholem uses Lodz as something of a derogatory term referring to Jews of Eastern European origin or *Ostjuden*. For more on the perception of Ostjuden by Jews of Central and Western European background see Aschheim, *Brothers and Strangers*, esp. 3–31.

that while the Zionist project had won the battle of exile, it had paradoxically lost its soul in Palestine. This insight appears for the first time in the private note cited above and resurfaces constantly with only slight variations in other private notes, letters, and in his public statements up to the early 1930s.[43] In August 1931, Scholem developed this idea into a more or less coherent thesis that draws upon the private sources, including the one discussed above. The essay devoted to this issue was published in *She'ifotenu* under the title "Be-may Ka Miflagi?," a recurring Talmudic formula that indicates a dispute and that translates roughly as "What is the debate about?"[44]

According to Scholem, the Zionist movement had divided into two parts. In exile, Zionism had realized much of its potential and had successfully rejuvenated the decaying spirit of Judaism. Most Zionists, he claimed, had been overwhelmed by their own unexpected success. And they had celebrated their victory by insisting that the rejuvenation of the Jewish spirit had always been the true end of the Zionist movement. "To most Zionists," Scholem claimed " 'Zion' is perceived as a tabernacle that could be erected anywhere. It is not, in any case, the 'Temple.' "[45] In other words, the Zionists living in exile had begun to regard the path leading to the destination as the destination itself. In a narrow sense, therefore, the Zionism of exile had triumphed, for it had achieved a victory of sorts by reviving the nation. But as it relished its victory, it had chosen to end the struggle, thus losing sight of the true objective of the Zionist movement.

In contrast to the Zionism of exile, a small number of Zionists, or as Scholem termed them, "the cult of Palestinian Zionists," had not forgotten that the real cause of Zionism was Zion, in the most concrete sense. But Zionism of Zion, Scholem asserted, was facing a catastrophe. For unlike exilic Zionism, Zionism in Palestine was obliged to appear on the political stage of history and to take an unambiguous political stance thereon. Its fatal mistake, Scholem argued, was to take the wrong political stance and to have completely misunderstood the importance of the historical hour. Rather than serving their own spiritual interest, he maintained, Zionists had chosen to serve the empire, eager to reap

43. See Scholem's letter to Benjamin reprinted in Scholem, *Walter Benjamin: The Story of a Friendship.*" Daniel Weidner tends to accept this argument, hesitantly placing it in the context of Scholem's debate with Jabotinsky's Revisionist movement, thus failing to perceive that this insight was, first and foremost, Scholem's attempt to reflect on the historical moment in Palestine and is at the same time a reflection of his own personal experience. See Weidner, *Gershom Scholem: Politisches, esoterisches und historiographisches Schreiben,* 111.

44. Gershom Scholem, "The Debate—What Is It About?," in *'Od davar,* 74–82.

45. Ibid., 78.

the "fruits of the First World War." In other words, Palestinian Zionism had sided with the imperial powers for the sake of mundane benefits and advantages. Yet in vying for some short-term gains, it had unwittingly surrendered its soul to these powers. Palestinian Zionism, Scholem scornfully observes, "sought to succeed through the intrigue of war. It has signed off on the Treaty of Versailles and the San Remo Conference, as well as the mandate of victory. And this victory now informs our destruction. It is the greatest obstacle of the entire movement."[46] In the long run, Scholem predicted, the imperial powers were destined to crumble, and the tiny Jewish community, which had staked its future on it, would be "burned by the flames" of the awakening East. According to Scholem, the Zionist movement in Palestine had parted ways with the Zionist movement of exile and was forced to assign itself new objectives. But crucially, the Zionist movement had dangerously and miserably failed to read the political map and to secure its own interests. In the long run, Scholem argued, it had therefore placed its very existence in jeopardy.

The irony is that Scholem's formula—according to which Zionism had succeeded in exile and failed in Zion—encapsulated his own experience arguably better than it captured the actual historical situation. In Germany, among his fellow Zionists, Scholem had enjoyed prestige and influence. He had maintained close contacts with the central figures of the Zionist youth movement, including its leaders Martin Buber and Siegfried Bernfeld. His outspoken critique had had an impact on many and was widely discussed among members of the movement.[47] Thus, in his own way, Scholem had left Germany victorious. In Palestine, on the other hand, he had lost almost everything he had. He was relegated to the margins of the most marginal political group, which at times was even denied the title "Zionist." Indeed, Scholem had lost not merely his influence but, more important, that which facilitates influence, namely, a sense of belonging. His thoughts and ideas had lost their relevance; they no longer appeared to touch the people or the things that were dearest to his heart. In a private note written in 1926, on the third anniversary of his immigration, Scholem appears perfectly aware that the reality of Palestine had led him to lose touch with the world. "During these three years I have learned much and seen much. But it is all unreal. It [the situation in Palestine] is unsustainable, because the Zionism that brought us to Palestine has here become a farce. And the few decent heads succumb to this fact, which they do not wish

46. Ibid., 81.

47. For more on Scholem's influence among the members of the Zionist youth movement, see Weiner, "Gershom Scholem and the Jung Juda Youth Group in Berlin."

to acknowledge."[48] And so despite everything he had said and done, he had felt more at home in exile than he felt now in Zion.

IS JERUSALEM THE NEW "ZION"?

Scholem's immigration to Palestine, as we have seen, transformed his political conceptions, his appreciation of the historical hour, the style of his writing, his social standing, and above all his sense of self and of belonging. These various transformations could be succinctly expressed by pointing to the fundamental issue at stake. Having sustained him throughout his years in exile, Scholem's concept of Zion did not survive the experience of immigration. Upon his immigration, Scholem reached the conclusion that Palestine was not "Zion" and could not be interpreted as the dawn of a new messianic age. To him, Jerusalem was ultimately only another kind of exile. Indeed, we have noted that upon his immigration Scholem replaced the ideal "Zion" with the mundane Jerusalem, and the dream of a perfectly harmonious society with something rather imperfect, a parliamentary democracy that would best represent the peoples living in Palestine. All the transformations discussed thus far may indeed be reduced to this one painful insight.

It is, however, imperative to note that allowing the reality of Palestine to crush the dream of "Zion" not only created the conditions for a certain existential situation, but reflected in itself a political determination. As we have seen, for Scholem this determination entailed exchanging the romantic metapolitical arguments of the youth movement for a pragmatic political struggle. But, more important, it inevitably pitted Scholem against those who did not share his insight about the nature of the land. To some, the land of Palestine could still become the locus of the messianic revival of the Jewish people. Indeed, the flawed reality served some as the justification to step up the struggle for "Zion," rather than as a reason to relinquish the idea altogether, as Scholem had done. Some in fact believed that Brith Shalom's call for negotiations was defeatist, not merely because they sought to appease the enemy, but also because their politics entailed forgoing the essence of the Zionist dream, namely, its messianic aspirations.

One such believer was the Zionist author Yehuda Burla, who in the aftermath of the 1929 riots wrote a scathing attack on Brith Shalom in the newspaper *Davar*, which was the mouthpiece of the Zionist Labor movement until it closed in 1996. Burla did not represent any radical faction in the Zionist

48. Heute vor 3 Jahren, Arc 4° 1599/277-1 Nr. 60, Gershom Scholem's personal archive, Archive of the National Library of Israel, Jerusalem.

political discourse of Palestine. Nevertheless, in an opinion piece titled "Brith Kishalon" (Covenant of Failure), Burla accused Brith Shalom of deeply offending the spirit of Zionism. Its members had, he claimed, offended "the heart of the ideal that beats in the folds of [the people's] soul; Brith Shalom's plan shatters its sense of self, its human (and not only national) consciousness and abuses its holiest of holies—the hope for complete redemption [*ge'ula shlema*]. In other words, the messianic historical hope exists in the heart of the new Israeli man in the form of political Zionism . . . and he who tries to lessen, sever, or stain the splendor of this hope—the hand of the people will reach him first to silence him [*yad ha'am tiheye bo barishona lehashtiko*]."[49]

In his reply, which also appeared in *Davar*, Scholem expressed his opinion of the messianic tendency in Zionism more clearly than anywhere else. "I completely reject the notion that Zionism is a messianic movement or that it has the right to employ religious language for its political ends. The redemption of the people of Israel, for which I strive as a Zionist, is not in any way identical to religious redemption, which I hope will one day come . . . The Zionist ideal belongs on one side and the messianic ideal belongs on the other. The one kingdom does not touch the other."[50]

Scholem indeed believed that Zionism would pay a terrible price for choosing to construe itself in messianic terms. He expressed the danger somewhat poetically in a letter to Franz Rosenzweig, written in December 1926. The letter was subsequently found by Stephan Moses, and gained fame most likely through Jacques Derrida, who wrote an essay on it.[51] Scholars have interpreted Scholem's text in different veins, as a reflection on language as such,[52] and as an exemplar in the debate about the politics of language in Jewish modernity.[53]

49. Yehuda Burla, "Brith Kishalon," *Davar*, November 27, 1929. See also item 12 in the appendix of Gordon, *Brith Shalom and Binational Zionism*.

50. Gershom Scholem, "On the Three Sins of Brith Shalom," in *'Od davar*, 85–90.

51. The letter was first discussed by Jacques Derrida in a lecture delivered at the School for Criticism and Theory at Dartmouth College in June 1987. See Derrida, "The Eyes of Language: The Abyss and the Volcano," in *Acts of Religion*, ed. Gil Anidjar (New York: Routledge, 2002), 189–227.

52. See, for example, Derrida's analysis, but also William Cutter, "Ghostly Hebrew, Ghastly Speech: Scholem to Rosenzweig, 1926," *Prooftexts* 10, no. 3 (September 1990): 413–33; Annabel Herzog, " 'Monolingualism' or the Language of God: Scholem and Derrida on Hebrew and Politics," *Modern Judaism* 29, no. 2 (2009): 226–38.

53. Andreas Kilcher, "Kafka, Scholem und die Politik der juedischen Sprachen," in *Politik und Religion im Judentum*, ed. Christoph Miething, Romania Judaica (Tübingen: Niemeyer, 1999), 79–115.

But as some scholars have also noted, the letter was, first and foremost, a reflection on the Zionist political-theological complex, the attempt to construe the Zionist endeavor as an expression of Jewish messianism.[54]

In essence, Scholem argued that the basic dilemma of Zionism was encompassed in the language, as nowhere else. As Galili Shahar suggests, "Scholem's text, which was rediscovered after his death, can be viewed as a document of esoteric writing on the New Hebrew and the future of the Zionist enterprise in Palestine."[55] The revival of the Hebrew language in the context of Zionism had, Scholem believed, created an intensely confused social, political, and historical situation that placed the Hebrew speakers of the Yishuv at a dangerous disadvantage. On the one hand, the Zionists in Palestine were using the language on a daily basis and for mundane purposes, thereby maintaining an active connection to the tradition in which the language had been formed. On the other hand, in order to apply it to daily life they were forced to repress its inner religious meaning. Thus, Hebrew speakers both commit themselves to religious thinking and deny themselves any real knowledge of its inner nature. This, Scholem believed, was an extremely dangerous situation. In fact, it constituted the gravest and most overlooked threat to the Zionist endeavor in general. To describe the danger, Scholem employed the metaphor of the 'volcano,' which was a common trope in the discourse of the Yishuv. In this discourse, the large Arab population of Palestine was referred to as a volcano about to erupt.[56] In contrast to accepted wisdom, Scholem argued in the letter, it was the problem of the "actualization" of Hebrew (and not the presence of a majority of Arabs in the population) that constituted the volcano alongside which the unsuspecting Yishuv was building its future. Eventually, Scholem thought, the deep layers of the language would turn on its users, who would be not merely surprised but also unable to defend themselves.

Whereas Scholem is very clear about the danger that stems from the profane usage of a messianic language, it might be difficult to foresee how exactly a language can physically erupt like a volcano and destroy everything in its path. Nevertheless, one may construe the danger that is lodged between the

54. See Galili Shahar, "The Sacred and the Unfamiliar: Gershom Scholem and the Anxieties of the New Hebrew," *Germanic Review* 83, no. 4 (Fall 2008): 299–320. See also Christoph Schmidt's introductory comments to *God Will Not Stand Still: Jewish Modernity and Political Theology* (in Hebrew), ed. Christoph Schmidt and Eli Schonfeld (Jerusalem: Van Leer, 2009), 7–17.

55. Shahar, "Sacred and the Unfamiliar," 300.

56. The image of the volcano, Anita Shapira shows, was often employed in this period to describe the security uncertainties of the Yishuv. See *Land and Power*, 79–80.

different levels of Hebrew as a danger of ignorance. David Biale has suggested something along these lines, arguing that "the apocalyptic dangers of which Scholem warned in his letter to Rosenzweig are . . . the result not of using a divine language in history but of invoking a human language that its speakers *think* is grounded in revelation."[57] Scholem, it may thus be argued, expressed the fear that the Hebrew speakers' ignorance of Hebrew's inner nature left the political field wide open to charlatans who could claim to possess a deeper knowledge of the profound religious meanings of the words. From Scholem's personal and political perspective this was not a theoretical danger.

One charlatan who seemed to Scholem to have manipulated the language in order to make it seem divine was the prolific historian and literary critic Joseph Klausner. Klausner was born in 1874 in the Russian Empire, submitted his dissertation on Jewish history at the University of Heidelberg in 1902, and settled in Palestine in 1919. He was also a publicist, a charismatic lecturer, editor of the journal *Ha-Shilo'ah*, a professor of Hebrew literature at the Hebrew University, and the author of dozens of books in the fields of Jewish history and literature, as well as a great number of articles, essays, and opinion pieces. Furthermore, he was an outspoken critic of the mainstream Zionist movement from his position on the right of the political spectrum. Klausner never joined the right-wing Revisionist party, but he expressed support for its cause and its leader, Vladimir Ze'ev Jabotinsky. Contemporary scholars consider him to be one of the intellectual pillars of the Revisionist party.[58]

Gershom Scholem first heard Klausner lecture shortly after arriving to Palestine. The event instilled in him a profound despair. In a private note written in late 1924, already quoted above, he wrote: "We inwardly believed in the fullness of the heart, and now this meager and cold petty bourgeois that brings together a *halutz* [pioneer] and a Klausner—I cannot forget his diatribe, which I once witnessed in 1923 as I accidentally stumbled into his lecture in Petah Tikva—is killing us."[59] Scholem's reaction to Klausner was, it appears, not unusual among the intellectuals of the nascent Hebrew University. As David Myers notes, several figures of different circles opposed nominating Klausner to a position in Jewish history at the newly established Institute of Jewish Stud-

57. David Biale, *Not in the Heavens: The Tradition of Jewish Secular Thought* (Princeton: Princeton University Press, 2011), 54.

58. See Jacob Shavit, *Jabotinsky and the Revisionist Movement, 1925–1948* (New York: Frank Cass, 1988), 127–31.

59. Scholem, "Der Zionismus wird seine Katastrophe überleben," Arc 4° 1599/277–1 Nr. 52, Gershom Scholem's personal archive, Archive of the National Library of Israel, Jerusalem.

ies (the precursor of the Hebrew University). As Myers writes, some "considered Klausner more a publicist and an activist than a scholar, a perception shared by a good number of . . . German colleagues in Jerusalem."[60] As a result of this criticism, Klausner was initially denied a position to teach in the history department, to which he was most suited. But in 1925, following the intervention of the chancellor of the university, Judah Magnes, and of the Zionist public figure Menahem Ussishkin, he was appointed professor of literature at the Hebrew University.[61] Scholem commented on Klausner's appointment in a letter to Ernst Simon: "I can't deny that I consider Klausner's appointment in the apparently 'harmless' field of literature a highly questionable blunder, motivated by the purest cowardliness (or in the long run, fear) . . . Yesterday I went to hear him lecture again. Take my word for it—it's obscene to allow such a second rate hack to teach at the university in Jerusalem."[62]

Joseph Klausner was a prolific, widely read, and well-known writer, and on this ground probably suitable for a position at the university. He published dozens of voluminous studies in Jewish history and literature and wrote hundreds of essays, articles, and opinion pieces on many other subjects as well. As David Myers notes, he was also a popular lecturer at the university. It is more than likely that the animosity toward Klausner among his colleagues was fueled also by his otherness, his being of Russian extraction and belonging to the other end of the Zionist political spectrum. Nevertheless, in style, substance, and mode of analysis, Klausner's work indeed differs significantly from that of his counterparts. His oeuvre is decidedly more popular and more approachable than the works of Gershom Scholem or of Samuel Hugo Bergman, for example. This, too, surely played a part in shaping Klausner's reputation among his colleagues and definitely also his standing in the eyes of the junior and aspiring faculty member Gershom Scholem.

Be that as it may, Klausner's importance and influence especially in the very small intellectual circles of Palestine of the 1920s cannot be over rated. And his field of expertise was one of special significance to the discussion here. Indeed, one of Joseph Klausner's central areas of study was the history of the messianic idea in Judaism, in particular during the First and Second Temple periods. In his voluminous work, and especially in his book *The Messianic Idea in Israel, from Its Beginning to the Completion of the Mishnah*, which appeared in three installments and subsequently as a single volume in 1925, he set out to describe

60. Myers, *Re-inventing the Jewish Past*, 94.
61. Ibid., 94–97.
62. Scholem, *Gershom Scholem: A Life in Letters*, 148.

the "original" Jewish messianic idea. More important, it is in this book that Klausner laid the historical foundation for the connection between Zionism and Jewish messianism. The crux of his historical analysis of the Jewish messianic idea was the link between the political and the spiritual aspects of the messianic endeavor. According to Klausner, Jewish tradition had never made the distinction between the political aspirations of the Jews as a nation and their spiritual yearnings as a religious group. In other words, Klausner claimed that the political desire to realize sovereignty and the theological desire to become whole were always the two sides of the coin of Israel. This idea appears already in Klausner's dissertation, later revised and republished as the third part of his book:

> In the course of the long evolution of the Jewish Messianic idea, two different conceptions were inseparably woven together: politico-national salvation and religio-spiritual redemption. These two elements walked arm in arm. The Messiah must be both king and redeemer. He must overthrow the enemies of Israel, establish the kingdom of Israel, and rebuild the Temple; and at the same time he must reform the world through the Kingdom of God, root out idolatry from the world, proclaim the one and only God to all, put an end to sin, and be wise, pious, and just as no man had been before him or ever would be after him. In short, he is the great political and spiritual hero at one and the same time.[63]

The conclusions that Klausner draws from his historical analysis for his contemporary political situation are not difficult to foresee. Essentially, if Zionism is to succeed it must fashion itself as the heir to the messianic idea in its entirety. It must therefore restore both Judaism's long-lost sovereign power and its forgotten spiritual perfection. Or in Klausner's own words, "In our own times and before our very eyes, the politico-national part which is in the hope for redemption has returned to life together with the spiritual-universalistic element which is in the Messianic expectation . . . Only when the two of them flow together to make one mighty stream can the most important Jewish movement, Zionism, consider itself to have come into possession of the inheritance of the Messianic idea."[64] That Zionism should indeed strive to "come into possession of the inheritance of the Messianic idea" was taken for granted by Klausner.

---

63. Joseph Klausner, *The Messianic Idea in Israel, from Its Beginning to the Completion of the Mishnah* (New York: Macmillan, 1955), 392.

64. Ibid., 10–11.

The notion of reaching a negotiated agreement between Arabs and Jews in Palestine that would satisfy both the material and the emotional needs of all sides to the conflict appeared to contradict the fulfillment of the messianic idea. Klausner made this point explicitly in his polemic against Brith Shalom. "*Brith Shalom,*" he wrote, "is nibbling away at the roots of the Zionist movement, at Hebrew Nationalism and the ideal of Israelite statehood, at the hope of *full redemption* [*ge'ula shlema*] and at the whole great national destiny." He consequently called for the waging of an "ideological war against the new assimilationism."[65]

Scholem, naturally, did not share Klausner's political conviction, much less his sentiment concerning the role of messianism in Jewish politics. A settlement agreed upon by the peoples of the region must necessarily be reached at the expense of the messianic ideology propagated by Klausner. And in order to impress upon his readers the urgency of the issue, Scholem employed a powerful trope in his above-mentioned reply to Burla, in the form of Sabbateanism. "The Zionist ideal belongs on one side and the messianic ideal belongs on the other. One kingdom does not touch the other except in the hollow clichés of town hall meetings that sometimes instill in our youth a renewed spirit of Sabbateanism, which is destined to fail. Its inner roots preclude the Zionist movement from falling under the jurisdiction of the Sabbatean movement, and the attempts to infuse it with such a Sabbatean spirit have already caused much damage."[66]

To some, Sabbatai Zevi was known as the false messiah who had stirred an entire nation into deluded action. In this context, therefore, the term Sabbateanism signified everything that was wrong and misinformed in Jewish messianic history.[67] By mentioning Sabbateanism in the context of Zionism, Scholem here expresses his profound unease about the very concrete attempts to align the messianic aspirations of the Jewish religion with Zionism. The hope that Zionism would fulfill messianic aspirations was, to Scholem, a mistake of "Sabbatean" proportions.

Yet, no one would listen to Scholem's insistent warnings. Brith Shalom was marginalized and eventually ceased to exist in the early 1930s. At the university,

---

65. Emphasis in the original. Quoted from Ratsabi, *Between Zionism and Judaism*, 146.

66. See note 50.

67. As David Biale shows, there are some rather positive readings of the history of the Sabbatean messianic movement. "Shabbtai Zvi and the Seductions of Jewish Orientalism," in *Jerusalem Studies in Jewish Thought*, ed. Rachel Elior (Jerusalem, 2001). These aspects are discussed in greater detail in chapter 5.

Joseph Klausner expounded his ideas to an enthusiastic crowd of students, ever more of whom spoke Hebrew as a mother tongue. To Scholem it would therefore have appeared that the political field was left wide open to right-wing thinkers, who took advantage of the ignorance of their public. The danger that Zionism would transform into a new Sabbatean affair must have appeared to him very real and palpable.

What happened next should therefore come as no surprise. In the late 1920s Scholem started a new research project, one that would make him famous. This was the study of the Sabbatean movement. It would prove to be far more successful than any other endeavor he had undertaken, certainly more than his political activism in Brith Shalom. Some commentators have read Scholem's Sabbateanism studies in the context of his disillusionment with the German idea of culture, as a romantic enthusiasm for iconoclasm and charismatic albeit deluded figures. While this may be true to some extent, I wish to suggest that through this field of study Scholem was seeking, originally and first and foremost, to address the political reality in Palestine and what he deemed at the time to present the gravest danger to Zionism: Sabbatean-like misguided messianic endeavor.

Scholem's early work on Sabbatai Zevi should therefore be understood as a plea, as the sounding of a warning bell. According to Scholem, the lesson of the deluded belief in the false messiah Sabbatai Zevi was that people should be cautious about wishing that the impossible would materialize and redeem their lives. For in fact, as the Sabbatean experience proved, such hopes end bitterly. Put differently, in his early studies of Sabbateanism Scholem shows that throughout history, the greatest hope of all, the yearning for a messiah, had never succeeded in creating a promised land; rather, it had brought about only new forms of suffering and new kinds of exile.

Furthermore, the results of Scholem's study of Sabbatai Zevi should likewise be read as a critique of the foremost scholar of Jewish messianism of the day, Joseph Klausner. Scholem's underlying methodological assumption was that messianism could not and should never be understood as an idea, an expectation, or a vision alone. Messianism was, essentially, an event in history. As a historical event, Scholem showed, messianism had rewarded its adherents with harsh disappointment. In fact, therefore, the appearance of the Messiah on the stage of history inevitably crushes the idea of messianism itself, regardless of how beautiful or convincing this idea may have appeared at first. This was something that Scholem knew all too well.

Finally, however, Scholem's study of the messianic movement of Sabbatai Zevi reflects the personal frustration that Scholem himself felt upon immigrating to Palestine. In his study, Scholem tells the story of a promise that was never fulfilled. Entertaining messianic expectations may be an invigorating experience; it stirs people to action. The problem lies in the realization of the vision, which is doomed to fall tragically short of the expectation. This neatly sums up Scholem's personal experience in Palestine. Gershom Scholem was a young radical who was prepared to risk all in the name of an ideal he had developed together with and in opposition to his friends in the youth movement. There was nothing inherently wrong with the vision, apart from the fact that it could never have come true. Indeed, when Scholem finally arrived in Zion, nothing was quite as he had hoped it would be. One may thus convincingly argue that no one could have taught the Sabbatean lesson in quite the same way as Scholem did. For, in fact, Scholem drew the lesson of dashed dreams, to which we now turn, from the disappointment he himself had experienced after immigrating to Palestine.

CHAPTER 5

Against All Odds:
Sabbatean Belief and the
Sabbatean Movement

The messianic phraseology of Zionism, especially at decisive moments, is not in the least that of Sabbatean seduction, which could bring the renewal of Judaism, the stabilization of its world from the unbroken spirit of language, to ruin.

[Die messianische Phraseologie des Zionismus, besonders in entscheidenden Momenten, ist nicht die geringste jener sabbatianischen Verführungen, die die Erneuerung des Judentums, die Stabilisierung seiner Welt aus ungebrochenem Sprachgeist, zum Scheitern bringen können.]

GERSHOM SCHOLEM, "The Theology of Sabbateanism
in Light of Abraham Cardozo," 1928

What happens when the events of world history take an unexpected turn and profoundly upset people's hopes and desires? Mostly, we would assume, people learn to cope and eventually return to their mundane routine, to their daily expectations and casual disappointments. But what happens if the hopes stored for a certain epoch, movement, or leader transcend the realm of wishful thinking and transform into a belief? What if people intensely believe that this time things will really change, that poverty will be overcome, pride restored, trust created, and promises kept? In some such cases, the most ardent believers do not despair even when they discover that society is polarized, that poverty persists, and that the leadership is corrupt. In certain instances, the hard facts of historical reality do not deter people from clinging to their unrealistic hopes. This is the conclusion that Gershom Scholem reached in his study of Sabbatean messianism.

People, Scholem observed, maintain their beliefs even in the face of every shred of historical or political reasoning and even when these beliefs are detrimental to their long-term interests. They might keep on believing in the integrity of a leader, for example, even when everything he has done suggests that he is corrupt and is abusing his power. This behavior, Scholem furthermore observed, might be condemned from a moral or political standpoint, but should be understood by the historian. The historian, and especially the historian of religion, should understand that belief does not obey the rules of historical reasoning. Belief, Scholem noted, cherishes the improbable, the strange, and what he called the paradoxical, that is, the impossible. We believe, in other words, in what cannot be rather than in what we see every day. Therefore, if the historian is bent on understanding the history of belief, in this case the history of Sabbatean belief, as well as its antecedents, structures, and impact, he or she should seek to reconstruct the internal reasoning of the belief and put aside moral judgment of it.

Scholem's call to understand belief rather than to judge it was especially poignant in the case of the messianic adventure of Sabbatai Zevi, which was often conceived of either as a dramatic act of bravery or as a direct affront to common sense. Born in 1626 in Smyrna (Izmir), Zevi was an unstable young man who studied the classical sources of Judaism but was especially drawn by the Kabbalah. He first declared himself to be the Messiah in 1648. In order to prove his vocation he pronounced the Tetragrammaton in public. A mortal sin for most humans, pronouncing the Tetragrammaton is considered in the Jewish tradition to be the unique prerogative of the High Priest in Jerusalem, who utters the explicit name of God on the Day of Atonement at the culminating moment of the day's ritual. Contrary to every expectation, Zevi did not die as a result of this action. He was, however, denounced for it by his community leaders and later expelled from the city. This did not hinder him from prophesying and declaring himself to be the Messiah. He gradually caught the attention of Jewish dignitaries and subsequently of the Jewish communities in Jerusalem, Salonika, and in Cairo. Eventually he was recognized by Jews throughout the Diaspora as the Messiah until he was called in 1666 to Istanbul by the Ottoman authorities for questioning. It was prophesied that the Sultan would submit to Zevi and would crown him with his own crown. Upon his arrival Zevi was arrested, imprisoned in Gallipoli, and finally summoned to Edirne, where, under the threat of death, he cast off his Jewish garment and donned a Turkish turban, thereby proclaiming his conversion to Islam. Sabbatai Zevi died in exile 1673, on a day of special significance in the Jewish tradition. According to an ancient Jewish legend, the ninth day of the month of Av, the day on which the Temple in Jerusalem was twice destroyed, was also the day on which the

Messiah was to be born.[1] It is said that Sabbatai Zevi was born and died on that day.

Some were impressed by the figure of the false messiah, by his prowess as well as his unorthodox and unruly behavior. In *Altneuland* (Old-New-Land), Theodor Herzl's vision of the future utopist Jewish state, 'Sabbatai Zevi' is an opera that enacts the dramatic events surrounding the Messiah and his failed mission to restore the world.[2] Zalman Rubashov (Shazar), a journalist historian and a leading Zionist politician, asked his readers in a column in the daily *Davar* to remember their spiritual forefather, Sabbatai Zevi, on the day of his death. He ended his comments, published in 1925 on the ninth of Av, with the following words: "distant is the man [Zevi], distant is the generation and foreign are the paths. But the eternal flame will not snuff out."[3] It is telling that Rubashov chose on this day to commemorate Sabbatai Zevi and not the destruction of the Temple, yet his admiration is perfectly understandable. Sabbatai Zevi was the first Jew in memory to walk proud as a king among the otherwise ruthless Ottoman rulers of the land, and to suffer no consequences, or so it at first seemed.

Other intellectuals, such as the influential historian Heinrich Grätz, portrayed Sabbatai Zevi in his monumental work *The History of the Jews* as dim-witted and mentally unstable.[4] Grätz's contempt was no less understandable. Sabbatai Zevi was a vulgar heretic who offended practically every Jewish religious sentiment, and whose celebrated pomp ended in a whimper.

Within this continuous argument about Zevi's role in Jewish history, Scholem took an entirely new position. His main concerns were informed by neither contempt nor enthusiasm. Rather, he argued, the most important aspect of the story is still largely unknown. Indeed, none of the many renowned historians and intellectuals who wrote about Sabbateanism had seriously entertained the idea that it might have been more than a mere infatuation, something more profound than an explosion of light and color in the otherwise tedious history of Jewish life in exile. For over a century and a half after the conversion of the "Messiah," Sabbateanism stirred emotions and fired the imagination of

1. This legend appears already in an early text, Midrash Rabbah, an interpretation of the Book of Lamentations (Eicha).

2. For more on the reception of Sabbatai Zevi among a generation of Zionists and Jewish reformers including Herzl, see Biale, "Shabbtai Zvi." See also Lazier, *God Interrupted*, 139–45.

3. Zalman Rubashov, "Shabbatai Sevi's Day" (in Hebrew), *Davar*, July 29, 1925. In the translation I follow Lazier, *God Interrupted*, 140.

4. Heinrich Grätz, *History of the Jews: From the Rise of the Kabbala to the Permanent Settlement of the Marranos in Holland* (New York: Cosimo, 2009), 118–66.

Jews throughout the world. It left a deep imprint on Jewish history and serious rifts in Jewish consciousness. Yet, Scholem claimed, no one had taken notice of the events that had taken place since the conversion of the Messiah. And neither had serious attention been paid to the fact that despite Sabbateanism's mistaken and perhaps outrageous beliefs, it nevertheless constituted a comprehensive system of thought. As a result, he asserted, historians had collectively failed to appreciate the importance of the Sabbatean movement in the history of the Jewish people and its impact on the evolvement of its religious thought.

In his own work, Scholem insisted that the Sabbatean movement had not become transformational merely because one individual had declared himself to be the Messiah and another had begun to prophesy that redemption and homecoming were imminent. It was true that Sabbatai Zevi had generated more excitement than most messiahs, and that Nathan of Gaza, his prophet, had reached out further and struck deeper than most prophets. But while the success of the leading figures of the Sabbatean movement was important, it alone could not account for its lasting historical effect.

The historical import of Sabbateanism, Scholem argued, stemmed from the decision of certain factions among its followers to retain the belief in Sabbatai Zevi's integrity even after he committed the worst sin a religious leader can commit. They clung to their Messiah, that is, even after he converted to Islam, thereby formally denouncing his religion and his office. In fact, Scholem argued, the believers had maintained their cherished belief not despite the conversion but because of it. All the evidence notwithstanding, they regarded the conversion as symbolizing the authenticity of their leader and the veracity of the prophecy. Furthermore, it was the very improbability of the belief that explained, Scholem argued, its lasting success. Belief in the unruly, converted, and later dead Messiah had proved more durable than many other systems of thought precisely because it was based on an elaborate fiction, because it was a figment of a desperate imagination.

The improbable belief in a converted Messiah was important, Scholem claimed, not only to appreciate the reasons for Sabbatean resilience but also to understand the conduct of its believers and their impact on Jewish history. According to Scholem, one hundred and fifty years of Sabbatean experimentation had left the Jewish body politic splintered and mainstream Jewish religious thought petrified. The integrity of the nation had been corrupted by groups that had broken off completely from the Jewish nation, by others who chose to lead a nihilistic and destructive way of life, and by enthusiastic reformers of different persuasions who had compromised the overall integrity of the Jewish faith. Some believers, Scholem showed, had kept their inclinations mostly to themselves, strictly observing the rituals of Jewish life while secretly devoting themselves to an apostate messiah. Nevertheless, although they appeared to be Jewish in the most traditional sense, they had relinquished the emotional aspect of their religion by consciously investing their thoughts, intentions, and beliefs in apostasy and in sin. They, too, had thus contributed to the widening chasm within the Jewish spirit. In his work, Scholem set out to trace the development of each of these social and ideological trends as they sprouted off the Sabbatean stem, but his overarching conclusion transcends the detailed recounting of the various trajectories of belief. According to Scholem, Judaism dramatically transformed as a direct result of the Sabbatean debacle. The Kabbalah in general and the mystical messianism of Sabbatai Zevi in particular played an essential role in shaping modern Jewish history by generating a fragmented, inauthentic, and confused type of Judaism.

GERSHOM SCHOLEM AND SABBATAI ZEVI

Scholem's study of the Sabbatean movement became the hallmark of his scholarly career, arguably his most provocative and compelling work. Joseph Dan writes that "no part of Scholem's voluminous works had a greater impact on modern Jewish historiography than his studies on the Sabbatean Movement."[5] Some scholars have sought even to find in these studies clues or a coded message regarding his political convictions. To a certain degree such attempts are justified. Scholem's own life and ideology can be viewed in relation to the Sabbatean past. Born in 1897, Scholem was heir to the political, spiritual, and social trends that were rooted, according to his own historical account, in Sabbatai Zevi's conversion. In other words, growing up in Germany around the turn of the twentieth century, he was intimately familiar with the different paths and the various pitfalls of Jewish life in the modern world, with the Jewish liberal movement, Hasidism, Orthodoxy, and Zionism. One may therefore justifiably argue that in his Sabbatean studies Scholem sought to describe the roots of the spiritual confusion that he himself had experienced as a young man. In a more direct way, Scholem's investigation of the Sabbatean past was also a reflection on the political situation in Palestine and his disappointment at what he had discovered there. As noted above, he started his studies of the Sabbatean history and published the results of his endeavors during the 1920s and 1930s, precisely, that is, as the Zionist movement appeared to him to be

5. Joseph Dan, *Gershom Scholem and the Mystical Dimension of Jewish History* (New York: New York University Press, 1988), 286.

veering dangerously away from historical reality in pursuit of unattainable hopes and unrealistic dreams.

During the first part of this period Scholem was fully engaged in the Zionist politics of Palestine. This will be discussed in more detail in the next chapter, but it may already be mentioned here that the 1930s witnessed radical changes in Scholem's political worldview. After immigrating to Palestine, Scholem argued polemically and powerfully against the unholy harnessing of religious thought to politics, and more specifically against what he perceived as the messianic delusions of Zionism in Palestine. As we have seen, already in 1929 Scholem wrote that "the Zionist ideal belongs on one side and the messianic ideal belongs on the other. One kingdom does not touch the other except in the hollow clichés of town hall meetings that sometime instill in our youth a renewed spirit of Sabbateanism, which is destined to fail." Scholem likewise warned against the dangers that Zionism was facing by choosing to align itself with what he considered to be unjust and therefore unsustainable British imperialism, and against what he believed to be the legitimate national aspirations of the Arabs in Palestine. He argued that this decision reflected the movement's deep and dangerous misunderstanding of world history and contemporary politics. The imperial project, he maintained, was about to crumble, and the Arab East was on the rise. Zionism, he believed, should carefully choose its allegiances, forgo imperialism, and form a lasting relation with its new neighbors in Palestine. Seen in this context, Scholem's history of Sabbateanism was an intense meditation on the dangers of ideology, historical blindness, and political disappointment, as well as an authoritative treatise on the role of politics in general and messianic tendencies in Zionism during the 1920s and early 1930s in particular.

Yet Scholem's political zeal gradually waned during the 1930s. The violent events in Palestine in 1929 led to a deep ideological crisis among the members of Brith Shalom, which began to disintegrate at that point and finally ceased to exist in 1933. These events had also shaken Scholem's convictions about the possibility of a peaceful solution for Arabs and Jews in Palestine. The Nazi rise to power in Germany likewise seems to have forced Scholem to reevaluate the direction of the Zionist enterprise in Palestine as well as the relations between the Zionist movement in Palestine and the Jews of the Diaspora. Under the pressure of these overwhelming historical currents, Scholem revised his historical consciousness during the latter half of the 1930s. This will be discussed further in the present and forthcoming chapters as Scholem's new outlook on history clearly played a significant role in his conception of the Sabbatean movement, its historical impact, and its ideology.

The fact that Scholem's studies on Sabbateanism reflected his personal engagement in Zionist politics and his historical consciousness was not lost on commentators and scholars. Most understood Scholem's reflection on the Sabbatean movement as a direct continuation of his Zionist ideology.[6] Sabbateanism, they suggested, provided Scholem with a historical and religious blueprint for Zionism, since both movements were heretical (or at the very least, nonorthodox) attempts to overcome exile and restore the national integrity of the Jewish people in the holy land. Baruch Kurzweil was the first to make this claim, and the ensuing debate between him and Scholem attracted considerable scholarly attention.[7] In 1957 Kurzweil wrote a review of Scholem's newly published book about Sabbatai Zevi in the daily *Ha'aretz* in which he noted: "G. Scholem makes use of Sabbatean ideology and its consequences in order to view it as the immanent link between ancient traditionalist Judaism and the modern national Jewish movement."[8] Scholem never explicitly enunciated such a connection, but the suspicion that a deeper political insight was lurking in the shadows of Scholem's works on the Sabbatean movement lingers to this very day. Since Scholem was a devout Zionist, and since the link between Sabbateanism and Zionism already existed in the Zionist imagination, it would seem only natural to conclude that in excavating the Sabbatean past he sought to discover the hidden forefathers of Zionism within the Jewish religious tradition. It is probably for this reason that articles such as *Jewish Modernism: The Hidden Meanings of Gershom Scholem's Sabbatai Zevi* continue to probe beyond Scholem's stated objectives.[9]

6. For more on identifying Scholem's Kabbalah studies and especially his interpretation of Sabbateanism with Zionism, see Christoph Schmidt, "Der häretische Imperativ"; Lazier, *God Interrupted*, 139–45; David Anthony Skinner, "Jewish Modernism: The Hidden Meanings of Gershom Scholem's Sabbatai Sevi," in *Jewish Studies at the Turn of the Twentieth Century: Judaism from the Renaissance to Modern Times*, ed. Judit Targarona Borrás, and Ángel Sáenz-Badillos (Leiden: Brill, 1999), 384–88. Some commentators, including Joseph Dan, totally reject the notion of such identification. See Dan, *Gershom Scholem and the Mystical Dimension of Jewish History*, 286–312. Other scholars have taken a more nuanced approach. See Biale, *Counter-history*, esp. 94–111.

7. See, for example, David Meyers, "The Scholem-Kurzweil Debate and Modern Jewish Historiography," *Modern Judaism* 6, no. 3 (October 1986): 261–85; Noam Zadoff, "In the Garden Rows of Nihilism: The Debate between Gershom Scholem and Baruch Kurzweil" (in Hebrew), *Kabbalah: Journal for the Study of Mystical Texts* 16 (2007), 299-360.

8. Kurzweil, "Remarks on 'Shabbtai Sevi.'"

9. Skinner, "Jewish Modernism."

Nevertheless, there are reasons to doubt the existence of covert ideological ties between Scholem's interpretation of Sabbateanism and his Zionist convictions. Although he was never one to refrain from expressing himself in broad and powerful terms, Scholem never expressed any relation between Sabbateanism and Zionism in general, or his own Zionist convictions in particular. Moreover, as Noam Zadoff notes, he was angered and offended by this interpretation of his works. In a private letter to Kurzweil, Scholem reacted angrily to the above-mentioned review article: "All those things that you attribute to me about the genealogy of the secular nationalism in the Sabbatean movement are all of your own . . . I have never expressed such folly and this is not the hidden reason for my interest in this affair . . . In my opinion, my scientific endeavor should be discussed in accordance to its stated objectives, not according to its hidden meanings."[10]

This is not a ploy. Scholem was obviously fascinated by Sabbatean history and theology, but in his studies of Sabbateanism Scholem never portrayed it as a positive element in Jewish history, nor did he provide any direct reference that would tie it to Zionism. In fact, he was mostly critical of Sabbatean heresy, condemning it as destructive and immoral.

More important, perhaps, neither Scholem's interpretation of Sabbateanism nor his Zionist convictions could be regarded as stable, absolute, or finite ideas. In fact, Scholem's conception of both ideas evolved and changed over time. As we have seen in chapters 2 and 3 above, Scholem's appreciation of Zionism in general and his own engagement with it changed according to the circumstances of place, influences, and current events. His Zionism reflected his personal situation—in Berlin and then in Jerusalem—and his personal convictions, as an uncompromising opponent of the First World War and of mainstream Zionism. As we shall see in the next chapter, Scholem's appreciation of Zionism would change again in the 1930s in the wake of the violent events in Palestine and the Nazis' rise to power in Germany.[11] Scholem's interpretation of Sabbateanism cannot therefore be understood as an integral and final one. He studied the Sabbatean movement and wrote about it over a period of over fifty tumultuous years. Written at different times, each study bears the marks of his ever-evolving historical knowledge and consciousness. Therefore, discussing Scholem's Zionism or his Sabbateanism as finite ideas and identifying

10. In Noam Zadoff, "In the Garden Rows of Nihilism," 342.

11. This is discussed below in greater detail. See also Noam Zadoff, "'Zion's Self-Engulfing Light': On Gershom Scholem's Disillusionment with Zionism," *Modern Judaism* 31, no. 3 (2011): 272–84.

the one with the other run the risk of anachronism at the very least, and of oversimplification at worst.

It is for this conceptual instability that the following discussion shies away from the term "neutralization." On several different occasions,[12] Scholem argued that Hasidism (which followed the Sabbatean eruption) neutralized the messianic forces by, as Biale puts it, "redirecting its energies towards the personal rather than the national realm."[13] "Neutralization" seems therefore to be a rather suggestive term. Not only does it describe Scholem's conceptualization of Hasidism but also it seems to bear important similarity to his view of Zionism. Thus Biale for example argues that Scholem "obviously conceives the Zionist movement as more revolutionary than Hasidism."[14] For Biale the term is obviously useful for certain ends, but it seems to me that it mostly obfuscates the complex issue at hand. For in fact, "neutralization" is relevant only for a very specific and rather narrow aspect of Scholem's outlook on Hasidism, Sabbateanism, and Zionism, which carried throughout his life different meanings at different times.

Reading Scholem's works on Sabbateanism and evaluating his political convictions demand a certain historical sensitivity. Just as Scholem's early Zionist activism differs profoundly from his Zionism during his later years, so too Scholem's earlier work on the Sabbatean movement differs from the works he wrote later in his life. The following discussion on Scholem's Sabbatean works concerns, first and foremost, Scholem's three most comprehensive studies, which he wrote and published prior to the end of the Second World War. These include his first article on the topic published in *Der Jude* in 1928; his best-known study, "Redemption through Sin," which appeared in 1937; and his most comprehensive study, initially delivered as part of lecture series in New York in 1938, and subsequently published under the title *Major Trends in Jewish Mysticism* in 1941. Analysis of these three major studies reveals that already in this early period, Scholem held a wide gamut of views and ideas about the Sabbatean movement, its causes and its effects, which in turn reflect dramatic transformations in Scholem's understanding of himself and in his political convictions. Never again did Scholem publish a comprehensive study of Sabbateanism, an attempt to comprehend Sabbateanism as a whole.

12. This point is made nowhere more clearly than in an article titled "The Neutralization of the Messianic Element in Early Hasidism," in Gershom Scholem, *The Messianic Idea in Judaism, and Other Essays on Jewish Spirituality* (New York: Schocken, 1971), 176–203.

13. Biale, *Counter-history*, 107.

14. Ibid.

His later work on Sabbateanism—most notably his thousand-page study originally titled *Sabbatai Zevi and the Sabbatean Movement during His Lifetime*, published in 1956—completes the cycle of Scholem's Sabbatean studies. As we shall see, this study substantially differs from the three earlier ones for being devoted to only one aspect of the Sabbatean story, the one that Scholem declared in his previous studies to be less important.

THE THEOLOGY OF SABBATEANISM

In retrospect, it seems more than fitting that Gershom Scholem published his first, bold, and mostly forgotten study on the Sabbatean movement, "The Theology of Sabbateanism in Light of Abraham Cardozo,"[15] in a special issue of an exceptional yet largely forgotten journal.[16] The March 1928 issue of *Der Jude* was dedicated to Buber's fiftieth birthday and therefore especially festive. Martin Buber was the editor of the journal, its founder and publisher. With the inauguration of this journal, perhaps the most daring of all German Jewish Weimar era publications, he had created a platform for discussion.[17] The festive issue, edited by Robert Weltsch, was not a rehearsed homage to the already legendary Buber, but rather includes cutting-edge articles in the spirit of the journal. Many of the major Jewish intellectual figures of the time including Arnold Zweig, Samuel Hugo Bergman, Leo Baeck, and Judah Magnes contributed to the issue. It included also a copy of a handwritten letter from Theodor Herzl to the young Martin Buber, written in 1903, as well as an

15. This study was, however, discussed at some length by Daniel Weidner, who also comments on its historical stature. See *Gershom Scholem: Politisches, esoterisches und historiographisches Schreiben*, 373–76.

16. A scanned version of the original publication, "Über die Theologie des Sabbatianismus im Lichte Abraham Cardozos," can be found in its original context, together with scans of practically all historical German Jewish publications, on the excellent website www.compact memory.de in the *Der Jude* issue of March 1928, 123–39 . All page numbers accord with this publication. The study was also reprinted in Gershom Scholem, *Judaica 1* (Frankfurt am Main: Suhrkamp, 1963), 119–46.

17. The title of the journal alone conveys a sense of the driving force behind it and the boldness of its publisher, who thus transformed the mostly derogatory term 'Jude' into a symbol of forward thinking and creativity. Paul Mendes-Flohr even suggests that "under Buber's deft stewardship, *Der Jude* became not only the most sophisticated journal within the Jewish community but one of the most engaging periodicals in the Weimar Republic." Mendes-Flohr, *Divided Passions*, 211. See also Eleonore Lappin, *Der Jude, 1916–1928: Jüdische Moderne zwischen Universalismus und Partikularismus* (Tübingen: Mohr Siebeck, 2000).

exchange of letters between Buber and Franz Rosenzweig titled "Letters to an Anti-Zionist by a Non-Zionist." In this company, Scholem appeared as an up-coming scholar among the giants of the previous generation.

In his study Scholem offered, for the first time, his insights into the history of the Sabbatean movement and his suggestions for how to proceed beyond everything that had previously been said about the topic. In retrospect, it is astounding to discover that some of his deepest insights into the movement's history already appear here in 1928. First and foremost, Scholem asserts that knowledge about the Sabbatean movement had been impaired by historians who had restricted themselves to the period before Zevi's conversion. Second, he argues, Sabbateanism had been misunderstood because of attempts to uti-lize the events for political leveraging. As a result, Scholem claims, the driving force of the Sabbatean movement had been obfuscated as had its true histori-cal impact. In order to unveil the real significance of the Sabbatean movement in Jewish history, it was thus necessary to set aside political judgment and to address the events that followed the Messiah's conversion. And this was the task that Scholem took upon himself already in this article from 1928.

Compared with much of the existing literature, Scholem's basic analysis of the Sabbatean movement is based on a rather radical claim, namely, that the driving force behind the Sabbatean movement was its basic set of ideas about the world, God, and man. The Sabbatean movement, therefore, was not driven by the figure of Sabbatai Zevi, who had dared to stand up and promise to lead the Jews to their homeland after more than fifteen hundred years of humilia-tion in exile. Neither was it motivated by the man, Sabbatai Zevi, who had so vulgarly offended every Jewish religious feeling in public and yet enjoyed the respect of Jews everywhere. Sabbateanism was not, Scholem claimed, a story about the Ottoman rulers in Alexandria, Jerusalem, Izmir, and Salonika, whose tardiness in reacting had allowed the movement to thrive. Nor was it about the charismatic prophet, Nathan of Gaza, who had disseminated the new gospel among the Jews. The story of the Sabbatean movement, according to Scholem, should be understood by the ideas that motivated it. Sabbateanism, he says, is first and foremost a theology: "What actually took place here in the inner heart of Judaism will continue to appear totally unclear and mysterious, as long as one fails to observe with objective seriousness the movement's *theology* and its relations to contemporary Judaism."[18]

Scholem's analysis of Sabbatean theology, to which the article is indeed dedicated, is, however, somewhat dense and incoherent. In this initial study, it

18. Scholem, "Über die Theologie des Sabbatianismus," 123. Emphasis added.

appears that Scholem had yet to master the material fully and that he had not fully developed his historical thesis. The argument clearly reflects his desire to pack all his findings about the causes, effects, ideology, developments, and belief of the Sabbatean movement into twenty-odd pages, and to express his astonishment at these findings. One sentence should suffice to demonstrate the perplexity that Scholem must have felt as he confronted his sources. In an underscored sentence on the third page Scholem states: "The theology of Sabbateanism transpires as the construction of a virtual Gnostic antinomianism within the world of Judaism and its order of life, devised from a dialectical collapse of the rudimentary concepts of the Lurianic Kabbalah in the spirit of Marranism."[19]

In this early study, therefore, Scholem shows signs of having difficulty in differentiating between the theological background of the Sabbatean development and the social causes that made it so popular, and the historical consequences of the movement and its ideological aftermath.

Notwithstanding these complexities, Scholem's basic historical insight was that the Sabbatean theology of Abraham Cardozo should be read against the backdrop of the decadent enthusiasm that, so Scholem believed early in his career, characterized the Lurianic Kabbalah. In stark contrast to his later descriptions, Scholem claimed here that Rabbi Isaac Luria and other sixteenth-century mystics of Safed had developed the basic intuitions of previous mystical systems into an overarching scheme of multiple forces and aspects. "In Safed," Scholem wrote, "the mystical world lost its simple constitution. The ten aspects [*sephirot*] of the divine were *contorted* into an endless mythological catalogue . . . that resists any overview."[20] This radical development had far-reaching consequences. As Scholem noted, "such a situation had, through dialectical necessity, to give rise to religious processes that sought to salvage the living relationship with God from such mythological entanglements."[21] The intricacy of the Lurianic model of the Godhead has, Scholem argued, distanced Him from the lives of his believers. He became, ironically, a philosopher's God, beyond the reach of everyday life.

---

19. "Die Theologie des Sabbateanismus erweist sich als die Konstruktion eines virtuellen gnostischen Antinomismus innerhalb der Welt des Judentums und seiner Lebensordnung, aus einem dialektischen Zerfall der Grundbegriffe der lurjanischen Kabbala im marranischen Geiste konzipiert." Ibid., 125.

20. Ibid., 128. Emphasis added.

21. Ibid.

The solution to this problem, Scholem argued, took two different routes. The first solution of the problem of the multiplicity of the Godhead was to recast the original mystical intuition in "the language of the heart,"[22] a project undertaken, according to Scholem, by the leaders of the popular eighteenth-century Hasidism movement. The second solution was the Sabbatean one. According to Scholem, Sabbatean theology radically separated the intensely complex structure of the Godhead, as created in the Lurianic Kabbalah, from the Being of God. While the Supreme Being was left intact, expressing the original completeness of the monotheistic god, the complex structure of the Lurianic Kabbalah portrayed the active aspect of divinity. This aspect, rather than God, was the dynamic force that maintained the world in its abundance. And once again, it was this complex being rather than God that was the living subject of everyday belief.

Ultimately, Scholem argued, Abraham Cardozo's Sabbatean theology had implanted an inverted Gnostic ideal at the heart of Jewish thought. As in the ancient Gnosis, so he maintained, God was understood not as essentially one being but rather as two. While one God was distant and cold, the other was active and responsive. However, whereas in the ancient Gnosis the active God, or God the creator, was essentially evil, according to the Sabbatean scheme the creator was essentially good and benevolent. Thus, Scholem asserted, Sabbatean theology had accepted the overarching idea of Gnosis but had inverted its value judgment.

Scholem's analysis of Sabbatean theology stood in stark contrast to almost everything that was assumed about monotheism and Gnosticism at the time.[23] Since the end of the nineteenth century, the idea of Gnosis had served as a central trope in an intense and ongoing discussion about the nature of religion, messianism, and theology.[24] In this discussion, Gnosis was generally situated between monotheism and polytheism. It belonged to an era in which the Christian dogma was not yet fully formed and accepted, and in which pre-Christian beliefs still circulated widely. Scholem's conception of Gnosis,

22. Ibid., 126.

23. As Guy G. Stroumsa shows, this notion that Kabbalah and Gnosis were linked existed long before Scholem. See "Gnosis and Judaism in Nineteenth-Century Christian Thought," in *Kabbala und Romantik*, ed. Eveline Goodman-Thau, Gert Mattenklott, and Christoph Schulte (Tübingen: Niemeyer, 1994), 43–58.

24. See Karen L. King, *What Is Gnosticism?* (Cambridge: Harvard University Press, 2005), esp. 71–110. For more on the contemporary reception of Gnosis, including Jonas's contribution, see also Lazier, *God Interrupted*, esp. 27–60. For more on Gnosis in Zionist thought, see Yotam Hotam, *Modern Gnosis and Zionism* (in Hebrew) (Jerusalem: Magnes Press, 2007).

therefore, participated in this discussion, which must have been familiar to his readers. Yet the proposition that this essentially heretical and ancient belief had taken a deep hold on the imagination of the Jewish people, the harbingers of monotheism, at the dawn of the modern age, was a revolutionary one. In his study, Scholem repeatedly stressed that Cardozo's radical speculation had raised fierce objections among his contemporaries. But it seems that with these remarks Scholem was also expressing his own astonishment at the utter improbability of the new theology and was conveying this astonishment to his readers.

Yet as offensive as Cardozo's theology might have been, it still fell short of becoming a driving force in history and a basis for religious and social practice. The social potential of Sabbatean theology, Scholem argued, had come to the fore once it was superimposed onto Jewish history. Cardozo, Scholem asserted, had argued that the historic exile of the Jews was reflected in their spiritual state. In exile Jews were deprived not only of a homeland and sovereignty but also of a true understanding of the forces that determined the world and their lives. For fifteen hundred years Jews had worshiped an immovable God rather than the God of creation and abundance. It thus followed that rediscovery of the truth in the guise of Sabbatean wisdom necessarily corresponded to the abolition of historical exile and the return of the Jews to their homeland. In this early work (which appeared almost fifteen years before *Major Trends*), Scholem evidently had a very different understanding of the role played by the symbol of 'exile' in Jewish tradition. Nevertheless, already in this early version he stresses the important symbolic role played by exile as well as the sudden appearance of a fundamentally new conception of the order of the world and the relationship between man and God, which arose against the backdrop of a fifteen-hundred-year-old misconstrued tradition.

The Messiah, in Cardozo's theology, was to be the propagator of the secret knowledge about the world, man, and God. As such, he must be unbound from the shackles of traditional Judaism, which was created in the darkness of exile and had therefore essentially misled believers for so long. The Messiah, it followed, was extraordinary inasmuch as he was able to overcome the mediation of tradition and experience the truth at first hand. Indeed, it was the power of his superior intuition, Scholem explained, and his pure, rational, and immediate perception of the truth that made the Messiah what he is, according to the Sabbatean formulation. As Scholem noted, "The Messiah will perceive God not through tradition or revelation as in the case of all others since King Hezekiah, but through his intuition [*ratio*], and this absolute intellectual permeation of the 'mystery of faith' is the actual and unmistakable identifying mark of the Messiah."[25] This dialectic and almost ironic turn appeared to Scholem to be essential to Sabbatean theology. "The collapse of an unlimited intuition-mysticism, as is the case in the Lurianic Kabbalah, leads to an almost Maimonidean notion of the redemptive power of the intellect . . .—that fundamentally illuminates the metaphysical stage of the Sabbatean movement."[26]

The idea that the Messiah could by virtue of his intuition perceive the bare truth directly and could thus penetrate the veil of tradition explained the behavior of Sabbatai Zevi. Sabbatai Zevi had done what no one else could do. He had uttered the explicit name of God in public and had felt nothing of God's wrath. And he had pronounced himself king of the Jews alongside the Ottoman rulers and had remained alive. Zevi could do these things precisely because he saw the truth: the world was about to transition from the present era of law and coercion to a new age of freedom. And this knowledge lent him his power and his unique stature vis-à-vis social norms and the edicts of Jewish law. His unruly behavior, therefore, did not merely confirm the authenticity of his messianic vocation but was also essential to his mission. Sabbatai Zevi, according to this account, had converted to Islam in order to do what no ordinary mortal could have done without inflicting great harm on himself and on others. Paradoxically, it was precisely this singular and outrageous act that proved conclusively that he was indeed the Messiah.

With this argument, Scholem now turned to formulate the interpretation that would become the foundation for his understanding of Sabbatean heresy. Sabbatai Zevi's conversion, he argued here for the first time, was construed by his believers as an attempt to restore the sparks of divine light that had fallen onto the exile of materiality during the process of the creation of the world according to the Lurianic myth. As discussed in chapter 3 above, the climax of the sixteenth-century Lurianic myth of creation was the breaking of the vessels. These vessels were designed to capture the divine light that emanated from the absolute endlessness of God into the empty space created by the initial act of *tsimtsum*, by the exile of God. However, they had failed to withstand the immense pressure of the light and had shattered. A limited number of sparks caught in the fragments of the vessels fell with those fragments into the shells of materiality, into the exile of the world. In the popular reception of this myth, Scholem asserted, the people of Israel were given the task of freeing these sparks from their material prison through pious behavior and by fulfilling the edicts

25. Scholem, "Über die Theologie des Sabbatianismus," 132.
26. Ibid., 133.

of Jewish law. Every good deed could free a spark, and once all the sparks were freed, it was further believed, creation would regain its original wholeness. God and man would then overcome the existential state of exile. In the original Lurianic version, Scholem would later argue, the Messiah was accorded a symbolic role. He was perceived not as a human figure but as an idea, encapsulating the possibility of joint action.

In Sabbatean theology, however, the figure of the Messiah was resurrected and allocated a precise function in the scheme of redemption. The Messiah was to undertake a mission that no regular human could undertake without risking his life and soul. According to Sabbatean dogma, so goes Scholem's interpretation, several sparks fell beyond the reach of regular human beings, deep into the lowest and most terrible part of the shells. Reaching down into the shells and freeing the sparks that had lodged therein was thus a task given to a superhuman figure, the Messiah, and this was how Zevi's deed was perceived. The Messiah, Sabbatai Zevi, had converted to Islam in the world of the senses, but the inner truth of this action was quite different. In fact, this conversion had given Zevi access to the place to which no ordinary person can go, into the deepest layers of evil, where the last sparks were to be found and freed.

But the connection that Scholem made between the Gnostic theology of Abraham Cardozo and Zevi's conversion is somewhat questionable. Gnostic theology, in fact, explained the conversion only in very general terms. Therefore, Scholem resorted to an interpretation of the Lurianic Kabbalah that he presented here for the first time in a few short sentences.[27] The relation between Cardozo's Gnosticism and Luria's Kabbalah is described here in unique terms, to which Scholem never returned. Scholem perhaps realized the inadequacy of his theological explanations and thus developed his theory in new directions. He certainly continuously developed his interpretation of the Lurianic Kabbalah until it became a pivotal factor in his account of the creation of the Sabbatean movement. As we have seen in chapter 3, the Lurianic Kabbalah would transform, in Scholem's later work, into a full-fledged ideology of the Jewish people. Simultaneously, Gnostic theology would transform into yet another curious element within the larger scheme of the Sabbatean configuration. These changes represent a gradual accumulation of knowledge and a greater focus rather than a revolution. Yet there is one important aspect that renders this early study— "The Theology of Sabbateanism in Light of Abraham Cardozo"—radically different from Scholem's later works on Sabbateanism.

27. Ibid.

In the very last lines of this study Scholem explicitly draws a parallel be-tween Sabbateanism and Zionism. These lines bring Scholem's study more in line with the forum in which it was published. Unlike his analysis of a for-gotten seventeenth-century mystic, the other studies in this special edition of *Der Jude* addressed current social and political issues. It is thus possible that Scholem concluded his study with a reference to current affairs in order to contribute to the contemporary discussion, although it seems even more probable that Scholem's remarks reflect his still combative political spirit, which would gradually moderate over the following years. In any event, the Sabbatean experiment was, according to Scholem, similar in a deep and im-portant way to Zionism.

Those familiar with scholarly discourse on Scholem's Sabbateanism, much of which has taken Baruch Kurzweil's position on this matter, may be sur-prised by the analogy he drew between Sabbateanism and Zionism. For this analogy has nothing to do with Sabbatean heresy, that is, with its essentially unorthodox attempt to restore Jewish pride and Jewish sovereignty. Heresy might have inspired other Zionist historians, but not Scholem, for whom the Sabbatean affair was a lesson in hubris. Sabbateanism, he rather argues, had allowed Jews to ignore historical reality and instead create an ideological mon-ster, a "chimera" that would threaten to ruin Judaism from within. To him, the study of Sabbateanism proved that a thoroughly corrupt "Jewish reality" had existed already in the seventeenth century. This comment explicitly referred, one should note, to Oskar Goldberg's book *Die Wirklichkeit der Hebräer* (The Reality of the Jews),[28] which had won acclaim in Jewish circles in Germany in the 1920s, much to Scholem's dismay.[29] Scholem argued that the Sabbatean affair proved that the vain and shallow declaration of Jewish prowess had not begun with Zionism nor died out with Sabbatai Zevi's demise. On the con-trary, the unholy approach of Sabbateanism, mixing piety with heresy, reli-gious sources with political aspirations, had persisted within the Jewish spirit ever since Cardozo. Scholem writes, "The messianic phraseology of Zionism, especially at decisive moments, is not in the least that of Sabbatean seduc-tion, which could bring the renewal of Judaism, the stabilization of its world by the unbroken spirit of language, to ruin. For however ephemeral, like all

28. Oskar Goldberg, *Die Wirklichkeit der Hebräer* (Wiesbaden: Otto Harrassowitz Verlag, 2005).

29. Scholem mentions Oskar Goldberg in his memoir. *From Berlin to Jerusalem*, 146–48. But a more poignant critique may be found in a letter he sent to his friend Rosa Okun, which was widely distributed and discussed. See Scholem, *Briefe I*, 235–39.

theological constructions, Cardozo's too might have been, the deepest and most destructive impulse of Sabbateanism—Jewish hubris—has remained."[30] It was with this harsh observation that Scholem concluded his first study of the Sabbatean movement.

REDEMPTION THROUGH SIN

Nine years elapsed between Scholem's article on Abraham Cardozo and the publication of what is perhaps his best-known study. During this period Scholem wrote prolifically about issues concerning the Sabbatean movement, but it was only in 1937 with "Redemption through Sin"[31] that he faced once again the challenge of describing it as a coherent whole. On the face of things, not much had changed. Sabbateanism still entailed a revolutionary theology, an attempt to explain the conversion of the Messiah. As in his previous study, Scholem here too stated that the events and ideology of the Sabbatean movement during the period preceding the conversion of the Messiah were fairly well known, whereas knowledge about the 150 years of activity that followed the conversion was extremely limited. Here he expresses himself even more poignantly on the matter than before: "In turning to consider the Sabbatean movement after Sabbatai Zevi's conversion to Islam, we find ourselves still standing before a blank wall, not only of misunderstanding, but also of an actual refusal to understand."[32] With these words Scholem again announced his intention of venturing beyond the period mostly associated with the Sabbatean movement, namely, the lifetime of Sabbatai Zevi. In reality, Scholem went far beyond describing the ideological or even theological aspects of Sabbatean thought. With this study Scholem undertook for the first time to lay out his thesis about modern Jewish history. It is here that Scholem first delved into the origins of

30. "Die messianische Phraseologie des Zionismus . . . ist nicht geringste jener sabbatianischen Verführungen, die die Erneuerungen des Judentums, die Stabilisierung seiner Welt aus ungebrochenem Sprachgeist, zum Scheitern bringen können. Denn so vergänglich in der Zeit, wie alle theologischen Konstruktionen, auch Cardozos . . . gewesen sein mögen—der tiefste und zerstörende Antrieb des Sabbatianismus: die Hybris des Juden ist geblieben." Scholem, "Über die Theologie des Sabbatianismus," 139.

31. In the following, I make extensive use of the English translation while introducing minor adjustments based on the original Hebrew. See Gershom Scholem, "Redemption through Sin," *Studies and Sources on the History of Sabbateanism* (in Hebrew) (Jerusalem: Mosad Bialik, 1974), 9–67. All page numbers accord with Gershom Scholem, "Redemption through Sin," in *Messianic Idea in Judaism*, 78–141.

32. Scholem, "Redemption through Sin," 78.

modern Jewish social history and described how it had unfolded from its beginnings. And it is here that Scholem became the kind of author who, through knowledge and audacity, leaves a distinct mark on culture.

Jewish modernity, Scholem claimed, had originated from a radical idea: redemption could be brought about through sin. It had begun, in other words, by providing a new interpretation to an old dilemma, indicated in the title of the article. In the article Scholem fails to mention that the formula—redemption through sin—appears in the classic Jewish sources, including the Talmud, in reference to a recognized legal principle.[33] Perhaps he thought this would be redundant. In any event, the title of the study, which reads in the Hebrew original "Mitzvah ha-Ba'a be-Avera," does not accurately translate to "redemption through sin" but should rather be translated—somewhat awkwardly—as "a commandment fulfilled while committing a transgression."[34] The word *mitzvah* refers in general to each and every commandment stipulated by the Jewish edicts, the *halakha*. A *mitzvah* is therefore not a redemptive act per se, and certainly not redemption itself, but rather the basic component of Jewish life. *Avera*, on the other hand, is a legal term denoting an illegal act. In this context it would include any transgression of the Jewish code and any sin, but it does not carry the theological weight of the term 'sin' (Hebrew: *het*).

The legal issue known as *mitzvah ha-ba'a be-avera* or "a commandment fulfilled while committing a transgression" belongs in the context of the intricate web of duties, principles, and laws of the *halakha*. Raised, as noted, already in Talmudic literature, it consists of the following fundamental legal dilemma: What happens if, in the process of fulfilling a certain commandment, one commits a transgression? For example, what is the status of bread baked with stolen wheat? Could such bread be used for ritualistic purposes? Or in other words, does the fact that a specific piece of bread is used for a holy purpose somehow condone the crime of stealing? The traditional answer is no. The Talmud stipulates that the end does not sanctify the means. That is, bread made with stolen wheat cannot be used even for devotional purposes.[35] In traditional legal thinking, that is, the crime, it seems, undermines the value of the

33. In a footnote that was not translated to English, Scholem pointed out that the Sabbatean awakening had already been denoted by the formula 'Redemption through Sin' in a source dated 1756.

34. Robert Alter beautifully suggested translating the title as "The Way of Holy Sinning." The word *sin*, however, carries a much heavier theological baggage than the Hebrew *avera*. See Alter, "Scholem and Sabbatianism," in *Gershom Scholem*, ed. Harold Bloom (New York: Chelsea House, 1987), 21.

35. Tractate Baba Kamma 94A.

ritual. The Sabbatean answer to this question, on the other hand, is yes. The end does sanctify the means. And with this new unorthodox answer, Scholem argued, a new chapter in Jewish history had been inaugurated.

Some commandments, the Sabbateans argued, were so important that a crime committed in the process of their fulfillment does not detract from their value. Moreover, some commandments are so radical and so dangerous that they can be fulfilled only by transgressing the law. One such commandment is the injunction to redeem the world, which was given to the Messiah. He, according to the Sabbatean belief described here, committed a terrible crime (his act of conversion), but he did this in order to rescue the sparks of good that were lodged in the deepest, most remote sphere of evil. Only the Messiah could venture into the heart of darkness, as it were, into Islam, and emerge intact. This was, therefore, the explanation for the behavior of the Messiah Sabbatai Zevi: the sin of conversion was, deep down, the fulfillment of a commandment, one so terrible that it bore the appearance of sinning. In the case of the Messiah, the Sabbateans believed, the end did sanctify the means, and a revolutionary legal principle was thus born.

According to Scholem, the path that led from this new legal interpretation to a social revolution was a direct one. The Messiah, Sabbatai Zevi, had successfully stirred unprecedented excitement among Jews throughout the world. Many believed that with his leadership the time of reconciliation had finally arrived. But, Scholem claimed, this in itself had not inaugurated the movement in its fullest sense. The movement, rather, had begun when, instead of leading his people to the Promised Land, Zevi went off to meet the Sultan and then converted to Islam. To many, this entirely unexpected turn of events had raised a social, moral, and existential question. As Scholem notes, " 'Heretical' Sabbateanism was born at the moment of Sabbatai Zevi's totally unexpected conversion, when for the first time a contradiction appeared between the two levels of the drama of redemption, that of the subjective experience of the individual on the one hand, and that of the objective historical facts on the other . . . One had to choose: either one heard the voice of God in the decree of history, or else one heard it in the newly revealed reality within."[36]

In other words, Sabbateanism as a social movement was launched by the ideological interpretation of the terrible and unexpected disappointment felt by the followers of the Messiah Sabbatai Zevi. "The essence of the Sabbatean's conviction . . . can be summarized in a sentence," Scholem argued; "it is inconceivable that all of God's people should inwardly err, and so, if their

36. Scholem, "Redemption through Sin," 88.

vital experience is contradicted by the facts, it is the facts that stand in need of explanation."[37] The Sabbateans, or, as they were also known, the "believers," were those who chose the internal reality rather than the external one. They chose to believe that the Messiah had converted in order to fulfill a terrible and daring commandment. They chose, in other words, to revolutionize a fundamental legal principle, according to which a transgression invalidates fulfillment of a commandment, or rather, that commandments cannot be fulfilled through crimes. And this choice, Scholem argued, instigated the implosion of the entire Jewish legal system, the *halakha*. If the law can be broken in the name of a higher principle, then every law of the Jewish code was suddenly open to debate. The essence of the matter, Scholem thus maintained, was that the Sabbatean believers had effectively called for the abolishment of the very system that governed Jewish life in exile. Moreover, they were compelled to act according to their legalistic insight. This, then, was how the Sabbateans had become a movement, not by contemplating theoretical problems, but by acting in the world, changing social conduct, and revolutionizing the accepted norms of behavior.

To the believers, the quandary posed by the conversion of the Messiah was not merely a theoretical or a theological issue but rather something that they had to face themselves. The question was, How did the actions of the Messiah affect the rule of Jewish law? Was the Messiah an example for all to follow? Or was sinning for the sake of redemption the prerogative of the Messiah alone? These were the questions, Scholem argued, that had torn open a schism in the core of the Jewish way of life. According to him, all Sabbateans had come to recognize the fact that traditional Judaism was a product of exilic life, and as such it was deluded. All those who retained their belief in the Messiah after his conversion accepted the idea that Sabbatai Zevi had a special prerogative to sin against Jewish law for the sake of the redemption of the Jews. He was considered by all believers to be the representative of a new age of freedom and pride, unshackled by the demands of law. Yet a fundamental question remained unresolved: What did this belief entail for the everyday life of practicing Jews? Had Zevi undone the legal system altogether as he undertook his monumental task? Or was the *halakha* still relevant for ordinary Jews? And even if it was relevant, this one act, so Scholem claimed, opened the question about its rigor, reasoning, and import.

Scholem's discussion of the various answers given by Sabbatean believers to these questions forms a deep yet implicit transition in "Redemption through

37. Ibid.

Sin." What was up to this point a discursive history of ideas transforms here almost seamlessly into a study in social history. Each solution to these problems informed a different social movement. And Scholem traces the history of the most important movements that evolved from the unorthodox solution offered to the problem posed by the converting Messiah. Recent scholarship, it should be noted, largely rejects Scholem's attempt to recast Sabbatean theology as a social historical phenomenon.[38] Nevertheless, after analyzing the main tenets of Sabbatean ideology, Scholem proceeded to address the social implications of this ideology for the lives and practices of real historical figures.

In "Redemption through Sin," Scholem defines two broad responses to the unexpected conversion of the Messiah. The moderate faction of Sabbateanism, according to Scholem, claimed that the conversion of the Messiah was his alone. Only he was permitted to undertake such a dreadful mission, and only for him does the end sanctify the means. This faction held, therefore, that their belief in the apostate Messiah should be expressed neither in the public sphere nor in everyday life. Thus, on the face of it, they remained ordinary observant Jews, even if in their heart they continued to believe in the integrity of the Messiah Sabbatai Zevi and in the holiness of his dreadful deed. The leaders of the radical faction, on the other hand, claimed that the dawning of the new age meant that every Jew must follow in the footsteps of the Messiah.

Both the moderate and the radical factions, Scholem argued, wrought terrible devastation. Ostensibly, moderate Sabbateanism had restricted its followers' behavior so that they remained in the fold and thus seemed not to cause extreme damage. But in fact, Scholem insisted, it had emptied traditional Judaism of its emotional content and replaced it with new, heretical notions. "Although the new sense of [messianic] inner freedom bore purely inner consequences," Scholem wrote poignantly, "we can nevertheless rely on the judgment of those anti-Sabbatean polemicists who saw perfectly clearly that the inward devastation of old values was no less dangerous or far reaching than its outward manifestation."[39] The route taken by radical Sabbateanism, on the other hand, amounted to an overt and shameless assault on traditional Judaism. In practice, the new moral code of radical messianism stipulated a systematic violation of the edicts of Jewish law. In its most extreme form, every rule broken was a commandment fulfilled. In this instance, Scholem contended,

38. Yehuda Liebes, *On Sabbateanism and Its Reception: Collected Essays* (in Hebrew) (Jerusalem: Mosad Bialik, 1995), 20–35; Jacob Barnai, *Sabbateanism—Social Perspectives* (in Hebrew) (Jerusalem: Shazar, 2000), 9–68.

39. Scholem, "Redemption through Sin," 102.

hidden psychological tendencies, which were normally kept in check by the social norms and by the dictates of the law, suddenly erupted in bizarre displays of sexual perversity and disruptive behavior. "The new sense of [messianic] freedom having been denied the political and historical outlets it had originally anticipated, now sought to express itself in the sphere of morality."[40] In other words, the identification of the believers with the acts of their leader, the belief that they must sin as he did, sowed the seeds of extreme religious nihilism in the soil of traditional, law-abiding Judaism. And as a result Jewish messianism transformed into nihilism.

The most outstanding example of radical Sabbateanism was, according to Scholem, the Frankist movement, which Scholem discussed here in some detail. Jacob Frank, the leader of the movement, took the radical ideology of Sabbateanism to its extreme by rereading and reinterpreting the symbols of traditional Judaism in a nihilistic vein. He argued that the systematic destruction of Jewish social norms—through defiance of the edicts of Jewish law, subversion of rabbinical authority, and negation of the principles of piety—would make way for messianic redemption.[41] Scholem's explanations of the nihilist Sabbateans were lucid, and while he appears to have divined the secret of their dark attraction, he nevertheless took a resolute stance against this trend: "Just as the 'believers' had deliberately chosen to follow that dangerous path along which nothing is impossible, so it was perhaps precisely this that attracted them to Frank, for here was a man who was not afraid to push on to the very end, to take the final step into the abyss, to drain the cup of desolation and destruction to the lees until the last bit of holiness had been made into a mockery."[42] The contempt that Scholem expresses throughout the text toward Frank and his followers could not be clearer or more trenchant.

Nevertheless, in both its moderate and its radical guises, Sabbateanism, Scholem claimed, had radically altered the social landscape of Judaism and its history. The idea that one could be a Jew while disregarding the legal code of Jewish life was introduced by radical Sabbateanism. And the notion that the emotional element of belief could be dissociated from the social-ritualistic aspect of the religion emerged from within the stream of Jewish religious life.

40. Scholem, "Redemption through Sin" (in Hebrew), 36.

41. During the time that has elapsed since Scholem's groundbreaking work on Sabbateanism, knowledge about the genealogy of the Frankist movement, its ideas, and its leading figures has, of course, increased dramatically. See Pawel Maciejko, *The Mixed Multitude: Jacob Frank and the Frankist Movement, 1755–1816* (Philadelphia: University of Pennsylvania Press, 2011).

42. Scholem, "Redemption through Sin," 128.

These discoveries played a pivotal role in Scholem's historical analysis. According to him, obedience to the code of Jewish life had been shaken to the core by the experiences of early Sabbateanism. When, in the eighteenth century, the ideas of religious reform and of enlightenment swept across Europe, and when the French Revolution broke out,[43] Jews were already well prepared to receive them. In fact, Jewish enlightenment, Scholem boldly claimed in this article, was the product of Sabbatean heresy. Ironically, therefore, by way of historical, social, and ideological dialectic, the most profound religious belief of all—the belief in the messianic miracle—had led to the complete breakdown of the Jewish religious way of life.

This was the essence of Scholem's social history of the Sabbatean movement, which he addressed here for the first time and which would become the cornerstone of his scholarly achievement. In "Redemption through Sin" Scholem offered a glimpse into his grand social narrative of Jewish modernity from the perspective of the Sabbatean movement. According to Scholem, the Sabbatean movement paved the way for the integration of new ideas about religion, science, and politics into the texture of Jewish social life. And although his writing exhibits deep fascination, he did not shy away from judgment. He clearly expresses dismay and moral disgust with those who took it on themselves to uproot traditional Judaism.

Drawn to the topic as he was, Scholem revisited it about a year later, this time as part of a series of lectures to be given in New York. This series, published in book form in 1941, marked the first and the last time that Scholem discussed the entire gamut of Jewish mysticism in sequential historiographical order. As we shall see next, while this account of the Sabbatean movement contains little new material, in *Major Trends* Scholem's thesis on it changes once again.

MAJOR TRENDS IN JEWISH MYSTICISM

The most remarkable element of the eighth lecture in the series on the major trends in Jewish mysticism, titled "Sabbateanism and Mystical Heresy,"[44] is not the new material that Scholem presented, but rather the context within which it is set. Here Scholem places the Sabbatean eruption in the context

43. On the relation between the French Revolution and the Sabbatean movement see, for example, Gershom Scholem, "Ein verschollener jüdischer Mystiker der Aufklärungszeit: E. J. Hirschfeld," *Leo Baeck Institute Yearbook* 7 (1962): 247–79.

44. Scholem, *Major Trends*, 287–324.

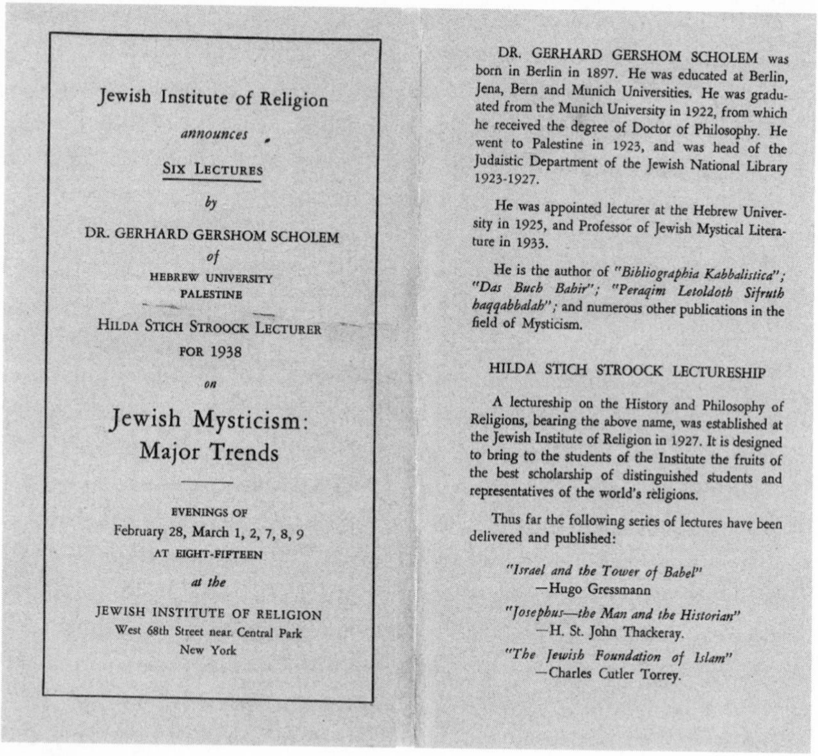

Jewish Institute of Religion

announces

SIX LECTURES

by

DR. GERHARD GERSHOM SCHOLEM

of

HEBREW UNIVERSITY
PALESTINE

HILDA STICH STROOCK LECTURER

FOR 1938

on

Jewish Mysticism:
Major Trends

EVENINGS OF
February 28, March 1, 2, 7, 8, 9
AT EIGHT-FIFTEEN

at the

JEWISH INSTITUTE OF RELIGION
West 68th Street near Central Park
New York

DR. GERHARD GERSHOM SCHOLEM was born in Berlin in 1897. He was educated at Berlin, Jena, Bern and Munich Universities. He was graduated from the Munich University in 1922, from which he received the degree of Doctor of Philosophy. He went to Palestine in 1923, and was head of the Judaistic Department of the Jewish National Library 1923-1927.

He was appointed lecturer at the Hebrew University in 1925, and Professor of Jewish Mystical Literature in 1933.

He is the author of "*Bibliographia Kabbalistica*"; "*Das Buch Bahir*"; "*Peraqim Letoldoth Sifruth haqqabbalah*"; and numerous other publications in the field of Mysticism.

HILDA STICH STROOCK LECTURESHIP

A lectureship on the History and Philosophy of Religions, bearing the above name, was established at the Jewish Institute of Religion in 1927. It is designed to bring to the students of the Institute the fruits of the best scholarship of distinguished students and representatives of the world's religions.

Thus far the following series of lectures have been delivered and published:

"*Israel and the Tower of Babel*"
    —Hugo Gressmann

"*Josephus—the Man and the Historian*"
    —H. St. John Thackeray.

"*The Jewish Foundation of Islam*"
    —Charles Cutler Torrey.

FIGURE 5.1. The invitation to Scholem's lecture series at the Jewish Institute of Religion in New York, 1938. Courtesy of The Jacob Rader Marcus Center of the American Jewish Archives, Cincinnati, Ohio.

of the entire history of Jewish mysticism, from its beginnings in the Second Temple era until its end (according to Scholem) at the dawn of modernity. This achievement should be attributed, first and foremost, to Scholem's diligent work and productivity during the time that had elapsed since he first took up the Kabbalah as a subject of inquiry. As Scholem wrote in 1935 to his friend Walter Benjamin, *Major Trends* proved indeed to be "a concise exposé of the results of my studies over the past 15 years."[45] Yet Scholem's deepening understanding of the textual sources went beyond a mere accumulation of knowledge. His studies revealed to him an entirely new perspective on Jewish history, from which he could evaluate these sources and endow them with meaning. And he was able to bring a special and deep insight to a certain view

45. Scholem, *Gershom Scholem: A Life in Letters*, 263.

of Jewish history that already existed elsewhere but had never received such thorough treatment.[46] Scholem himself never expressed his position on Jewish history as comprehensively as in this lecture series turned book.

Since Scholem had published his first study on Sabbateanism the world had changed and so had Scholem. In 1928 he had been an active member of the Brith Shalom organization. He had believed firmly that Zionism should lead to the spiritual rejuvenation of the Jewish people. At the same time he had also realized that Zionist settlement in Palestine had forced the Jewish people onto the stage of history and into the realm of politics. Jewish politics, Scholem contended, must serve the Zionist end and should therefore support the legitimate aspirations of the Arabs rather than promoting the interests of the superpowers in the region. By 1938, however, Scholem realized that his visions of Zionism and his prescriptions for Zionist politics had been rendered impossible by events in Palestine and abroad. The already tense relations between Jews and Arabs in Palestine had violently erupted on several occasions, and a full-scale war seemed to many virtually inevitable. As noted above, many indeed believed that the Jews of Palestine were living on the slopes of a volcano. Worse still, Europe was embroiled in one of the deadliest conflicts known to man. Jewish life was being destroyed with brutality and according to a dreadful design. Under these circumstances, it was hard to imagine Palestine as a spiritual safe heaven but only as a rescue raft for the drowning. Scholem seems to have understood the meaning of the historical hour quickly, and this realization is expressed in *Major Trends in Jewish Mysticism* and particularly in his study of Sabbatai Zevi.

By placing the Sabbatean movement within the context of the entire history of the Kabbalah, Scholem expressed a startling new realization about the movement. According to Scholem's *Major Trends*, the entire history of Jewish mysticism had led directly and indirectly to the Sabbatean movement of the seventeenth century. The Sabbatean movement, it is thus implied, was not an accident of fate. It had erupted from the latent energies that had lain dormant within the Kabbalistic tradition at least since the Spanish expulsion. Scholem

46. A very concise version of the historical narrative discussed here (describing the developments since the Spanish expulsion through the Lurianic Kabbalah to the Sabbatean movement and its aftermath) can be found already in Martin Buber's early discussion of Jewish mysticism. See Buber, *The Tales of Rabbi Nachman* (Atlantic Highlands, NJ: Humanities Press International, 1988), 3–18. On this see also Boaz Huss, "Martin Buber's Introduction to the Stories of Rabbi Nachman and the Genealogy of Jewish Mysticism" (in Hebrew), *By the Well: Studies in Jewish Philosophy and Halakhic Thought, Presented to Gerald J. Blidstein*, ed. Uri Ehrlich, Howard Kreisel, and Daniel Lasker (Beer Sheva: Ben Gurion University, 2008), 97–121.

makes this claim explicitly. The very first sentences of the eighth lecture read: "The development of Jewish mysticism from the time of the Spanish exodus onwards has been singularly uniform and free from cross currents. There is only one main line."[47] The "line" leading from the expulsion of the Jews from Spain to the Lurianic Kabbalah was described in some detail in chapter 3 above. Succinctly, Scholem argued that Luria's Kabbalah was a direct response to the profound spiritual crisis experienced in the wake of the sudden and cruel destruction of medieval Spanish Jewry, the most prosperous and fully integrated Jewish community in history. The Sabbatean eruption, in turn, was nothing but a consummation of Luria's theory of exile. According to Scholem's interpretation in *Major Trends*, the Lurianic Kabbalah had instilled in the heart of every Jew the belief that exile could be overcome. Therefore, he maintained, it was only a matter of time before this belief would transform into an uncontrollable fervor, and the fervor into a massive delusion. As he argues, "A people which had suffered from all the tribulations that exile and persecution could bring and which at the same time had developed an extremely sensitive consciousness of life actually lived between the poles of exile and redemption [expressed in the Kabbalah], needed little to take the final step to Messianism."[48]

The Sabbatean movement, according to Scholem's *Major Trends*, was therefore a natural, practically unavoidable culmination of an entire history of Jewish thought and of Jewish life in exile. "The appearance of Sabbatai Zevi and Nathan of Gaza," Scholem argued, "precipitated this [messianic] step by liberating the latent energies and potentialities which had gradually accumulated during the generations immediately preceding them."[49] This is an entirely new realization. It means that the Sabbatean eruption occurred not because of a unique set of ideological and historical circumstances or because of the singular personalities that were involved. It was, rather, the culminating moment of the mystical Jewish tradition, which had reached breaking point as a result of the expulsion from Spain. This accumulation of so many layers of latent energy could have led, Scholem argued, to only one outcome: "the eruption of the volcano, when it came, was terrific."[50]

But Scholem traced Sabbateanism not only to historical and political conditions but also to intellectual ones. Indeed, in *Major Trends*, Scholem insists

47. Scholem, *Major Trends*, 287.
48. Ibid., 287–88.
49. Ibid., 288.
50. Ibid.

that the roots of the Lurianic Kabbalah lay in a far more distant past. Everything that had occurred in the history of Jewish mysticism prior to the eruption of the Lurianic Kabbalah was mostly accidental. Scholem regarded even the Kabbalah's most canonical work, Sefer ha-Zohar (Book of Splendor), as elitist and therefore historically inconsequential.[51] Yet for the sake of his argument, Scholem was keen to note that the Lurianic Kabbalah of the sixteenth century was firmly rooted in the Kabbalah of Rabbi Moshe Cordovero, and was thus connected to the classic work of medieval Kabbalah, the Zohar, to medieval Jewish asceticism, to Talmudic literature, and to the Torah itself.[52] In other words, in this series of lectures Scholem traced the way in which the Lurianic Kabbalah had absorbed and thus bore the entire weight of the multilayered Jewish mystical tradition.

To drive home the point that Sabbateanism had been inevitable, Scholem now turned to discuss Sabbatai Zevi and Nathan of Gaza for the first time. In his previous studies he had emphasized that the movement had begun only with the conversion of the Messiah in 1666 and the reluctance of certain believers to accept the fact that the Messiah had failed in his mission. Rather than reconciling themselves to the disappointment, they interpreted it symbolically as an internal mystical struggle. In this earlier scheme, therefore, the Messiah himself and his prophet had played only a marginal role, and Scholem had discussed them, their ideas, and their actions only insofar as they pertained to the mystical Sabbatean theology. However, in this lecture series delivered in 1938 and published in 1941, Scholem profoundly altered the overall thrust of his analysis by slightly shifting the focal point of his historical account.

The Sabbatean movement began, Scholem proclaims in lecture 8 of *Major Trends*, long before the conversion, when Sabbatai Zevi met Nathan of Gaza for the first time. And it was already during the Messiah's lifetime that Nathan of Gaza developed the new and socially potent theory of redemption and sin. Nathan's theory about the sanctity of sin, Scholem argues here, was triggered by the Messiah's evident psychic condition: "[A] mass of documentary evidence now available shows that [Zevi] . . . was constitutionally

51. This may explain why Scholem did not fully appreciate the messianic content of this book, as later scholarship has shown. See Yehuda Liebes, "The Messiah of the Zohar: On R. Simeon Bar Yohai as a Messianic Figure," in *Studies in the Zohar* (Albany: State University of New York Press, 1993), 1–84. For more on Scholem's reception of the Book of Zohar, see Boaz Huss, "Admiration and Disgust: The Ambivalent Re-canonization of the *Zohar* in the Modern Period," in *Study and Knowledge in Jewish Thought*, ed. Haim Kreisel (Beer Sheva, 2006), 227–28.

52. Scholem, *Major Trends*, 259. Further references in the text.

a manic-depressive, that is to say, he belonged to a type whose lack of mental balance displays itself in alternate fits of deepest gloom and most uncontrollable exuberance and exaggerated joy" (290). In his exuberant moods, Zevi's outrageous and deliberately aberrant behavior offended the most profound tenets of Jewish life. In this mode, furthermore, he mustered the charisma to place people under his spell.

The self-aggrandizing spirit and proclamations of divine insight, Scholem argued, were hardly unique to Zevi. "Had it not been for Nathan of Gaza he would undoubtedly have remained one of the many anonymous enthusiasts of the generation who, in the years after the Chmielnitzky persecution of 1648, entertained vague dreams of messianic vocation, without anyone paying attention to him" (294). Sabbatai Zevi approached Nathan of Gaza as a patient approaches a doctor, Scholem claimed (295). Nathan was a mystic who enjoyed a reputation for being able to gaze into the depths of one's soul. And Sabbatai Zevi, who suffered from wildly undulating moods, sought help. Yet instead of healing Zevi, Nathan of Gaza was overwhelmed by the stature of his patient. He believed that Zevi's radical behavior was not an affliction but furnished proof of his true calling.

The basic principle of Sabbatean theology concerning the sanctity of sin was inspired, first and foremost, not by the urgent need to make sense of the Messiah's conversion, as Scholem had asserted in earlier essays, but rather by Nathan's mystical interpretation of Zevi's emotional predicament. According to Nathan's Kabbalistic interpretation, the struggle between the moments of gloom and the moments of exuberance constituted the external manifestation of the perpetual struggle between good and evil, in which the Messiah's soul was engaged. "According to Nathan, there exists a certain relationship between the Messiah and the course of all those intrinsic processes [of the Lurianic Kabbalah]: *tsimtsum, shevira,* and *tikkun*" (298). The metaphysical interpretation of Zevi's moods encapsulated, Scholem argued, the Sabbatean theory of "redemption through sin." "The subsequent heretical doctrine of Nathan and the other Sabbateans concerning the mission of the Messiah, and in particular concerning his apostasy as a mission, is contained *in nuce* in this astounding document [concerning Zevi's psyche]" (299).

As in his previous studies on Sabbateanism discussed above, here too Scholem argues that the source of Sabbatean theology was the Lurianic Kabbalah. Yet whereas in his essay on Cardozo's theology Scholem maintains that Sabbateanism was motivated by questions about the world, God, and man, and in his essay "Redemption through Sin" he argues that Sabbateanism was the product of a deep rift between experience and belief, here the motivating factor for Sabbatean theology was psychological. In his first substantive appearance in Scholem's work, Sabbatai Zevi is portrayed as a stricken and suffering man whose delusions and transgressions should be understood rather than judged. And Nathan of Gaza appears as a misguided but well-intentioned healer who believed that Zevi's behavior was a sign of his exceptional calling rather than an indication of an affliction to be pitied.

In Scholem's psychological interpretation, Nathan of Gaza harnessed the Lurianic Kabbalah, and with it the entire history of Jewish mysticism, to the cause of Sabbatai Zevi. Scholem does not portray this as the cynical exploitation of a sick man or of a popular belief, but as an authentic expression of a vital desire for messianic awakening and true redemption. Viewed in this vein, Zevi's choice of conversion rather than death appears quite natural. Zevi was, after all, not a hero but a man who suffered from a mental illness. Finally, Scholem's application of Nathan's theory of the Messiah's soul to Sabbatai Zevi's conversion appears to be part of a logical progression. Zevi's conversion was but the theological manifestation of the Messiah's psychological profile and therefore marked a new phase in the movement's historical development but not a substantial transformation.

The description of Sabbatai Zevi and Nathan of Gaza marks a decisive turn in Scholem's interpretation of Sabbateanism. In *Major Trends* Sabbateanism is no longer portrayed as an outrageous, immoral, and destructive force within the annals of Jewish belief. Rather, it is discussed as an almost normal, and in any case foreseeable and comprehensible, progression of events that may be regrettable but were not tainted by malice or ill intent. This impression is created first and foremost by the context in which Scholem places the Sabbatean conflagration. It was, as we have seen, a consummation of energies that had lain dormant in the Lurianic theory of action, which in turn was based on a long history of subversive thought. In the historical sense alone, Sabbateanism appears as a practically inevitable phenomenon. Scholem enhances this impression of the predictability of Sabbateanism by shifting the focal point of the discussion from ideology to psychology. Ideas may be right or wrong and are thus the stuff of political debates. But psychology is a given fact, and psychological ailments are to be pitied rather than argued against. By describing the actions and thoughts of Nathan of Gaza and of Sabbatai Zevi in the way he does here, Scholem creates the impression that Sabbateanism had a human face. It was the reaction of deluded but nevertheless honest people to the circumstances in which they found themselves.

It is not only the rise of Sabbatean theology that is portrayed in *Major Trends* as an inevitable historical necessity, but also the history of the movement and its consequences. As he did in "Redemption through Sin," here too Scholem surveys the different factions of Sabbatean heresy. Now, however, even the nihilistic faction of Sabbateanism becomes the object of cool historical observation. "Mere condemnation of this doctrine," Scholem says of Jacob Frank's radical Sabbatean sect, "leads us nowhere. Attention must be given also to the positive side. "The religious, and in some cases moral, nihilism of the radicals is after all only the confused and mistaken expression of their urge towards a fundamental regeneration of Jewish life, which under the historic conditions of those times could not find a normal expression" (318). In *Major Trends*, therefore, Scholem exhibits understanding, almost forgiveness, toward those he fiercely repudiated in previous articles. On the one hand, his moral judgments of the Frankist movement remain as forthright as before, but on the other hand, even the Frankists, he now appears to argue, acted under the pressure of forces by far superior to their own, and certainly beyond their control.

The Jewish enlightenment movement and even the reform movement are likewise rooted, Scholem argues, in Sabbatai Zevi's messianic movement. But in contrast to what he does in "Redemption through Sin," the connections Scholem traces here are not ideological but rather historical in nature. In his earlier essay, Scholem asserted that the inherent apostasy of Sabbatean theology had prepared the hearts of the believers to accept the new doctrines of reason and tolerance once these became popular in the eighteenth century. While he still alludes to this notion in *Major Trends*, Scholem now stresses not the ideas but the circumstances of the subversive belief in Sabbatai Zevi. "The attempt of a minority to maintain, in the face of persecution and vituperation certain new spiritual values, which corresponded to a new religious experience, facilitated the transition to a new world of Judaism" (301). Thus, it was not so much what the Sabbatean actually believed but rather the historical fact that they clung to this belief against all odds that suddenly became crucial.

The eighteenth-century Hasidism of the Ba'al Shem Tov, to which Scholem dedicates the ninth and final lecture in *Major Trends*, was also a direct continuation of the Lurianic Kabbalah as well as a response to the Sabbatean conflagration, and as such was a practically inevitable development. Hasidism, according to Scholem, did not develop a unique theology but rather aspired to create a new social structure based on older ideas and in response to the Sabbatean eruption. Therefore, "Lurianic Kabbalism, Sabbateanism, and Hasidism are after all three stages of the same process" (327). Like Sabbateanism, Hasidism, too, had departed from the rabbinical scale of values, "replacing the ideal human type of the scholar [*talmid hakham*] with a charismatic leader and the illuminate, the man whose heart has been touched and changed by

God" (333–34). The movement also drew heavily, albeit perhaps unwittingly, from Sabbatean sources, specifically from Rabbi Heshel Hazoref, whom Scholem described as "without doubt one of the outstanding prophets of moderate Sabbateanism" (331–33). But most significantly, Hasidism, so Scholem maintained, had sought to retain the broad appeal of the Kabalistic doctrine of spirituality without descending into the chaos of messianism: "Hasidism represents an attempt to preserve those elements of Kabbalism which were capable of evoking popular response, but stripped of their messianic flavor . . . This seems to me to be the point—Hasidism tried to eliminate the element of Messianism—with its dazzling but highly dangerous amalgamation of mysticism and the apocalyptic mood—without renouncing the popular appeal of later Kabbalism" (329).

Scholem's discussion of the Sabbatean movement in *Major Trends* is remarkable not only because of what it offers but also for what it omits. On the face of things, it offers a far more comprehensive view of the Sabbatean conflagration. As noted, Scholem traces the Sabbatean eruption directly to the Spanish catastrophe and indirectly to a far older tradition, going back to the time of the Second Temple in Jerusalem. However, seen from this distance, the circumstances under which Jews lived in exile appear far more crucial than the actions of any individual, and as a result the overall sequence of events appears to have been almost inevitable. Indeed, in *Major Trends* the revolutionary zeal of individual actors is all but discounted, and belief in the impossible is no longer mentioned. Here, Scholem no longer asserts that people acted contrary to every shred of historical reasoning. Therefore, although Scholem's analysis of Sabbateanism remains more or less constant, the definitive argument of his previous studies now fades into the background, and he exhibits far greater understanding toward the main players in the drama. In his 1941 book, Scholem observes Sabbateanism as a more or less value-neutral historical event as he downplays the ideological and theological aspects of the Sabbatean affair as well as the political potency of this radical movement.

SABBATAI ZEVI AND THE SABBATEAN MOVEMENT DURING HIS LIFETIME

Published almost three decades after he first started to study the annals of the Sabbatean movement, Scholem's last major work on the topic seems to promise a culminating analysis. This promise is supported already by the physical appearance of the book. The original Hebrew version, titled *Sabbatai Zevi and the Sabbatean Movement during His Lifetime*, appeared in two volumes in 1956. The English translation, which was published in 1973 with the title *Sabbatai Sevi: The Mystical Messiah, 1626–1676*, is a mammoth thousand-page book. The promise is further supported by the reception it had. When it was first published, the book was hailed as one of the most important works in Jewish history and a monumental achievement. It was discussed in daily newspapers like *Davar* and the *New York Times*,[53] in professional journals,[54] and in general-interest magazines such as the *New York Review of Books*.[55] The book also helped to solidify Scholem's global reputation as a leading intellectual in religious and Jewish studies. The English translation, which appeared in the distinguished Bollingen series of Princeton University Press, is still in circulation today. These facts too seem to further support the impression that this book finally exhausted the matter of Sabbateanism. This is not the case.

In fact, *Sabbatai Zevi and the Sabbatean Movement during His Lifetime* is a unique undertaking in Scholem's oeuvre. Not only for the stature it achieved, but also for its style and tone, and most important for its subject matter, this book stands out from much of his other writings and from his other works on Sabbateanism. *Sabbatai Zevi* is a biography that primarily offers an account of the comings and goings, successes and misgivings of one person. When compared with historical events and the actions of men and women, highly complex Kabbalistic texts and theological reflections receive only little attention. Also in its style and tenor, this book represents a complete reversal. Here is, for example, a description of the events in Smyrna during the high tide of the movement.

Smyrna was in a festive mood, and the believers moved in dizzy whirls of legends, miracles, and revelations . . . Hardly had the report arrived from Aleppo that Elijah had appeared in the old synagogue there, and Elijah walked the streets of Smyrna. Dozens, even hundreds, had seen him: he was the anonymous beggar asking for alms as well as the invisible guest at every banquet.[56]

53. Chaim Wershuvsky, "Heresy through Belief" (in Hebrew), *Davar*, May 24, 1957; Cynthia Ozick, "Slouching towards Smyrna," *New York Times*, February 24, 1974.

54. Jacob Neusner, "Review of *Sabbatai Sevi: The Mystical Messiah, 1626–1676*, by Gershom Scholem," *Journal of Modern History* 48, no. 2 (June 1976): 316–20.

55. D. P. Walker, "Mystery in History," *New York Review of Book*, October 4, 1973.

56. Gershom Scholem, *Sabbatai Sevi: The Mystical Messiah, 1626–1676* (Princeton: Princeton University Press, 1976), 417.

In contrast, this is how Scholem describes in *Major Trends* the no less agitated community of Safed in which Luria was active.

> The Kabbalistic propaganda, through which the new messianism sought to win its way, gained directness and popularity . . . There was a passionate desire to break down the Exile by enhancing its torments, savoring its bitterness to the utmost . . . and summoning up the compelling force of the repentance of a whole community.[57]

The second description has very little of the vividness and brilliance of the first one. Indeed, the colorful narrative of the *Sabbatai Zevi* book is almost nowhere else to be found among Scholem's writings.

The handling of the textual sources in this book is also unique. Despite Joseph Dan's characterization of Scholem's early works as "mystical," it appears that Scholem was always a careful and meticulous researcher.[58] Even his dissertation, his 1922 translation of the first book of the Kabbalah, *The Book Bahir*, carries all the external and essential markers of an academic research work.[59] Clearly, Scholem's professional integrity was beyond dispute. In his works, nevertheless, Scholem often refrained from describing his sources or his editorial decisions. This is an especially poignant problem in his description of the Lurianic myth of exile, where, as noted in chapter 3 above, no single source can account for Scholem's fluent interpretation. This is not mentioned as a critique but merely in order to point to the peculiarity of the *Sabbatai Zevi* book. In contrast to his other large-scale synthetic works, in this book Scholem makes a continuous effort to describe the various sources and discuss their importance and reliability. The extremely authoritative voice present in so many of his works makes way for a more cautious tone here.

But the most glaring difference between the *Sabbatai Zevi* book and his earlier studies of Sabbateanism is the inverted ratio between the length of the book and the historical scope it covers. While in *Redemption through Sin*, Scholem discussed the entire 150-year arch of the Sabbatean conflagration in about fifty pages, the thousand pages of densely written text of the *Sabbatai*

57. Scholem, *Major Trends*, 250.

58. See Joseph Dan, "The Book in Which the Scholar and the Mystic Parted Ways," *On Gershom Scholem*, 57–61.

59. Gershom Scholem, *Das Buch Bahir: Ein Schriftdenkmal aus der Frühzeit der Kabbala* (Berlin: Schocken Verlag, 1933).

Zevi book are devoted, as the title suggests, only to Sabbatai Zevi's life and to
the Sabbatean movement during his lifetime. In other words, what appears to
be Scholem's most comprehensive book on the issue actually discusses only
a small segment of Sabbatean history. This book does not even come close to
fulfilling the promise it seems to make by its size, reception, and publication
record. In truth, it was never intended to do so.

In the preface to the English translation, Scholem acknowledges some of
the unique aspects of this book. "I myself was surprised by the wealth of unknown material which shed new light on all phases of Sabbatai Sevi's career,
and it soon became apparent that the entire picture of the movement's history
had to be reconstructed from the start."[60] There is no reason to doubt this
statement, for it is indeed more than possible that what Scholem deemed to be
thoroughly researched in 1937 appeared partial two decades later. Nevertheless, one must take Scholem's remark that he has changed his mind regarding his overall understanding of the history of the Sabbatean movement with
some caution. Despite the many stylistic differences between this book and the
previous essays, the overall historiography remains precisely as it was before.
This fact seems to be reflected in another comment Scholem makes in the English preface: "I have not hesitated to change the opinions I expressed in earlier
publications on specific points when a renewed consideration of the sources
required a new interpretation of the documents of historical process reflected
in them."[61] This study diverges from previous essays mostly on certain specific
points. Scholem also addresses the fact that this book discusses one part of a
much longer historical narrative. "The present work . . . offers a comprehensive history of the [Sabbatean] movement up to the deaths of Sabbatai Sevi
and his prophet . . . and I hope that I will be able to complete at a later time
a sequel covering the history of Sabbateanism in its various forms after the
death of Sabbatai Sevi."[62]

The *Sabbatai Zevi* book poses something of a riddle. On the one hand, one
could argue that this book represents nothing but an elaboration of Scholem
previous studies, not a shift in his understanding. One can also argue that any
critique of Scholem's work should be based on its actual content and not on
what it lacks.[63] Scholem had too much material and thus he might have never
quite "gotten around" to completing his project. And yet, on the other hand,

60. Scholem, *Sabbatai Zevi*, x.
61. Ibid., xi.
62. Ibid., x.
63. See Joseph Dan, "Between History and Historiography," *On Gershom Scholem*, 62–105.

it is in this case rather compelling to argue that Scholem's choice to avoid the more explosive and complex theological aspects of Sabbateanism and to focus mainly on the standard historiographical depiction of the movement is rather telling. I tend toward the second option.

The particularity of this book is, I argue, more than a product of Scholem's insistence on details. It points toward a complete shift in his emphasis and in his understanding of Sabbateanism. Strikingly, this book is devoted precisely to those aspects he deemed in his previous essays to have been more or less exhausted by previous scholarship. In his essay about Abraham Cardozo's theology, Scholem argued that the most important and least-known aspect of the Sabbatean debacle was the radical theology it developed. In his 1937 essay "Redemption through Sin," Scholem insisted that the untold story of the Sabbatean movement starts with the conversion of Sabbatai Zevi. He makes a very similar claim again in *Major Trends*. And yet twenty years later he has changed his mind. The Sabbatean theology receives relatively little treatment, and the account of the events following the conversion of the Messiah, the most terrible and awe-inspiring aspects of the tale, is cut short with Zevi's death only ten years later.

By narrowing its field of inquiry, this book continues the overall trend that is exposed above. As the years went by, Scholem's concentration on the raw radicalism of Sabbatean thought gave way to a more measured historical appreciation. The *Sabbatai Zevi* book completes the trend by hardly attending to what made Sabbateanism, according to Scholem himself, such a dangerous movement. More important, this book completely refrains from discussing the 150 years of activity that, according to Scholem, emptied the Jewish political body from the inside and left it dry and splintered. The fact that Scholem never wrote a detailed history of the Sabbatean movement after Zevi's death could have been the result of circumstance, of a too busy schedule, or of bad luck. But if the comparison of Scholem's studies shows anything, it is that this would be an unlikely explanation. On the contrary, it seems rather appropriate that in 1957 Scholem should write a thousand-page book about the Messiah and never even begin to write its sequel.

The narrow scope of the book was overlooked by most scholars. In his review in *Davar*, Wershuvsky noted that "for the first time in Jewish historiography, the chronicles of the most important messianic movement in Jewish exile have been written in their full dimension."[64] The achievement of this book notwithstanding, this particular characterization seems rather inaccurate. It

64. Wershuvsky, "Heresy through Belief."

is possible that the size of the book, its fluent narrative, and the meticulous research it exhibits convinced Wershuvsky that this was indeed Scholem's concluding statement on Sabbateanism. The fact that it was published a decade and a half after *Major Trends*, at the height of Scholem's career, must have enforced this impression even further. The universal praise of the book surely contributed to this effect. Today, it would indeed seem that *Sabbatai Zevi and the Sabbatean Movement during His Lifetime* entails Scholem's most detailed and comprehensive work on the topic, but the truth is more complex. *Sabbatai Zevi* is indeed the most comprehensive book about the time period in question, but it is also the most confusing book about Scholem's conception of Sabbateanism in general. It obfuscates the fact that Scholem himself first argued that Sabbateanism only started with the conversion of the Messiah and was only in its initial phases when he died.[65]

JEWISH MYSTICISM AND THE QUEST FOR CONTINUITY

Scholem never wrote the sequel to *Sabbatai Zevi*, and he never returned to question the overarching historical thesis presented in *Major Trends*. And even if he was not the only historian to advance this historical narrative, it remains singularly audacious.[66] According to Scholem, practically the entire gamut of Jewish life at the end of the eighteenth and on the brink of the nineteenth century—Hasidism, Frankism, the Haskalah, and later the Reform movement—was the historical product of Sabbateanism, the Lurianic Kabbalah, and the mystical tradition that precipitated it. In other words, the character of modern Judaism as a whole was the amalgamation of the various attempts to make sense of the conversion of a self-proclaimed messiah. But as *Major Trends* draws to a close with a discussion of the last phase in Jewish mysticism, Hasidism, one outstanding question remains unanswered. What happens next? If, indeed, modern Judaism is a product of the Jewish mystical tradition, then how has the all-consuming energy of mysticism and mystical messianism

65. The reading of Scholem's earlier essays on Sabbateanism in light of this later book is the only reason I can find for certain remarks and misunderstandings about these earlier works by otherwise astute scholars. It explains, for example, the following statement by Benjamin Lazier, "In retrospect, the essay ["Redemption through Sin"] is a promissory note. But what exactly did it promise? It is difficult to say." In Lazier, *God Interrupted*, 144.

66. On this issue see also Huss, "Martin Buber's Introduction." On the context of Scholem's historical narrative, see Myers, *Re-inventing the Jewish Past*, esp. 151–76.

evolved since the late eighteenth century? It seems unlikely that this two-millennia tradition, which erupted with such vigor and desire for renewal, would simply evaporate, even under the inhospitable conditions of modernity. One would expect to see a theory of "neutralization" of some kind, but Scholem never offers one.

At the very end of *Major Trends* Scholem discusses the possibility of the continuation of the mystical tradition in the modern age in a somewhat nebulous manner. On the final page of his magnum opus he recounts a fable about the degeneration of the magical powers of the Hasidic rabbis, which has been retold by several of the greatest authors of modern Judaism including Martin Buber and S. Y. Agnon.[67] Scholem's version proceeds roughly as follows: When the Ba'al Shem Tov, the founder of the Hasidic movement, faced a difficult challenge he would head to a specific location in the forest, light a fire, and meditate in prayer until he found a solution. In the generation following the Ba'al Shem Tov, it became impossible to light the holy fire, but the magic was still maintained by praying at the secret location in the forest. The generation after that forgot the words of the prayers but accessed the esoteric knowledge by returning to the secret location in the woods. When, in the following generation, the location too was forgotten, the masters of Hasidism conjured up divine inspiration by telling the story of the Ba'al Shem Tov and his mystical deed in the forest. This is where the short fable comes to an end, and Scholem offers a few short lines of explanation. "That is the position in which we find ourselves today, or in which Jewish Mysticism finds itself. The story is not ended, it has not yet become history, and the secret life it holds can break out tomorrow in you or in me."[68]

With these words, Scholem clearly argues that although the mystical tradition has all but disappeared, it can still be reincarnated. He further suggests that the historian plays a unique role at this juncture, between the imminent demise of mysticism and its potential regeneration. On the one hand, historical analysis necessarily precludes the magical element of mysticism and thus brings it to an end. On the other hand, this transformation constitutes the natural and therefore inevitable progression of the tradition. In the end, even mysticism is reduced to historiography. Only in the dry and factual form of analysis, Scholem seems to imply, might mysticism survive in today's disenchanted world. In short, at the end of *Major Trends* Scholem suggests that the

---

67. Levi Cooper, "'But I Will Tell of Their Deeds': Retelling a Hasidic Tale about the Power of Storytelling," *Journal of Jewish Thought and Philosophy* 22, no. 2 (2014): 127–63.

68. Scholem, *Major Trends*, 350.

historian, who transforms all that is left of mysticism into historiography, bears the mystical tradition into a new era in which even the magical power of the fable has worn off completely.

On the final page of his most important work Scholem in fact reiterates the ideas he articulated in his famous letter to Zalman Schocken of 1937, titled "A Candid Word about the True Motives of My Kabbalistic Studies." In this letter he notes: "For today's man, that metaphysical totality of truth [*Des Systems*], whose existence disappears particularly when it is projected into historical time, can only become visible in the purest way in . . . the singular mirror of philological criticism . . . My work lives in this paradox."[69] As in the final section of *Major Trends*, in this letter Scholem lays bare the paradox that shapes his own work as a historian who stands at the end of the chain of mystical reception. On the one hand, mysticism must transform into historiography in order to retain its relevance in today's world. But on the other hand, it is precisely this transformation that renders it relative and transitory. It is precisely this transformation, in other words, that undermines the very essence of the mystical endeavor: its ability to access truth in its totality. While this paradox cannot, of course, be resolved, Scholem's makes his intentions perfectly clear: all the difficulties notwithstanding, it is the historian who is charged with carrying the mystical tradition onward in a disenchanted modern world.

Moreover, although Scholem never articulated this argument explicitly, he seems to suggest that at the end of the long chain of efforts to renew the Jewish spirit from within, we would find the Zionist movement. The role of Zionism, from this perspective, was to pick up the mantle of spiritual Jewish renewal from where it had been left by the mystical tradition. This precludes any simple identification of Zionism and Sabbateanism, as I have argued above. Nevertheless, Scholem's work offers a faint yet profound sense of continuity that leads the reader beyond mysticism and beyond the eighteenth century. This continuity is suggested by the historical scope of the work and the conceptual similarities between mysticism and Zionism. In *Major Trends*, Scholem traces the history of the mystical tradition from its roots in an "original" Temple-era Judaism up to what he conceived to be its demise in the modern era. Thus, the historical narrative of the book comes to an end precisely as Zionism is about to appear on the stage. This seems hardly a coincidence.

Furthermore, both historically and ideologically, Jewish mysticism created the spiritual conditions for the appearance of Zionism. Jewish mysticism, Scholem claims, gave rise to an urgent and acute sense of agency among the

69. Quoted from Biale, *Counter-history*, 76.

Jewish people. For the first time in memory, it was the Lurianic Kabbalah that instilled in Jews the belief that they could overcome exile. The mystical tradition was also responsible for the rupture within Judaism, from which the Jewish Enlightenment and all the other splinter traditions within Judaism ostensibly emerged. It was thus also the mystical tradition that created the need for a unifying and active force within Judaism that might render it relevant by solving the problem of exile once and for all. Indeed, the basic impetus of Zionism to renew the spiritual life of the nation and revolutionize its living conditions did not begin with Herzl. As Scholem notes at the end of *Major Trends*, "Abulafia, the Zohar, the book *Peliah*, the Kabbalistic systematizers of Safed—they all no less than the Sabbateans and Frankists, plead the coming of the dawn as the justification of what was new in their ideas."[70] Described in these terms, mysticism finds common ground with Zionism in general and in particular with the Zionist convictions of the young Gershom Scholem.

As we have seen in chapter 2, the young Scholem believed that the true vocation of Zionism was to renew the Jewish spirit after almost two millennia of stagnation in exile. His convictions could therefore likewise be described in these words, as an attempt to plead "the coming of the dawn" as a justification for new ideas.

THE HISTORY OF MYSTICISM AND ZIONIST POLITICS

The notion that the thirst for renewal, so characteristic of Scholem's interpretation of the Kabbalah, might have found continuation in Zionism endows the historiographical work with special significance. For if, indeed, the mystical impetus has yet to reach its end; if, indeed, the historian carries the mystical knowledge onward into the modern era; and if Zionism retains the mystical impetus toward spiritual regeneration in Judaism, then Scholem's history of the Kabbalah is also an authoritative statement about Zionism. First and foremost, it is a statement about the origins of Zionism and the path along which it emerged. Scholem's most consistent argument concerning the relation between Zionism and mysticism appears to assert that if Zionism is to know itself, it must learn the lesson of the mystical tradition that generated it. And if there is one lesson to be learnt from the history of Jewish mysticism, it is the Sabbatean lesson. Throughout the two-thousand-year history of Jewish mysticism, the Sabbatean eruption, so Scholem believed, represented both its

70. Scholem, *Major Trends*, 321.

highest and lowest points, its most suggestive and most intimidating aspects. Scholem's Sabbateanism is a story about the terrible devastation wrought by mass movements and ideologies. He made this point especially clear in his 1928 study on Abraham Cardozo and in *Redemption through Sin* of 1937. But at the same time, the Sabbatean affair was a story about the honest desire to reform a petrified religion and to fundamentally change the living conditions of a nation, which had inevitably erupted in a display of open rebellion. He made this point especially clear in his discussion of Sabbateanism in *Major Trends* in 1941. In short, Scholem's Sabbateanism was about an exiled nation yearning to find a home and about the terrible consequences of wanting this too much. And at the same time, it mirrors Scholem's own life's story.

The competing impulses within Sabbatean history, to rebel and to reinvigorate, are also reminiscent of Scholem's Zionism. In fact, it is in Scholem's discussion about the history of the Sabbatean movement in *Major Trends* that he formulated a central thesis on Jewish mysticism, which he would subsequently apply to Zionism. Moderate Sabbateans, he claimed, had been motivated by the competing desires to reinvigorate Judaism and yet to maintain it as a viable spiritual option. To this end, they developed the mystical interpretation of messianic sin. "Only a mystical interpretation of the fundamental categories of the Law and the Redemption," Scholem argued, "was capable of preparing the ground for antinomian tendencies which *strove to maintain themselves within the general framework of Judaism.*"[71] The mystical solution of Sabbatean heresy, in other words, reflected the competing desires to rebel against the petrified religion of law and to contain these changes within the existing Jewish social constellation.[72] Zionism faced a similar predicament. According to Scholem, it too struggles to define itself as it seeks both to revolutionize traditional Judaism and stay a part of it. In an interview with Ehud Ben Ezer conducted in 1970, Scholem stated: "Zionism has never fully recognized itself—is it a movement of continuity or a revolutionary movement . . . As long as Zionism was not realized in practice, both tendencies could live side by side . . . it is obvious and remarkable that these two tendencies determined the essence of Zionism as a living entity, developing according to its own dialectics. They have also determined the trouble we are facing today."[73] This is the deepest similarity one may find within Scholem's thinking between Sabbateanism and

71. Ibid., 314 (emphasis added).

72. Scholem developed this idea further in an essay titled "Revelation and Tradition as Religious Categories in Judaism."

73. See "A Dialectic of Continuity and Revolt," in Shapira, *Continuity and Revolt*, 34.

the Zionist endeavor. If Zionism is to divine its future, Scholem effectively claims, it should look into the past and discover that the competition between continuity and rebellion has existed in Jewish history for generations. More precisely, in looking back it would observe the salutary case of Sabbatean heresy, which operated within these contradicting desires and took the entire edifice of Judaism to the brink of collapse. And this was the undertaking Scholem had taken on himself: to find the roots of the Zionist impulses—between continuity and revolt—within the Jewish mystical past. It can be no coincidence that being a Zionist, he found what he was looking for.

However, while Scholem reconstructs spiritual Jewish mysticism as the spiritual antecedent of Zionism, he studiously refrains from offering any prescriptive statement about the path that Zionism should take into the future. He thus completely avoids the most obvious and pressing question: How did he, the undisputed authority on the history of Jewish mysticism, comprehend Zionism and its path in the world? How did he think it might resolve the tension between continuity and revolt? Did he believe that the Jews must break free from their religious past in order to survive as a nation among nations? Or did he believe that Jewry could retain its spiritual impulse without succumbing to Sabbatean-like folly? Many commentators and readers have found answers to these questions in Scholem's work.[74] But these were always teased from between the lines, and thus based more on impressions than on quotations. Many of these impressions are not categorically wrong. One cannot doubt the attraction Scholem must have felt to the curious, contradictory, and unlikely notions of redemption, sin, and revolt that he found in the manuscripts and texts of the Sabbatean movement. Nevertheless, to the questions about the future of Zionism, Scholem offered no concrete answers. One may, I venture to say, quite plausibly conclude that like most of us he simply had none.

Ultimately, therefore, Scholem's studies on Sabbateanism reveal more about the author and the transformations he underwent from the time of his immigration to Palestine to the outbreak of World War II than about the Zionist movement. In 1928 Scholem was a political activist, a member of the "radical coterie" of Brith Shalom, who believed in the power of ideas to change the world. He believed that Zionism should fulfill its destiny as a spiritual sanctuary for

74. One interpretation—clearly misinformed—was offered by the right-wing extremist Geula Cohen. See Nitzan Lebovic, "The Jerusalem School: The Theopolitical Hour," *New German Critique* 35, no. 3 105 (September 21, 2008): 97–120. This is also the context in which one should read the polemic with Baruch Kurzweil about the Sabbatai Zevi book. Much to Scholem's chagrin, Kurzweil sought to interpret the significance of the Sabbatean past for the Zionist present.

the renewal of the Jewish spirit. He also felt that the course taken by Zionism in Palestine, in the form of a political entity that strove for recognition by the European superpowers in opposition to the will of the local people, was misinformed and dangerous. In 1928, Sabbateanism was likewise largely an idea to Scholem. It was a dramatic and improbable idea that had moved people to engage in dangerous and deluded action. It was furthermore a product of Jewish hubris, which still existed, Scholem argued, in the form of Zionist messianic folly. He did not shy away from making this comparison explicitly. In 1928, his historical study of Sabbateanism was also a gambit in a larger political argument and as such played a part in Scholem's overall struggle for a better future for Jews in Zion, on which he expounded in the most progressive Jewish journal of the time, *Der Jude*.

By 1941 Scholem's political and historical conception had collapsed under the pressure of historical processes vastly more powerful than his activism, and far more intricate than his own struggles. The violent riots in Palestine of 1929 instigated an ideological crisis among the members of Brith Shalom. Many of its members, including its founder, Arthur Ruppin, began to doubt that a peaceful solution to the Arab-Jewish conflict was still possible.[75] In this respect Scholem was no different from the others.[76] Brith Shalom effectively ceased to exist in 1933. The Nazis' rise to power further strained Scholem's beliefs about Zionism. As a result of the events in Germany, the Jewish presence in Europe was suddenly in jeopardy, and this time the danger was not spiritual. Under these new circumstances Palestine would become more than a spiritual sanctuary; it was to become a life raft. Scholem was keenly aware of the significance of these developments, and his Sabbatean studies reflect this fact. By 1941 he no longer thought of Sabbateanism in terms of revolutionary idealism, but accepted it gravely and discussed it in a spirit of understanding. While in 1928 Sabbateanism had served Scholem as a lesson in Jewish hubris, by 1941 it had become the consummation of the historical trends that preceded it. Effectively, between 1928 and 1941 Scholem had gradually cast off the garb of an activist and donned the mantle of a historian.

Gershom Scholem of the postwar period, to which we now turn, was a radically different person from that described in the previous chapters. He was no longer an activist or a romantic dreamer. After the war Scholem learned

75. On the disintegration of Brith Shalom, see Yosef Heller, *From Brith Shalom to Ichud: Yehuda Leib Magnes and the Struggles for a Binational State* (in Hebrew) (Jerusalem: Magnes Press, 2003), 58–75.

76. Ibid., 107.

to accept the Jewish state and even campaigned on its behalf. But this does not mean that he had become a centrist Zionist and a representative of the establishment. As we shall see in the next chapter, Scholem kept hoping for a peaceful solution of the Israeli-Arab conflict and continued to aspire to a spiritual future for the Zionist movement even as he now accepted the necessity to resort to force of arms. We may conclude, therefore, that Scholem's desire to renew Judaism was tempered by historical events. Yet it can likewise be argued that what he sought to teach in his mature years was deeply rooted in the lessons he had learned. This is certainly true of the conclusions he drew from the Holocaust, as we shall see next.

CHAPTER 6

For the Love of Israel:
The Turn from the Fringe to the
Mainstream of Zionist Thinking

I consider Ben Gurion's political line disastrous, but nevertheless it is far nobler—or
even less evil—than the one we would have had we followed your advice.

[Ich halte Ben Gurions politische Linie für ein Unglück, aber immer noch für ein edleres
und sogar kleineres als das, was uns bevorsteht, wenn wir Ihnen folgen.]

GERSHOM SCHOLEM TO HANNAH ARENDT, 1946

Scholem's political worldview and style of political engagement changed radically again in the years before the Second World War. The historian of the
Kabbalah who became famous for his work in Western Europe and in the
United States was rather different from the man described in the chapters
above. Indeed, during the 1930s Scholem gradually withdrew from political action, and in the few instances he did talk about Zionism, he tended to express
rather mainstream positions. This is a strange turn of events. We have seen in
chapters 2 and 4 how Scholem placed himself in exile, adopting the stance of
an outsider. He castigated the Zionist youth movement and later the Zionist
establishment for disastrously neglecting the real objectives of Zionism. He
had no qualms, for example, about ridiculing Martin Buber, the father figure
of Zionist youth. And he eventually took his leave of the movement, despairing
of its actions in the present and of its capacity to lead Zionism in the right direction in the future. Scholem's struggle against mainstream Zionism reached
its peak with his activity in Brith Shalom. As we have seen, at that time he
expressed views that were considered so radical and outrageous that he could
barely have them published in the Zionist press. He argued forcefully against,
for example, the resolutions of the sixteenth Zionist Congress, as we shall see
below. And he was quite prepared to claim that the Zionist dream was, in fact,

shattered by the actions of the Zionist establishment. Then, during the 1930s, things changed. Scholem retreated from political activism and recanted his outsider's position to become an insider. Both actions should be interpreted as part of a single process, namely, the realization that his vision of Zionism had reached a dead end.

Scholem's turn away from political action and toward the mainstream introduces certain challenges for anyone who seeks to understand and describe them. The realization that one's own political worldview, vision, and hope will never materialize happens silently. This is mostly because any discussion of failure becomes a critique and as such a political statement. And any continuous reflection of the political reality remains within the realm of the political even if it is undertaken in private. Scholem demonstrated this point powerfully with his farewell letter to the youth movement discussed in chapter 2. This letter was overtly political. And, as we have seen, it did not signal an end to Scholem's political engagement. The farewell to the political that Scholem bid in the 1930s is therefore of an entirely different nature. Indeed, unlike his 1917 farewell letter to Siegfried Bernfeld and the readers of his journal *Jerubbaal*, his 1930s retreat was gradual, silent, and thus essentially nonpolitical.

The objective of this chapter is therefore to describe Scholem's silent turn away from politics and his acceptance of mainstream Zionist position despite the lack of hard and clear evidence. In order to do so the following discussion will consign itself to traces of evidence, interpretation, and some speculation. It is more than likely to assume, for example, that Scholem's process of depoliticization was related to the monumental events that took place in Palestine and in Europe in 1929 and 1933 respectively. In August 1929 Palestine erupted violently in a series of bloody events that would shape the relation between Jews and Arabs in the region for the time to come. In 1933 a virulent anti-Semitic party came into power in Germany and changed the course of Western history. Both events, it would seem, suggested to Scholem that the path toward a Jewish-romantic social-spiritual entity in Palestine—like the one Scholem advocated when younger—was unrealistic. Scholem's response to these events will be discussed below. But as we shall see, this response is documented somewhat sparingly.

In order to gain a more systematic understanding of Scholem's turn and his response to current events during the 1930s, it is necessary consider the issue of the Jewish state. For it is the discussion of the question of the state that contains as in a nutshell the description of Scholem's turn, its reasons, and context. Ultimately, Scholem adopted mainstream Zionist positions on many

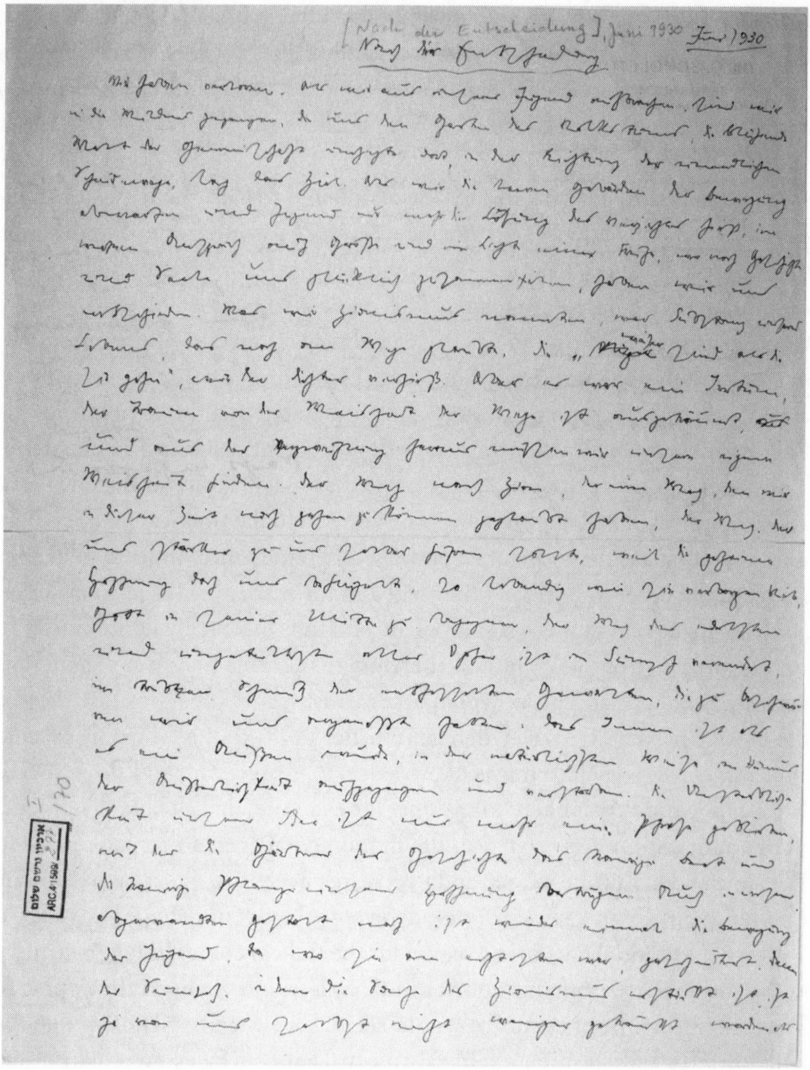
[Nach der Entscheidung], Juni 1930 Juni 1930

FIGURE 6.1. "After the Decision" (Nach der Entscheidung), 1930: A short think-piece about Zionism, which was never published as such. Courtesy of The National Library of Israel, Jerusalem.

of the most fundamental questions under discussion, including on this radically controversial issue.

The issue of the state occupied, in Zionist discourse as well as in Scholem's own political writing, an essential and a symbolic role. The Zionist establishment decided to define the Jewish state as the ultimate objective of the Zionist movement only about fifty years after this movement was first convened in Basel in 1897. It was, as we shall see, a highly controversial decision. In the tradition of German romanticism, Scholem's understood the state as everything that was wrong about being in exile. It was a mechanical, inhuman, and inorganic way of organizing society. And it was a problem that Zionism, according to Scholem, was to solve. As we shall see, Scholem ended up embracing the idea of a Jewish state and later the Jewish state itself. How, then, did Scholem progress from being a radical Zionist who operated on the margins of the Zionist political discourse, to identifying with the mainstream position of the Zionist establishment later in his life?

Scholem's revised position on the Jewish state and change of attitude toward his community always remained implied and must be intuitively divined. Nevertheless, two sources bear witness to his reversal on the question of the state. The first source is the emotional dispute he had with his longtime friend Hannah Arendt. The friendship between Arendt and Scholem, which was based on a long-held mutual respect and appreciation,[1] came to an abrupt end with the publication of Arendt's controversial reportage on the Eichmann trial in Jerusalem and Scholem's renowned open letter responding to it. It is less well known, however, that this friendship had experienced previous tensions. Of most importance in this context is the debate between the two that ensued upon publication of Arendt's essay "Zionism Reconsidered" in the *Menorah Journal* in October 1944. In this essay Arendt sharply criticized the decision of the Zionist Organization of America to define the Jewish state as its ultimate objective. Scholem was astounded by Arendt's critique and wrote to her about his reservations in a long and detailed letter, to which Arendt replied.

The second source that elucidates Scholem's acceptance of the basic tenets of political Zionism is his 1948 essay on the Star of David, the *Magen David*. Ostensibly, this was an academic essay on the history of the Kabbalah, dealing with one of Judaism's principal and most recognizable symbols, the Star of David. But it was, in fact, much more. Published shortly after Israel won its independence, this essay is Scholem's way of symbolically baptizing the Jewish state. In his essay he offers a historical justification for the need for a Jewish state that is not only very reminiscent of the prevalent justification for the state and very much at odds with his previous thoughts on the matter, but also deeply personal. This essay is, in other words, a highly personal account of

1. This friendship is documented in the recently published exchange of letters between the two. See also Marie Louise Knott, "Hannah Arendt—Gershom Scholem, Die Konstellation," in *Hannah Arendt / Gershom Scholem, Der Briefwechsel: 1939–1964*, ed. Marie Luise Knott assisted by David Heredia (Berlin: Jüdischer Verlag, 2010), 608–42.

a deep transformation, explaining why it was necessary for him, in the given historical circumstances, to accept Jewish sovereignty despite all his previous misgivings. These two sources will be discussed below.

It is also important to note that, all these changes notwithstanding, Scholem remained a critical thinker and astute observer of political reality throughout his life, who inhabited a position on the margins. This was clearly the case until the 1930s. But also much later in his life, as a well-known public intellectual Scholem would comment on issues of political and social concern. Shortly after the end of the Six Day War, Scholem signed a petition calling for immediate negotiations with the Arabs on the future of the occupied territories and protesting the de facto annexation of lands.[2] He subsequently expressed concern about the use of messianic vocabulary in Israeli political discourse, and compared Gush Emunim (the ideological nucleus of the settler movement) to the Sabbatean movement.[3] Thus, even after what must have appeared to him to be an endless chain of bloody conflicts with the Arabs, he continued to believe that a negotiable and just peace was possible. At the same time, however, Scholem was a proud citizen of Israel, a key member of its academic establishment, and an unofficial ambassador of the state to intellectual circles around the world. To judge by his public appearances, especially those made abroad, it is clear that he grew to love the Jewish state, which he came to call home.[4]

TRACES OF WITHDRAWAL

The first stirrings of doubt in Scholem's mind, so it seems, can be traced to the aftermath of the violent events of 1929, which mark a watershed in the

---

2. *Ha'aretz*, December 15, 1967. The petition reads: "The Six Day War was a justified defensive war of the people of Israel [Am Yisrael]. We believe that an unconditional withdrawal from the territories held today by the Israeli Defense Forces would not pave the way for peace but would return us to the pre-war situation and for this reason we reject it. However, we observe the campaign to unilaterally annex the territories that were occupied in the war that was forced upon us with concern. We see this as a distortion of the war's objectives. It also endangers the Jewish identity of the state, its humanistic and democratic character, or both of these at once. The first objective must be to pursue every opportunity for peace. Every action or deed that diminishes the chance for peace appears to us to be completely irresponsible toward the future of the Jewish people and the State of Israel."

3. David Biale, "The Threat of Messianism: An Interview with Gershom Scholem," *New York Review of Books*, August 14, 1980.

4. See, for example, Gershom Scholem, "A Speech about Israel," in *Devarim be-go*, 128–32.

region's history.[5] These events also hastened the disintegration of the fledgling peace organization Brith Shalom, whose members could not agree on how to interpret what had happened. Hans Kohn, for example, became so disillusioned with the belligerent reaction of the Zionist establishment and of the general public that he resigned from his job at the United Israel Appeal (Keren Hayesod) and eventually immigrated to the United States, thus bidding an unhappy farewell to Zionism, which had shaped his life up to then.[6] Scholem's reaction to these same events was very different. He appears to have forgone not Zionism, but rather his own political convictions.[7]

Traces of Scholem's political transformation first appear in a letter that he and two other prominent members of Brith Shalom wrote to Robert Weltsch, editor of the *Jüdische Rundschau*, shortly after the violent events of 1929. In this letter Scholem, Ernst Simon, and Shmuel Hugo Bergman report on their meeting with the leadership of the Haganah, the Zionist movement's paramilitary organization. Scholem, who but a few weeks previously had blamed the Jewish leadership for kindling the conflict between Arabs and Jews, was deeply impressed by his meeting with the military command of the Zionist movement. The Haganah's actions "must be judged positively," wrote the three men.[8] They summarized their impressions of the meeting as follows: "Given the prevailing psychological and political conditions, we are acutely aware of how difficult it will be to achieve a viable political arrangement with the Arabs while securing our defenses against the kind of attack we have experienced. To us, however, there appears to be no other way."[9]

Even if the three Brith Shalom members were not fully aware of it at the time, this message coveys a startling realization. The Haganah was a military organization and an executive branch of the Zionist movement, and its leaders necessarily believed that the conflict with the Arabs was a given fact for

5. See note 31 in chapter 4 above.

6. This episode is brilliantly captured in Adi Gordon, "Nothing but a Disillusioned Love: Hans Kohn's Break from the Zionist Movement," in *Brith Shalom and Binational Zionism*, 67–92.

7. Although Scholem's conclusions about the path of Zionism in light of world political events seems reasonable, it is important to note that other Zionist intellectuals, like Hannah Arendt, Judah Magnes, Mordecai Kaplan, and Hans Kohn, drew completely different conclusions from the same events. See for example Noam Pianko, *Zionism and the Roads Not Taken: Rawidowicz, Kaplan, Kohn* (Bloomington: Indiana University Press, 2010), 95–177; Gordon, "Nothing but a Disillusioned Love"; Heller, *From Brith Shalom to Ichud*, 69–118.

8. Scholem, *Gershom Scholem: A Life in Letters*, 176.

9. Ibid., 177.

which they needed to prepare. Brith Shalom, on the other hand, was a political organization driven by a vision and a set of ideas. Accepting the idea that the Haganah must "secure our defenses" meant accepting, at least nominally, its view of the conflict and acknowledging that violence was and would probably continue to be an inevitable aspect of life in Palestine. This contradicts everything that Brith Shalom was working for. The basic premise of Scholem's political consciousness was that the conflict between Arabs and Jews in Palestine was essentially an artificial conflagration and that there was in fact nothing that these two groups could not peacefully share. Asserting that the Yishuv must be prepared both for military action and for negotiations is the fundamental position of Zionism and is even expressed in Israel's declaration of independence.[10] And this was the position that the three members of Brith Shalom now adopted, and by so doing signaled a significant transformation of Brith Shalom's stance. If the association now upheld, more or less, the same fundamental position as the Zionist establishment, its role in the political discourse was, at the very least, less clear and less urgent. It seems that Scholem gradually came to realize this state of affairs.

Another trace of Scholem's feelings of hopelessness is to be found in an unpublished private document from June 1930. In style and grandeur, this two-page handwritten text bears much resemblance to Scholem's earlier pieces about Zionism. But there is also a difference. It is here, possibly for the first time, that Scholem seems to recognize the forces of history in the shaping of reality. As we have seen, Scholem in earlier phases of his life always poignantly ascribed the failures of Zionism to the mistakes of the Zionists themselves. It was they who misunderstood the Arabs, the Germans, or even themselves. Scholem never minced his words when he argued that they were deluded and misinformed. He might have been correct on many occasions, but it is nevertheless telling that in this document, written a year after the bloody events in Palestine, history makes a debut.

The document, titled "After the Decision," opens with the ominous words "We have lost."[11] This sentiment is of course not completely new. It echoes

10. The image commonly associated with Israel's unwavering willingness to find common ground with its neighbors is that of a hand extended in peace. This phrase appears in Israel's Declaration of Independence of 1948 and remains part of the country's political discourse to this day. Its original formulation is this: "We extend our hand to all neighboring states and their peoples in an offer of peace and good neighborliness, and appeal to them to establish bonds of cooperation and mutual help with the sovereign Jewish people settled in its own land."

11. "Nach der Entscheidung," Arc 4° 1599 07 277.170, Gershom Scholem's personal archive, Archive of the National Library of Israel, Jerusalem.

Scholem's experiences upon arriving in Palestine, discussed in chapter 4. However, here his tone and style are less polemic and angry and more sad and resigned. "That which we called Zionism . . . still believed in paths, which, as the poet promised, are wiser than the one who walks them. But it was a mistake. The dream about the wisdom of the paths was dispelled, and now we must discover our own wisdom out of despair. The path to Zion, the only path we believed at the time to have had, the way that should have led us to ourselves . . . the path of the noblest and most exceptional sacrifice perished in the quagmire."[12]

More than the general sentiment of this document and even more than its unique style, it is this metaphor—the quagmire—that is interesting. Scholem's basic argument is that Zionism, which was pure and noble, ran into trouble, drowned in a swamp. This was a process, Scholem notes. However, even in its changed form, that is, even in Palestine, "the movement of our youth, exactly where it was truest, failed. This is because the quagmire in which the concerns of Zionism drowned was watered by us no less than it was watered by the external cruelties of history."[13] Here too, much of the blame is placed on the shoulders of the Zionists. However, history played a critical role in making the land too boggy to walk on.

In 1942, Scholem rejected an invitation to join a political organization that sought to persuade the Zionist leadership in Palestine to take more concerted action on behalf of Europe's Jews as news of the catastrophe began to arrive.[14] Responding to the proposal, Scholem wrote: "At the time of catastrophe there are no teachings [Torah], and words were given only to those who could observe from a certain distance, and the one standing at the eye of the storm must always be silent."[15] He concludes his letter thus: "Excuse me if I tell you that in my opinion the historian will have to speak in a different way in the future."[16] By 1942, it seems, Scholem had abandoned political activism and consigned himself to scholarship. Admittedly, by providing historical knowledge and by enriching the debate with facts, he might have indirectly affected or even shaped the minds of decision makers. But such indirect influence was largely beyond his control. The historian's responsibility, as he conceived of it, was not to think about the future but to be loyal to the past, and this is what

12. Ibid.
13. Ibid.
14. Noam Zadoff, "Zion's Self-Engulfing Light."
15. Ibid., 276.
16. Ibid., 277.

Scholem was. The mature Scholem was a responsible historian who carefully avoided drawing parallels between the past and the present.

Scholem's withdrawal from politics was likewise evident in his academic work, especially in his studies of the Sabbatean movement discussed in chapter 5. His first study on the history of Sabbateanism, which appeared in 1928, was replete with political polemics. In it, Scholem criticized the concrete social and political situation in Palestine. In *Major Trends*, his most comprehensive analysis of the history of the Sabbatean movement, he all but ignored its political potency, portraying it as a culmination of prior historical forces. The movement thus appears as an unavoidable set of events, transcending the agency of the individuals involved, and therefore transcending politics. As noted in chapter 5, Scholem's tendency toward stripping the Sabbatean lesson of its political content extends to his most extensive study on Zevi, *Sabbatai Sevi: The Mystical Messiah*. As the original Hebrew title—*Sabbatai Zevi and the Messianic Movement during His Lifetime*—conveys, this meticulous, thousand-page project barely even touches upon the aspect that rendered Scholem's previous research so politically charged, namely, the Sabbatean ideology that emerged following Sabbatai Zevi's conversion. In his post–World War II work, Scholem not only evaded the more troubling and political aspects of Sabbatean history but highlighted those elements of the story that largely corresponded with the Zionist interpretations of Sabbateanism.[17] Scholem's book on Sabbatai Zevi, which appeared in 1957, thus represents a further stage of the overall process of depoliticization that Scholem had undergone.[18]

17. Ostensibly, therefore, Baruch Kurzweil's critique of Scholem's book, discussed in chapter 4, does not entirely lack substance. Kurzweil accused Scholem of portraying Sabbateanism as the spiritual precursor of Zionism. He in fact mistook Scholem's depoliticization of the Sabbatean affair as a positive judgment of the contribution of Sabbateanism to Jewish culture and history, which culminated in Zionism. However, inasmuch as Scholem actively avoids taking a political stance in this study and eschews discussion of the political developments in the wake of the "Messiah's" conversion, he effectively aligns his interpretation with the political status quo and with a Zionist interpretation of history.

18. Scholem's *Sabbatai Sevi* was planned as the first volume of a series of three books, which were to address the entire history of the Sabbatean movement and thus also cover the events after the conversion. But, as noted in chapter 5, Scholem never wrote the second and third volumes. His later work on the Sabbatean movement engages with the less controversial and less politically charged elements of its history. It addresses, in fact, those elements that Scholem, even in *Major Trends*, deemed less important and better known. As noted, this was, apparently, hardly a coincidence.

ZIONISM AND THE QUESTION OF
THE JEWISH STATE

In order to gain a better understanding of Scholem's attitude toward the idea of the Jewish state, it is imperative to address the context in which this debate took place. Unlike other national movements, the Zionist movement did not envision a Jewish sovereign state as its ultimate objective during the first half century of its existence.[19] Theodor Herzl, who coined the term "the Jewish state" in his renowned book of 1896, had a socialist-utopist vision in mind rather than an outline of a nation-state as such.[20] Several of Zionism's key figures, such as Ahad Ha'am and Martin Buber, rejected the idea of a state entirely and regarded the spiritual and cultural renewal of the Jewish spirit to be the Zionist movement's top priority. Others figures, including Ber Borochov and A. D. Gordon, argued that a state would hinder the revolutionary trans-formation of the Jewish social structure through labor and the creation of an authentic working class.[21] Even Chaim Weizmann, who had been instrumental in securing the Balfour Declaration of 1917 and who was the preeminent leader of the Zionist movement in the 1920s and 1930s, studiously avoided declaring statehood to be the ultimate goal of the Zionist movement. He believed that to do so would be a blunt provocation of the Arab population in Palestine, which would feel threatened by the prospect of Jewish sovereignty. Such a declaration would, furthermore, be interpreted as an act of defiance against the British Empire, whose presence in Palestine was part of its strategic hold on the region. The idea of a Jewish state was therefore held in abeyance and hardly ever publicly debated by the mainstream Zionist establishment until the early 1940s.[22]

19. Ben Halpern, *The Idea of the Jewish State*, 2nd ed. (Cambridge: Harvard University Press, 1969), 20–27.

20. See Shlomo Avineri, *The Making of Modern Zionism: Intellectual Origins of the Jewish State* (New York: Basic Books, 1981), 88–100. More recently this position was disputed by, for example, Yoram Hazony, "Did Herzl want a 'Jewish' State?," *Azure* 9 (2000), accessed May 3, 2011, http://azure.org.il/article.php?id=288. This criticism stems from a narrow perspective and thus avoids interpreting "the Jewish state" within the larger context of Herzl's work. It therefore strikes me as unconvincing.

21. Avineri provides by far the best source on the various ideas that made up the Zionist movement in its earliest phase. See *Making of Modern Zionism*.

22. The important exception to this rule is Ze'ev Jabotinsky and his Revisionist party, which regarded a Jewish state that confronted the Arab population as the only viable solution for the Jewish future in the region. For this reason, Jabotinsky clashed with Weizmann and eventually

As we have seen in chapters 2 and 4, Gershom Scholem was a vocal adherent of the cultural approach to Zionism, which believed in the precedence of the spiritual renewal of the Jewish people. Already as a young youth movement activist, Scholem rejected the political aspirations of the Zionist movement, including those implied by Herzl himself. For example, at the end of a long and emotional entry in his personal diary dated January 20, 1915, Scholem makes the following comment: "We as Jews know more than enough about the hideous idol called the state to bow down and offer up our prayers to it . . . We Jews are not the people of the state . . . We do not want to go to Palestine to found a state, thereby forging new chains out of the old . . . We want to go to Palestine out of a thirst for freedom and longing for the future."[23] Rather than striving to establish a state, Zionism, according to Scholem, should take a route entirely different from that of other national movements in Europe, namely, a spiritual one. He strenuously argued his case among fellow members of the Zionist youth movement in Germany and subsequently among the Zionist political establishment in Palestine.

Scholem continued vehemently to oppose the creation of a Jewish state in later years, as a member of Brith Shalom following his immigration to Palestine. In an editorial in Brith Shalom's journal *She'ifotenu* titled "Our Final Goal," Scholem wrote: "We, the members of Brith Shalom, have called all these years for a new orientation for the Zionist movement that would include an unambiguous and clear renunciation of the 'Jewish State.'"[24] He made this statement in response to the resolutions of the sixteenth Zionist Congress held in Zurich in 1929, which gave top priority to the Zionist project in Palestine by creating the Jewish Agency for Palestine and delegating to it a wide authority on issues such as immigration, land distribution, fundraising, and labor. Thus, it defined the creation of a self-sustaining Jewish social and political body in Palestine as the ultimate priority of the Zionist movement, even if it did not express its objective quite as such. This today mostly forgotten resolution seemed to contemporary observers to be as significant as the constitutive moment of the Zionist movement at the first Zionist Congress of 1897 in Basel.[25] To Scholem

---

left the Zionist movement, at least for a while. For more on this issue, see Halpern, *Idea of the Jewish State*, 31–39.

23. Scholem, *Lamentations of Youth*, 48.

24. Scholem, "Final Goal," 68.

25. Thus, for example, the editorial page of the *Jüdische Rundschau* of August 20, 1929, noted: "Die naheliegende Vergleich zwischen dem ersten Zionistenkongreß und der ersten Tagung der Jewish Agency ist in diesen Tagen oft gezogen werden.".

this resolution amounted to an implicit but fully intended endorsement of the Jewish state, for which the Zionist movement, he believed, would pay a bitter price, and he attacked this decision in no uncertain terms: "if this is the Zionist dream, numbers and 'borders,' and if it cannot exist without this dream, then Zionism is destined to fail, or rather, it has already failed."[26]

The Zionist movement defined a Jewish state as its ultimate goal for the first time in its history at the Biltmore Conference in May 1942. Only six months after the United States entered the war, the delegates to the conference in New York seem already to have realized that the war in Europe would end with a major shift in global power, or at least were willing to bet on such an outcome. Its resolution, known as the Biltmore Plan, called upon the nations of the world to recognize that a "Jewish Commonwealth" must be a part of any just postwar arrangement. This resolution thus signified a departure from the Zionist movement's traditional position, which until then had refrained from including the founding of a Jewish state in its official policy. The conference also marked the ascendance of a new leader in the Zionist movement, David Ben-Gurion, who was to become the first prime minister of the independent State of Israel, and a decline in the influence of the pro-British leader Chaim Weizmann.[27]

Two major factors led the Zionist movement to adopt the nation-state solution. First was the exacerbation of the violent conflict with the Arabs in Palestine that began in 1929 and took a more threatening turn with the Arab revolt of the years 1936–39. The violence in Palestine prompted the Zionist leadership to strengthen its protomilitary organizations and to forgo its reliance on the British colonial forces for the maintenance of security. The second was related to the violent events in Europe. The systematic disenfranchisement of the Jews of Europe, their forced uprooting and brutal extermination intensified the call to British authorities to open the floodgates of Palestine to the mass immigration of Jews. This call eventually became a demand for full control over immigration. In other words, the events of the 1930s and 1940s in Palestine and Europe had generated and justified a fundamental reorientation on the part of the Zionist movement.[28] It now defined itself in light of a radically new

26. Scholem, "Final Goal," 70.

27. See Shlomo Aronson, *David Ben-Gurion and the Jewish Renaissance* (Cambridge: Cambridge University Press, 2010), 168–78.

28. Halpern, *Idea of the Jewish State*, 39–41; Tom Segev, *The Seventh Million: The Israelis and the Holocaust* (New York: Hill and Wang, 1994), 67–112. Hannah Arendt, who was present at the Biltmore conference, repeatedly suggested that this and later policies were motivated by

goal, namely, the creation of a Jewish state that would be able to welcome persecuted Jews from around the world, house them, and offer them protection and sustenance. Zionism thus now came to define itself in terms of a goal that only a decade earlier would have been unthinkable even to many of the most visionary and daring Zionist thinkers and political leaders.

Although it is impossible to know for certain, it is more than likely that Gershom Scholem came to accept the idea of a Jewish state for similar reasons. He too witnessed with horror not only the events in Palestine but, more crucial, perhaps, also those in Germany. And he too came to realize, it seems, that cultural and spiritual Zionism could not offer solutions to the problems created by these events. He too, therefore, came to accept the idea of a Jewish state as a solution. Nevertheless, this turn did not dictate a fundamental change in Scholem's understanding of the Jewish-Arab conflict. When asked about his political stance, Scholem steadfastly avowed his belief in a peaceful solution to the conflict with the Arabs in Palestine and later in Israel, and continued to stress the importance of the spiritual and cultural transformation of the Jewish people. Ostensibly, therefore, these elements of his political stance had not changed. In fact, however, his acceptance of the Israeli state represented a profound transformation in his outlook. It meant that all his reservations notwithstanding, Scholem saw himself as a Zionist and as a part of the emerging Israeli community. While things had not turned out in the way he had hoped, in the face of what he perceived as grave existential dangers he identified with his community, in which he felt more or less at home.

Scholem's endorsement of the Jewish nation-state, however, meant not only that the physical preservation of Jewish lives took precedence over all other considerations, but also that the spiritual renewal of the Jewish people had become a less urgent matter. It also meant that, in essence, Scholem had surrendered his dissenting political position to the prevalent ideology. Given these changed circumstances, with the rise of the Nazi regime and the annihilation of Jewish life in Europe on the one hand and the intensification of the conflict with the Arabs on the other, the concerns that had driven Scholem to political action up to that point took a back seat. And it appears that he had little to say about this matter.

This, then, may explain Scholem's silent withdrawal in the thirties. It was anything but a political act and therefore bears no comparison to his previous

---

opportunism rather by a genuine political consciousness. See Arendt's column in *Aufbau*, her articles on Jewish politics in the 1940s, and especially her article "Zionism Reconsidered," in Arendt, *Jewish Writings*, 125–407, which is discussed below.

retreat, when he took his leave of the Zionist youth movement. As we have seen in chapter 2, Scholem's debate with the Zionist youth movement culminated in a bitter letter of resignation published in the youth movement's journal *Je-rubbaal*.[29] This farewell letter was an acerbic political statement and hardly marked the end of Scholem's political activism. Upon immigrating to Palestine he plunged himself into the most politically active period in his life. As a member of Brith Shalom, Scholem criticized not merely the local youth organization but the leadership of the Zionist movement itself, thereby pitting himself against the very tenets of mainstream Zionism. This time, his activism came to an end not in some defiant act of opposition. Unlike certain other intellectuals who disavowed their links to Zionism in a final and desperate response to its increasingly nationalistic tendencies,[30] Scholem adapted, or rather changed his mind. As his correspondence with Hannah Arendt demonstrates, he, like the Zionist movement itself, learned to accept the notion of the Jewish state.

ZIONISM RECONSIDERED: HANNAH ARENDT'S CRITIQUE OF ZIONISM

Scholem's debate with Hannah Arendt is revealing precisely because politically and socially, literally and metaphorically, they both come from the same place. Arendt was born almost a decade after Scholem, but they both grew up in Germany at around the same time to parents of similar means and social background. Both began their intellectual pursuits at a young age and studied at the finest academic institutions in the world, where they were both singled out for their exceptional ability and talent. Both grappled with the question of Jewish life in the modern world, albeit by very different means. Like Scholem, Arendt dedicated herself to Zionism, albeit for a far shorter period of time. During the 1930s and 1940s Arendt was familiar with Jewish national politics down to the finest and most intricate detail.[31] Both Scholem and Arendt belonged to similar and at times overlapping political and social circles. The Jewish experience is more salient in Scholem's work than in Arendt's, but as Jerome Kohn notes in his preface to Arendt's volume *Jewish Writings*, "even

29. Scholem, "Farewell."
30. See note 7.
31. Beyond her work on behalf of Zionist youth immigration in France before the war and her contribution to Jewish cultural reconstruction in the United States after the war, it is the sheer volume and depth of Arendt's writing on Zionism that display her commitment to this cause. See for example Arendt, *Jewish Writings*, 125–452.

on its most abstract level" Hannah Arendt's work "cannot be fully grasped without recognizing its poignancy as originating in [her] experience as a Jew living in the twentieth century."[32] In short, in their life and in their work Scholem and Arendt confronted similar questions in a similar environment, even if they ended up with radically different answers.

It was therefore only natural that Scholem and Arendt not only knew each other but were also friends. They corresponded with each other, respected each other greatly, and collaborated on several projects. They both developed a special relationship with Walter Benjamin and collaborated to reintroduce his works to the general public after the war. There were certainly also important differences between Arendt and Scholem, especially when it came to politics. Scholem was a fierce believer in the overriding importance of a cultural and spiritual Jewish revolution. Arendt, on the other hand, was more skeptical about the spiritual regeneration of Judaism and tended to focus on political solutions to Jewish problems, including the establishment of a Jewish army. But both Arendt and Scholem believed that an increasingly nationalistic and chauvinistic Zionism posed a great threat to the integrity of the movement and that a just arrangement with the Arabs in Palestine was an urgent necessity, and certainly more urgent than brokering a deal with the imperial powers. Both thinkers had shared these opinions for many years, but then one of them changed his mind. Nevertheless, they belonged to the same political, social, and cultural camp. Among other things, it is indeed this fact that could explain the depth and bitterness of the disputes between them.

One of the climactic moments of Hannah Arendt's involvement with Zionism was the publication of her essay "Zionism Reconsidered," written in reaction to the resolutions adopted at the conference of the Zionist Organization of America held in Atlantic City in October 1944. Like the Biltmore program, these resolutions called for the creation of a "Jewish commonwealth" after the war. Yet unlike the Biltmore program that reaffirmed in its final clause the "readiness and desire" of the Jewish people to cooperate with the Arabs, the Atlantic City resolution failed even to mention the Arab population of Palestine. In "Zionism Reconsidered," Arendt argued that this later resolution thus implicitly left the Arabs with the choice between "voluntary emigration [and] second class citizenship."[33] As such it dealt, she argued, "a deadly blow to all

32. See Jerome Kohn, "Preface, a Jewish Life, 1906–1975," in Arendt, *Jewish Writings*, ix–xxxiii.

33. Arendt, *Jewish Writings*, 343.

those . . . who tirelessly preached the necessity of an understanding between the Arab and the Jewish peoples,"[34] including, therefore, Scholem himself.

At the same time, Arendt argued, the Atlantic City resolutions expressed the movement's willingness to trust its fate to the bayonets of foreign powers. The future Jewish commonwealth to be created without the approval of the local Arab population would be unsustainable without external support and protection. This was a terribly dangerous gambit, Arendt asserted: "The big nations that can afford to play the game of power politics had found it easy to forsake King Arthur's round table for the poker table; but small powerless nations that venture their own stakes in that game, and try to mingle with the big, usually end up sold down the river."[35]

In short, Arendt argued that the resolutions adopted at Atlantic City proved that the Zionist desire for statehood had now finally overshadowed its commitment to its immediate cultural and social environment, namely, to the Arabs. And this aspiration had placed the Zionist movement in a double bind. On the one hand, without an agreement with the Arabs the settlement enterprise in Palestine would inevitably face a hostile reaction. On the other, it meant risking everything for a lopsided bargain with a foreign power whose interests might well turn it against Zionism at some point in the future.

This was the point that Arendt made in the first section of her essay: in its vain rush to achieve recognition, the Zionist leadership's political judgment had been clouded by opportunism, which had led it to take the wrong decisions on some of the most critical issues at hand. Arendt devoted the following nine sections of her article—some thirty-odd pages of dense writing—to an attempt to explore the reasons that had led the Zionist movement to make this fatal decision. Scholem largely acquiesced with Arendt's portrayal of the state of affairs. Atlantic City was, he concurred, a sham. But he vehemently rejected her analysis of the evolvement of the Zionism movement. In a letter to Arendt penned in 1946 he noted: "While I basically agree with your starting position in Section 1, I read the elaboration of your argument while vigorously shaking my head."[36] This is hardly surprising. As we shall see, Arendt's conclusions about the attraction of young men and women to Zionism could be read as

34. Ibid.

35. Ibid., 345.

36. Scholem, *Gershom Scholem: A Life in Letters*, 330. "Während ich mit dem Ausgangspunkt in Absatz I mich noch im Wesentlichen in Übereinstimmung befinde, kann ich die weiteren Ausführungen nur mit dem größten Kopfschütteln lesen." *Hannah Arendt / Gershom Scholem, Der Briefwechsel*, 92.

a particularly unflattering commentary on Scholem's own youthful Zionist enthusiasm.

How, then, had Zionism, according to Arendt, come to try its hand at the card game of power with the international entities against its neighbors? And what was it that prompted Scholem to respond with such dismay? Staking its future on the big powers was, Arendt argued, the "political consequence" of a fundamentally "unpolitical attitude" that had emerged within the Zionist movement. In "Zionism Reconsidered" she essentially argued that Zionism had failed to develop a genuine political consciousness during its fifty years of existence. As a result, it had systematically avoided taking a clear political stance on any of the crucial questions it had faced. Arendt spared none of the internal strands of Zionism from her critical analysis as she inveighed against cultural Zionism, Labor Zionism, the political Zionism of Chaim Weizmann, as well as the version of Zionism that had developed in the United States. She asserted that all these strands had been preoccupied with themselves, developing in an inward-looking manner, and had consequently failed to recognize the political implications of their actions. But the crux of her argument and probably its most hurtful aspect had to do with the essential "unpolitical" nature of Zionism's evolution.

According to Arendt, Zionism was nothing but the product of a frustrated and alienated generation of Jewish intellectuals who could find no place for themselves in the existing Jewish social world and were therefore bent on creating a new Jewish home. The very existence of Jewish intellectuals was a new phenomenon, she argued. The world had never before seen young Jewish men and women with a broad academic education and of middle-class background. These young men and women were neither rich nor poor, and this, Arendt claimed, was the problem. They did not belong anywhere in the Jewish charitable world, which, Arendt argued, came "very near to organize world Jewry into a curious sort of body politic." Had they been rich, they could have become philanthropists, the leading members of this curious international Jewish social structure. As poor people, they could have relied on this system for sustenance. Jewish intellectuals were members of the middle class and as such rich enough to support themselves, but not quite so well to do that they could support others. They were thus neither beggars nor patrons, and therefore they did not belong. Neither were they businessmen, and they were thus unable to utilize the extensive Jewish network that was spread across Europe. Alienated from the Jewish world, young secular Jewish intellectuals were desperate to assert their place. Zionism was the solution they found to their predicament. It functioned as an attempt to rebuild the Jewish social world around their personal aspirations and would, so they hoped, relieve the sense of alienation that they felt toward their old home, the home of "their fathers."

At the same time, however, Zionism was an attempt to escape the modern predicament of alienation. It was also defined by its promise of personal and existential salvation. But the promise of "community" was, so Arendt maintained, steeped in indifference toward the political aspect of the endeavor. It had, for example, envisioned the very real land of Palestine "as an ideal place, out of the bleak world, where one might realize one's ideals and find a personal solution for political and social conflicts."[37] In other words, young Zionists were more interested in "Zion," onto which they projected their hopes and fears, than in the actual land of Israel, or rather of Palestine. Indeed, Arendt asserted, the Zionist settlers in Palestine were, from a political standpoint, totally and woefully naive. The existential motivation of their project had blinded them to the ways in which their actions might affect their Arab neighbors, as they simply assumed that nothing they did could disturb the political status quo. Furthermore, Arendt added, the Jews in Palestine had no inkling of and harbored no curiosity about the way in which their new position as the vanguard of a new Jewish society could affect the lives of Jews living anywhere else.

Nevertheless, Arendt distinguishes, within this attempt to overcome alienation, also an ideological argument about the Jewish world. And it was in the context of this internal debate that Zionism had, she claims, committed its decisive political error. In arguing their cause, Zionists had fashioned their emerging movement as the ultimate solution to anti-Semitism. In their polemics they presented anti-Semitism "as the natural reaction of one people against the other, as though they were two natural substances destined by some mysterious natural law to antagonize each other to eternity."[38] This explanation served the internal political end of the Zionists, as they underscored the seriousness of the Jewish problem and the urgency of implementing its new solution. Yet, Arendt claims, by making this argument, they completely failed to understand the concept they were using. In fact, she argues, modern anti-Semitism was not a direct continuation of its medieval religious predecessor, nor was it a monolithic or a natural force. It was, rather, part of the creation of modern European nationalism, and as she later elaborated in her monumental work *The Origins of Totalitarianism* (1951), it had played a fundamental role

37. Arendt, *Jewish Writings*, 355.
38. Ibid., 358.

in the political history of Europe. Along with other factors (most importantly imperialism), it was modern anti-Semitism that ushered in the totalitarian regimes of the twentieth century.[39]

The insistence on the part of the Zionist leadership on ignoring modern anti-Semitism's political dimensions and on interpreting it as a force majeure had had, Arendt claimed, lasting consequences for the formation of the Zionist movement. To Arendt, this was nothing but a wholesale denial of the role that Jews had played in the creation of modern anti-Semitic myths, which tied them to the broader historical and political processes that had played out in Europe. Arendt argued that denial of the political significance of anti-Semitism and with it the denial of the roles of Jews in the formation of modern Europe were tantamount to cutting off "Jewish history from European history and even from the rest of mankind."[40] While this in itself was an ominous deed, signifying a thorough depoliticization of the Zionist movement, the true significance of the Zionist reluctance to reflect on the essence of modern anti-Semitism went beyond cutting the link between Jews and Europe.

This notion that anti-Semitism was inevitable undermined the link between the Zionist movement in Palestine and the rest of the Jewish people, on the one hand, and created the condition for a precarious and shortsighted alliance between Zionism and anti-Semitism, on the other. For, indeed, both parties seemed to agree on the fundamental principle, according to which Jews had no place in Europe.[41] The inner Jewish political stance of Zionism had on anti-Semitism, Arendt argued, led to "an utter confusion in which nobody could distinguish between friend and foe, in which the foe became a friend, and the friend the hidden, and therefore all the more dangerous, enemy."[42] At the same time, this position also pitted Zionist Jews, especially those who had fulfilled the ultimate Zionist aspiration and had migrated to Palestine, against non-Zionist Jews, who chose to stay in the land of their fathers and forefathers. The Zionist "doctrine of the inevitable decline of Jewish life in Galuth, the

39. As a previously unpublished draft of her essay "Antisemitism" proves, Arendt started working on a political interpretation of anti-Semitism already in the late 1930s. The essay appears in Arendt, *Jewish Writings*, 46–123. See also Hannah Arendt, *The Origins of Totalitarianism* (Orlando: Harcourt, Brace, Jovanovich, 1973), 3–122.

39. As a previously unpublished draft of her essay "Antisemitism" proves, Arendt started working on a political interpretation of anti-Semitism already in the late 1930s. The essay appears in Arendt, *Jewish Writings*, 46–123. See also Hannah Arendt, *The Origins of Totalitarianism* (Orlando: Harcourt, Brace, Jovanovich, 1973), 3–122.

40. Arendt, *Jewish Writings*, 358.

41. Arendt fully develops this controversial argument in her reportage from the Eichmann trial, in which she argues not only that Eichmann supported the Zionist effort to transport Jews from the regions under his control, but also that he had read Herzl and admired his book *The Jewish State*.

42. Arendt, *Jewish Writings*, 359.

Diaspora," Arendt argued, "made it easy for the consciousness of the *Yishuv*, the settlement in Palestine, to develop its attitude of aloofness. Palestine Jewry, instead of making itself the political vanguard of the whole Jewish people, developed a spirit of self-centeredness."[43]

This doctrine had led, Ardent asserted, to a political absurd. The Zionist leadership in Palestine believed that by building Zion they were strengthening the Jewish people against its enemies. Their endeavor, however, had shifted all the political resources of the Jewish people away from Europe where they were most desperately needed. And it had thus widened the gap between the Jews of Palestine and those of the Diaspora, leaving the latter to face their most implacable enemy virtually alone in the hour of their greatest need.[44] Owing to this blunder, furthermore, the real enemy, anti-Semitism, was reduced to a perennial cause and had in essence and in effect been almost entirely forgotten.

ZIONISM RECONSIDERED: THE DEBATE BETWEEN GERSHOM SCHOLEM AND HANNAH ARENDT

Gershom Scholem was flabbergasted by Arendt's essay, and yet he tried to maintain at least a semblance of respect, so as not to ruin the friendship. "My dear friend," he began his letter of January 1946, "I find myself in the extraordinarily unpleasant position of having to give you my opinion on the essay 'Zionism Reconsidered' though I don't in the slightest wish to have a fatal falling out with you."[45] Scholem's response was indeed harsh, although it appears that he did not quite understand the thrust of Arendt's critique, and he suggested as much himself. "In vain I asked myself what sort of credo you had in mind when you wrote it. Your article has nothing to do with Zionism."[46] To Scholem, Arendt's essay appeared to be no more than "a lovely assortment of anti-Zionist arguments"[47]

43. Ibid., 361.

44. This is the context in which Arendt's advocacy for a Jewish army should be understood. Jewish interests really lay, Arendt believed, in galvanizing their political and national courage in order to fight the war as Jews in a Jewish army and as representatives of the Jewish people. In this way, the Zionists of Palestine could indeed literally become the vanguard of the Jewish people. On the other hand, mobilizing Jewish opinion in favor of the creation of a future state was essentially a self-absorbed reactionary and irresponsible response.

45. Scholem, *Gershom Scholem: A Life in Letters*, 330.

46. Ibid.

47. Ibid.

Scholem's response was therefore itself, not surprisingly perhaps, something of an assortment, a mixed bag of attacks, refutations, and apologetics.
His attack on Arendt's character was direct and unrelenting. The only reason
Scholem could think of to explain Arendt's critique of Zionism in Palestine
and the notion that it was an answer to anti-Semitism was that she had developed "a serious anti-Palestine complex."[48] Elsewhere in his letter, he accused
Arendt of being a closet communist: "Your article has nothing to do with Zionism but is instead a patently anti-Zionist, rewarmed version of Communist
criticism [*Neuauflage kommunistischer Kritik*]."[49] This was one of the allegations that Arendt addressed in her reply to Scholem in April 1946, in which she
somewhat ironically noted: "The claim that this article is 'a rewarmed version
of Communist criticism' would appear, if I may, somewhat curious if you are
familiar with the relevant literature."[50] Yet Scholem's most scathing personal
attack was probably his insinuation that Arendt was, in fact, worse than David
Ben-Gurion. "I never dreamed that it would be easier for me to agree with Ben-
Gurion than with you!"[51] It is quite telling that he did, eventually, align himself
with Ben-Gurion rather than with Hannah Arendt.

Scholem proceeded to refute some of Arendt's assertions on the grounds
that they were factually inaccurate. In her essay, Arendt furiously criticized
the kibbutz establishment for being completely self-absorbed and showing no
interest in the world beyond its narrow confines, neither in the political effect of its presence in Palestine, nor in its relations with the rest of the Jewish
world. To this Scholem retorted: "Who told you that the people in Palestine
or even in the kibbutzim are not concerned about the Jewish people outside
of Palestine? I would like to be introduced to him. He must be a great fool."[52]
Arendt's claim that the Jewish Agency was not committed to creating a Jewish army likewise appeared to Scholem completely false. "The facts [known
to] anyone who has read newspapers in Palestine over the past six years are
precisely the opposite of what you claim."[53] Yet most significantly, Scholem
sought to refute Arendt's accusation that the Zionist leadership had forsaken
its attempt to reach a peaceful solution with the Arab population in Palestine.
To this Scholem responded in a manner that has characterized the mainstream

48. *Hannah Arendt / Gershom Scholem, Der Briefwechsel,* 96.
49. Ibid., *Gershom Scholem: A Life in Letters,* 330.
50. Ibid., 333.
51. Ibid., 332.
52. *Hannah Arendt / Gershom Scholem, Der Briefwechsel,* 95.
53. Ibid., 97.

Zionist movement from the beginning of its settlement in Palestine to this very day.[54] The fact of the matter was, so Scholem suggested, albeit in a somewhat allusive manner, that while the Jews had reached out to the Arabs, the latter had never taken up the offer: "I am not presumptuous enough to think that the politics of Brith Shalom would not have encountered precisely the same Arab opponents, who are primarily interested not in the morality of our political convictions but in whether or not we are here in Palestine at all."[55]

More than anything else, it is this statement that demonstrates Scholem's transformation and his acceptance of political failure. The onetime Brith Shalom member acknowledges here that the association's political aims were, in fact, unattainable and that there was very little that he, his associates, or even the Zionist establishment could have done differently. The problem was that there was simply no partner on the other side with whom to negotiate. And it is this statement that best signifies the prevalent mood in Scholem's letter to Arendt.

While Scholem was clearly angered and disturbed by Arendt's critique, the tone of his letter is predominantly apologetic and very similar in spirit to the common discourse of mainstream Zionism. It is true, Scholem admitted in his letter, Zionists did try to cut deals with the Nazis, and this was hardly something to be proud of. However, he insisted, subsequent experience had vindicated this action. "I would like to know," Scholem asked Arendt, "if we would not have saved the life of Walter Benjamin through such a transaction, had his life depended on it." And besides, Scholem argued, those who had undertaken this unpleasant task were merely doing their duty.[56] Indeed, Scholem furthermore confessed, there was something thoroughly reactionary about the Zionist movement, which like every movement had developed dialectically throughout its history. Nevertheless, he noted, "I feel free enough in my thinking not to be overly disturbed when I am accused of holding reactionary opinions."[57]

Finally, and most important of all, the issue of the Jewish state was, Scholem confessed, not that important after all. Were Scholem ever to have penned a letter of resignation from the political position he had once held so dearly, it might have looked like this: "I don't give a rap about the problem of the state

54. See note 10.

55. Scholem, *Gershom Scholem: A Life in Letters*, 332.

56. *Hannah Arendt / Gershom Scholem, Der Briefwechsel*, 96.

57. Scholem, *Gershom Scholem: A Life in Letters*, 332; "ich fühle mich in meinem Denken frei genug, um von dem Vorwurf reaktionärer Gesinnung ungerührt zu bleiben," *Hannah Arendt / Gershom Scholem, Der Briefwechsel*, 94.

[*Mir ist das Staatproblem vollkommen schnuppe*], because I do not believe that the renewal of the Jewish people depends on the question of their political or even social organization."[58]

Scholem did not go quite so far as to endorse the state, but neither did he rule it out. He moved, so to speak, beyond it, setting himself above the—now suddenly not so important—political question of the Jewish state. It is therefore most fitting that it was here that Scholem confessed to Arendt his political "belief." He was, he stated, an anarchist. In principle, therefore, he opposed the powers of the state, of any state. But in fact, so it seems, the state simply did not interest him. It is hardly surprising that having adopted this stance, Scholem now endorsed, albeit somewhat reluctantly, the leader of the Zionist organization and the future first prime minister of the State of Israel, David Ben-Gurion. In his closing remarks to Arendt, Scholem wrote, "I consider Ben Gurion's political line disastrous, but nevertheless it is far nobler—or less evil—than the one we would have had we followed your advice."[59]

As this letter to Arendt makes abundantly clear, Scholem had by then renounced his previous political stance and reversed his position on the question of the Jewish state. Furthermore, he now saw himself as an insider who had spent years reading the newspapers in Palestine and who felt sufficiently at home in Yishuv society to be dismayed at Arendt's characterization of the attitude of Jewish Palestine toward Jews who lived outside of it. This is the crux of the difference between him and Arendt. While they agreed on many issues, they parted ways when it came to their basic disposition toward the problems at hand. "Of course," Scholem concedes, "there are many points on which Zionist politics is completely wrong, and you focus quite rightly on these points. You do this, however, not from a Zionist perspective but from one propped up by obviously Trotskyite anti-Zionist arguments."[60]

In other words, Scholem criticizes Arendt for maintaining an outsider's position and thereby reveals that he himself has changed and has now, after so many years of bitter struggle, become an insider. As an insider, the question of the state appeared to Scholem of lesser importance, particularly since

58. Scholem, *Gershom Scholem: A Life in Letters*, 331. "Mir ist das Staatproblem vollkommen schnuppe, da ich nicht glaube, dass die Erneuerung des jüdischen Volkes von der Frage seiner politischen, ja sogar von der Frage der sozialen Organisation abhänget. Mein politischer Glaube ist, wenn er irgendetwas ist—anarchistisch." *Hannah Arendt / Gershom Scholem, Der Briefwechsel*, 94.

59. Scholem, *Gershom Scholem: A Life in Letters*, 332.

60. Ibid.

the decision had already been made. Scholem had become a pragmatist, and he asked Hannah Arendt to follow him. "Repent [*Umkehr*]," Scholem wrote Arendt in the closing lines of his letter. It is the best solution, he seems to imply, and the one he has already embraced.

Arendt did not take this advice. Nevertheless, the cordial relations between Arendt and Scholem withstood their profound disagreement. In a short postscript to his letter, Scholem informed Arendt of a planned trip to New York, expressing the hope that they would meet. In her response, Arendt assured Scholem that "I bear you no grudge because of your letter, not in the least. But I do not know how you are going to react to mine. When all is said and done, you are *masculini generis* and for this reason naturally (perhaps) more vulnerable."[61] Scholem, for his part, was not unduly dismayed by Arendt's refusal to change her ways. Their relationship, in fact, endured for a further seventeen productive years, that is, until the publication of Arendt's report on the banality of evil.

ABOUT THE LOVE OF ISRAEL

The debate between Arendt and Scholem erupted once more in 1962 over Arendt's book about the Eichmann trial in Jerusalem titled *Eichmann in Jerusalem: A Report on the Banality of Evil.*[62] In it, Arendt sharply reprimands the Israeli legal and political establishment for the way in which it staged the trial. She furthermore levels criticism at the Jews under German occupation for the manner in which they collaborated in the process of their own extermination, citing the willing participation of Jewish leaders and the councils that administered the lives of the Jews in the ghettos and the meek obedience of individuals. The book furthermore portrays the accused, Adolf Eichmann, not as some archvillain, but rather as a less than impressive state bureaucrat, more concerned with his status in the eyes of his superiors than with the deportations of the Jews, for which he was responsible and which he tried to conduct as efficiently as possible. Arendt portrays the prestate Zionist functionaries who negotiated with Eichmann for the lives of Jews rather unflatteringly. She then proceeds to show how Nazi interests coincided with those of Zionism, as the former sought to free Europe from the Jews while the Zionists strove to free the Jews from Europe. In short, there was hardly an element of the

61. Ibid., 334.

62. Hannah Arendt, *Eichmann in Jerusalem: A Report on the Banality of Evil* (London: Penguin Classics, 1994).

entire multifaceted Zionist world that Hannah Arendt did not deeply offend with her report on the Eichmann trial.[63]

Gershom Scholem was also deeply offended by Arendt's book and wrote her a long and detailed letter, which was subsequently published together with Arendt's reply and sparked considerable discussion.[64] In our context, the exchange is informative not because of what it tells us about Arendt's book or about the major issues that it raised, but rather because of what it reveals about Gershom Scholem. Scholem's letter to Arendt unveils some of his most deeply seated political assumptions during the latter period of his life. It consequently also reveals the personal and psychological mechanism underlying his acceptance of political Zionism, the Jewish state, and his willingness to surrender his previous beliefs about the Zionist endeavor.

In his letter to Arendt, Scholem's prime concern was her analysis of the behavior of Jewish individuals and of the Jewish councils during the war. The interesting point about Scholem's letter to Arendt is that he tended to accept her analysis. While he did not believe that it was entirely free of historical and analytical errors, he appears to acquiesce that the questions she raised in her book were indeed the most troubling and poignant. "The question that the young people in Israel are asking has real merit: 'Why did they [the Jews] allow themselves to be killed?' The answer that one always starts to give cannot be reduced to a formula." And later in the letter he furthermore acknowledged that "the problem you pose is genuine."[65] To Scholem, therefore, the problem with the Eichmann book was not primarily grounded in the integrity of

63. Some of the most poignant critiques of Arendt's book were collected in Friedrich A. Krummacher, ed., *Die Kontroverse: Hannah Arendt, Eichmann und die Juden* (Munich: Nymphenburger Verlag, 1964). For a more recent look at the controversy this book generated, see Gary Smith, *Hannah Arendt Revisited: "Eichmann in Jerusalem" und Die Folgen* (Berlin: Suhrkamp Verlag, 2000).

64. See, for example, David Suchoff, "Gershom Scholem, Hannah Arendt, and the Scandal of Jewish Particularity," *Germanic Review: Literature, Culture, Theory* 72, no. 1 (1997): 57–76; Eric Jacobson, "Ahavat Yisrael: Nationhood, the Pariah and the Intellectual," in *Creation and Re-creation in Jewish Thought: Festschrift in Honor of Joseph Dan on the Occasion of His Seventieth Birthday*, ed. Rachel Elior and Peter Schäfer (Tübingen: Mohr Siebeck, 2005); Etienne Balibar, "'God Will Not Remain Silent': Zionism, Messianism and Nationalism," *Human Architecture: Journal of the Sociology of Self-Knowledge* 7, no. 2 (Spring 2009): 123–34; David Kaposi, "To Judge or Not to Judge: The Clash of Perspectives in the Scholem-Arendt Exchange," *Holocaust Studies: A Journal of Culture and History* 14, no. 1 (n.d.): 95–119; Dagme Barnouw, "The Secularity of Evil: Hannah Arendt and the Eichmann Controversy," *Modern Judaism* 3, no. 1 (February 1, 1983): 75–94.

65. Scholem, *Gershom Scholem: A Life in Letters*, 395.

Arendt's judgment, or in the accuracy of the analysis. The dismay with which he greeted it was a matter of its style, its overall mood, and the sentiments that it aroused in the reader. He asked Arendt to explain: "Why then does your book evoke such a feeling of bitterness and shame . . . indeed not toward the author's subject matter but toward the author herself?"[66] This was, of course, a rhetorical question, and the answer Scholem famously offered was as simple as it was direct: "It is the heartless, the downright malicious tone you employ in dealing with a topic that so profoundly concerns the center of our life. There is something in the Jewish language that is completely indefinable, yet fully concrete—what the Jews call *ahavat Israel*, or love for the Jewish people. With you, my dear Hannah . . . there is no trace of it."[67]

Scholem's accusation, according to which Arendt's critique was driven by her emotional disposition toward her subject, was not far removed from that he had made in response to Arendt's "Zionism Reconsidered" of 1944. Then, he had charged her with offering anti-Zionist arguments and harboring an anti-Palestine complex. Arendt's response to these allegations is telling. In her 1946 reply to Scholem she wrote: "Actually it seems to me impossible to overlook the fact that my article was not written out of an 'anti-Palestine complex' but rather out of an almost panicky anxiety for Palestine [*nahezu panischen Angst um Palästina*]."[68] It was not, Arendt in other words claimed, her unhealthy attitude toward the subject that had sparked her sharp criticism; on the contrary, it was her deep and abiding concern about the issues at hand that had informed her writing. In 1963, on the other hand, Arendt confessed to an emotional indifference on her part toward the Jewish people, or toward any other group of people. In her reply to Scholem she wrote: "How right you are that I do not have such love . . . I have never in my life 'loved' a nation or a collective . . . The fact is that I love only my friends and am quite incapable of any other sort of love."[69]

The transformation Arendt underwent—from expressing a panic-stricken concern for the Jewish settlement in Palestine to confessing emotional indifference toward it (and toward any other group of people)—is revealing. Perhaps this transformation was the result of the blunt rejection she had encountered on the part of those she had cared so much about, namely, Zionists in Palestine such as Scholem. But more important, Arendt's transformation underscores

66. Ibid.
67. Ibid., 395–96.
68. *Hannah Arendt / Gershom Scholem, Der Briefwechsel*, 108.
69. Scholem, *Gershom Scholem: A Life in Letters*, 399.

the difference between the two friends and the essential point of division between the two scholars: their emotional relation to 'Zion,' the idea and particularly the place. Whereas Scholem had migrated to Palestine and wedded his
future to the land and its inhabitants, Arendt had chosen not to do so, even
when she was forced to flee her own country, Germany. The difference between living in one location and living in another is, in the context of Zionism, clearly ideological.

Arendt refused to accept the fundamental creed of the Zionist movement.
She refused to immigrate to Palestine, to make *aliyah*. Worse still, she sought
to continue her political Zionist activism from abroad. In her writing she insisted that Zionism should tackle anti-Semitism for what it was and where it
mattered the most, in Europe, rather than concentrating its entire effort in
Palestine. Despite his close personal affinity with her, Scholem flatly rejected
Arendt's assertions. Zionism was, for him, centered in Zion and was inextrica-
bly connected to the cultivation of its land, to its university, and even to its agri-
cultural settlements. He regarded his choice to live in Palestine to be the logical
conclusion of his Zionist ambition. Furthermore, unlike Arendt, Scholem had
over the years developed a deep emotional attachment to the Jewish people as
a collective. He possessed, as he insinuated in his famous letter, *ahavat Yisrael*.
And his love of Israel had determined not only his choices but also his political
convictions. This meant that at times of dire need and great upheaval, he would
accept Zionist positions even if he did not always agree with them. Scholem
had not changed his mind about the conflict with the Arabs and about the true
objective of Zionism. Like Arendt, he was, one imagines, also deeply troubled
by the negotiations of the Zionist leadership with Nazi officials. And like many
others, he was torn by the dilemma of cooperation, which was, and continues
to be, intensely debated. Yet his emotional disposition toward these dilemmas
is markedly different from that of Hannah Arendt.

Scholem's loyalty to the people of Israel was paramount. These, he seems
to argue, were not matters deserving of unrelenting and bitter criticism, or
of irony. Rather, they should be addressed with the utmost care, bearing in
mind that empathy, loyalty, and love precede analysis or critique. This is what
Arendt, so Scholem maintained, had misunderstood. And this was the reason
that Scholem's political principles, which had guided his thinking in his youth,
had become secondary in light of the events he had experienced. This was
the reason that Scholem preferred Ben-Gurion to Arendt. Indeed, Scholem
learned to accept the State of Israel and its leader, David Ben-Gurion, albeit
reluctantly but nevertheless without hesitation. This was the lesson he had

learned from historical experience, which he portrayed nowhere more poignantly than in his essay on the Star of David written in 1948.

A SYMBOL OF UPHEAVAL AND
REGENERATION: THE STAR OF DAVID

Gershom Scholem published his essay on the Star of David (*Magen David*) in the annual literary supplement of the daily newspaper *Ha'aretz* in October 1948. In the essay, the Star of David serves as a symbol on two distinct levels. On the literal plane, it is an emblem or a sign that appeared in Jewish history and symbolized slightly different things at different times and in different contexts. At the same time, however, the Star of David allegorically represented the State of Israel. Only several months separated Israel's declaration of independence and the publication of the essay. There is no doubt that during this period the symbol on the state's flag was constantly present in the imagination of everyone living in Israel. Literally, therefore, the essay explored the transformations of an idea, a symbol in the history of the Jews. Yet allegorically, the essay reflected on the role that the new Jewish state was to play in respect to the Jewish past and its religious tradition.

How, then, is the place of the Jewish state in Jewish history allegorically represented by the symbol of the Star of David? Scholem's answer to this question, offered in October 1948, is direct and simple and thus rather startling. In his essay, Scholem maintains that throughout Jewish history the Star of David was largely devoid of meaning and acquired a powerful emotional charge by having been able spontaneously to represent the upheaval of the Holocaust. The allegorical interpretation contained in the essay therefore suggests that even though the Jewish state played no role in Jewish history and was from this perspective utterly meaningless, it was charged with importance and acquired its legitimacy because it consolidated the emotional reaction of the Jews to the horrific events in Europe. On some intuitive level, Scholem argued, the state had explained the tragedy of the Holocaust and had rendered it tangible. And for this reason, the state had also become historically important, meaningful, and legitimate.

Symbols, Scholem asserts at the beginning of his essay, have the power to explicate the inexplicable.[70] They instinctively express a certain truth about

---

70. Scholem follows here a long tradition of describing and debating the nature of the symbol, which was especially prevalent around the turn of the nineteenth century in German

the intensely complex relations that appear on the plane of history and in people's lives. In other words, symbols possess the power to crystallize, as Scholem puts it, "the variegated phenomena of this world into simple, unitary and characteristic forms." For this reason, scholarly discussion of symbols tends, according to Scholem, not only to overlook their main characteristics, but to also go astray in complex attempts to unpack what is already self-evident in the form of a symbol. In his essay Scholem introduces the idea that symbols such as the Star of David are not a product of deliberation but rather occur spontaneously and emanate from an emotional need. And this is why they can express something endlessly complex and emotionally charged in the simplest form, one that is immediately recognizable.

To the surprise of those who see the Star of David as the symbol of Judaism, historically, Scholem claimed, it played only a marginal role. It did not appear in rabbinical literature, or in the Kabbalah. At times, it was used for decorative purposes, "in keeping with the tradition of ornamentation so beloved by the Arabs."[71] But it had never evolved into a symbol; it had never, that is, captured the emotional content of Jewish life. The six-pointed Star of David was, however, prevalent in magic talismans, and it appeared alongside a further emblem that is nowadays more associated with magic, the pentagram, the five-pointed star. As a vessel for magic powers, the Star of David gained some popularity, Scholem claimed, among the members of the Sabbatean movement, who were thus the first to make extensive use of this symbol, which they associated with secrets and magic. The Star of David represented their movement and the imminence of redemption. In this, Scholem ironically noted, the Sabbatean movement was the precursor of Zionism.

The Star of David gained prominence as a symbol of Judaism only in the modern age, and only vis-à-vis the Christian cross. When the two religious groups appeared alongside each other, such as during special parades, the Christian cross was matched by the Jewish Star. This initially occurred, according to Scholem, on the occasion of a special procession welcoming the Emperor Ferdinand I to Prague, during which the Jews marched "under their own flag." Later, in Vienna, the boundary of the Jewish section in the cemetery

---

literature, philosophy, and philology. For more see Engel, "Gershom Scholems 'Kabbala und Mythos' jenseits deutsch-jüdischer Romantik."

71. Gershom Scholem, "The Star of David: History of a Symbol," in Scholem, *Messianic Idea in Judaism*, 267.

was marked by a Star of David carved in stone next to the cross that signified the boundary of the Christian section. The Star traveled with the Jews as they were expelled from Vienna and gradually spread across Europe. Only in the nineteenth century, however, did the Star of David ascend to prominence as it came to adorn synagogues, which were themselves built, Scholem asserts, as Jewish churches. Yet intrinsically, Scholem repeatedly maintains, the symbol was mostly devoid of any authentic emotional meaning. In fact, its vacuity reflected the true state of Judaism at the time, which, he believed, was a petrified religion that served no spiritual role. Even during the nineteenth century, although it was widely used, the Star of David conveyed no religious significance and captured none of the emotional turbulence of the Jewish people. And even the Zionist movement, which adopted the Star of David for its own purpose in 1897, could not breathe life into the moribund symbol. It was only in the 1940s during the Holocaust that the symbol came to life.

Scholem discusses the resurrection of the Star of David only in the very last paragraph of the essay. After about twenty pages describing the emptiness, the inaptness, and the circumstantial meaning of this symbol in Jewish history, Scholem's style and arguments shift. In the last paragraph of the essay, the text becomes somber as it recounts the creation of a symbol.

> Far more than the Zionists have done to provide the Shield of David with the sanctity of a genuine symbol has been done by those who made it for millions into a mark of shame and degradation. The yellow Jewish Star . . . has accompanied the Jews on their path of humiliation and terror . . . Under this sign they were murdered; under this sign they came to Israel . . . The sign which in our own days had been sanctified by suffering and dread has become worthy of illuminating the path to life and reconstruction. Before ascending, the path led down into the abyss; there the symbol received its ultimate humiliation and there it won its greatness.[72]

Scholem's conclusion is debatable. Most important, it raises the question of the integrity of this symbol. Should the symbol of Jewish unity and hope, of its political success and social future accept the definitions imposed on it by its enemies? Yet such a debate is beside the point in this context. Symbols, Scholem stressed, were spontaneous and emotional objects and were, for this reason, hardly a matter of deliberation. The Star of David, according to Scholem, became a symbol in the full sense of the word for the first time in

72. Ibid., 281.

Jewish history by representing Jews in their darkest hour and in their most jubilant moment in recent memory. It represented the terrible suffering of Jews at the hands of the Germans and the destruction of European Jewry, and, at the same time, it came to represent the glorious achievement of the Zionist movement in the land of Israel, through its settlements, agriculture, factories, its army, and its university in Jerusalem. Moreover, it mysteriously came to capture the unimaginable emotional tension created by these two momentous events as a symbol of what Scholem called "simple, unitary, and characteristic form." And these, Scholem claimed, were simply the facts of the matter.

Scholem's descriptions of the Star of David does therefore closely describe his relation toward the Jewish state. Indeed, Gershom Scholem's life was woven into the story of Zionism and into the history that supported the symbol of the state. He rebelled against what he believed to be a petrified Jewish religion and devoted his life to Judaism through a lifelong study of its past and through active engagement in Jewish politics as a Zionist. This devotion paved his way from Berlin to Jerusalem. And from this vantage point he saw the world he once knew transform. He witnessed from afar how German anti-Semitism turned into an organized campaign to destroy Jewish life. He observed how conflicts with the Arabs evolved into a seemingly never-ending series of wars. He took part in the gradual creation of a Hebrew University from its very beginning as a fledgling institute into a fully fledged university. And he even lived to see the descendants of his political opponents, the Revisionist party, gain control of the Israeli government. At first he believed that a Jewish state was an abomination. But as his polemics with Arendt make clear, he chose the love of Israel. And as his essay on the Star of David implies, this position was forced on him as the Star of David was forced on Jewish history. For Scholem, the Jewish state became a meaningful object only in relation to the destruction of Jewish life in the Holocaust. It was, in other words, the historical circumstances that dictated his loyalty and overcame his critique, astute as it may have been.

CHAPTER 7

The Man and the Image

The very first pages of this book introduced the "Scholem enigma." Something about Scholem, it often seems, lay always beyond reach. One world-renowned scholar, with whom I spoke, used the term "coquettish" to describe Scholem's writing. Other examples are adduced in the first chapter above. Scholem is indeed an enigmatic figure. Especially mystifying, I argue, is his lasting influence and universal allure. Why, I asked at the outset, was Scholem so much more than a historian of a decidedly narrow field of knowledge? And how is it that he is well-known so far beyond the narrow confines of his own academic discipline? In the pages above, I sought to unravel the mystery.

This study essentially argues that the reasons for Scholem's unusually wide reception are rooted in his two stories. Scholem did not make novel use of concepts. Rather, he told stories that wrestle with key questions about Jewish life and European life in the twentieth century. We have seen, for example, how Scholem's stories about the Lurianic myth raise many questions about community, destiny, nationalism, homecoming, and exile. Following this line of argumentation, the chapters above opened up Scholem's stories, analyzed them, and pointed out common threads and interactions. Told together, the different plotlines of Scholem's life and work offer a more or less coherent narrative.

The story about Gershom Scholem, told in the pages of this book, is ultimately about a unique individual in the twentieth century. It is devoid of any mystical or mythical allusions. Some may find it befitting while others might be surprised or disappointed. For indeed much of the existing literature paints Scholem with some rather unusual colors. Harold Bloom, it was noted already

FIGURE 7.1. Scholem in his apartment, 1950s. Photo by Werner Braun. Courtesy of the Hebrew University.

in the first chapter, suggested that Scholem only "worked behind the mask of a historian" but that he in fact was "the secret theologian of Jewish Gnosis of our time."[1] Franz Rosenzweig used no less dramatic terms in a letter he wrote two years before Scholem's immigration to Palestine. "I have never seen anything like it among Western Jews," Rosenzweig noted; "he is perhaps the only one there is who actually returned home."[2] And Martin Buber famously claimed that Scholem "created an academic discipline." Such assertions find no room in this book.

This book, therefore, takes a radically different approach. Scholem, I show, was swayed by the winds of history, was rattled to the core by loss, and was often found on the losing side of the argument. In a deep sense, he was no more and no less a human being than most people. Of course, he was also singularly talented, diligent, and bright and had a phenomenally successful career. But Scholem's career developed gradually and knew many disappointments. The concluding chapter of this book is dedicated to considering this demystified

1. Bloom, "Scholem: Unhistorischer oder jüdischer Gnostizismus," 70.
2. Quoted in Biale, *Counter-history*, 78.

figure of Scholem. And it reflects upon the radical gap between his image here and the way he is often conceived.

To be sure, the demystification of Scholem undertaken in the pages above was an unintended result. The original determination, which then grew to become this book, was to study a commanding figure that had squared up to and answered many fundamental questions of religion and its scientific rendition, and its political dimensions. However, as I immersed myself in the sources, I found a much more complex character. It became clear that Scholem changed his position on several key issues. His political convictions changed over time, and so did his descriptions of, for example, the Sabbatean heresy. More careful consideration helped me realize that these changes follow a certain pattern or historical logic. Placed upon the timeline of European history, these patterns became almost self-evident.

Seen from a distance, the contours of Scholem's life and the changes exhibited in his work follow a somewhat predictable course. Scholem was born just before the turn of the twentieth century. He became engaged in politics, as many of us do, at around the age of seventeen. In Scholem's case this occurred shortly before the outbreak of World War I. Scholem reached the zenith of his engagement shortly thereafter. He immigrated to Palestine precisely as the new postwar world order was being shaped. In other words, his immigration can be seen as part of a larger shift of power, territory, and influence that took place in the aftermath of the war.[3] Scholem was in his mid to late twenties at the time. Yet the process of immigration proved to be more difficult and complex than he imagined. This, of course, would not surprise anyone who ever attempted to immigrate anywhere, nor would it surprise anyone who is able even vaguely to imagine interwar Berlin and interwar Jerusalem. Even at the age of twenty-six, immigrating from Berlin to Jerusalem is bound to be an existentially difficult undertaking. It therefore may be of little surprise that Scholem found the reality in Palestine to be entirely unsatisfactory, and it may be only natural that he then devoted himself to an ideological struggle. In the 1930s things changed radically again both in the Middle East and in Europe, and then again in the 1940s as a result of the Second World War. After the war, Scholem disengaged from political activism and learned to accept the prevailing political dogma.

3. Scholem immigrated to Palestine in the last phases of what is known as the Third Aliyah, that is, the third Zionist immigration wave to Palestine (1919–23). This fact is even carved onto his gravestone. The literature of the Third Aliyah unequivocally attributes the reasons for this wave to the emergence of new postwar power structures. See, for example, Yehuda Erez, ed., *The Third Aliyah* (in Hebrew) (Tel Aviv: Am Oved, 1964).

He still had serious reservations, but he kept those mostly to himself. Thus the fifty-year-old professor from Jerusalem who witnessed the Holocaust became, not only older, but also more cautious, more reserved, and more conservative.

A disenchanted view of Scholem would see him therefore as a human being trying to find a footing in the increasingly violent world around him. Indeed, it may be more or less expected that Scholem's views, convictions, and interpretations would be influenced by the rather dramatic circumstances. It would be in fact surprising if they had not differed according to place and time, between Berlin and Jerusalem, and between pre–World War I and post–World War II. It also seems natural that the radical spirit of Zionism, which motivated the seventeen- and eighteen-year-old's youth movement activism, would give way to the careful conservatism of the forty- or fifty-year-old professor. He struggled against Zionist politics when he was younger, and then gradually withdrew from political action once he realized that the barriers he faced were insurmountable and that his political desires would never materialize. The effects that these changes had on his scholarly writing are also something to be expected. And indeed Scholem's understanding of Sabbateanism changed after immigrating to Palestine, after Hitler's rise to power, and after the State of Israel gained independence.

All this is not to suggest that Scholem was an average individual or that he had to take the route that he did. The contrary is the case. Scholem was an exceptional figure, and his choices were often unusual and many times courageous. He was an outspoken critic of mainstream thinking and often expressed widely unpopular positions. He held a courageous position both against World War I and as a member of Brith Shalom. His choice to dedicate his life to the study of obscure Jewish texts in the 1920s in Germany is no less than remarkable. And his tenacity as a scholar, his productivity, memory, hard work, and dedication were nothing less than phenomenal. These facts, however, do not allot him a position outside history, nor do they make him a mystic. The violent events of the so-called short twentieth century, which Scholem witnessed, did affect his views, understandings, and actions. And it is this fact that paved the way for the present study, an intellectual biography of Gershom Scholem. For it is only in the form of a biographical study that it is possible to account for the ideological changes and shifts that occur over the lifespan of an individual.

This biographical study of Scholem identifies two major transitions in its subject's life. The first transition can be neatly demarcated. When Scholem left Germany and resettled in Mandatory Palestine in 1923, his entire existence was radically affected. This was not a forced immigration, but its impact can nevertheless be felt throughout Scholem's writing. Scholem's move from Berlin to Jerusalem that took place in October 1923 denotes a clear fault line in his life and work. The second transformative period in Scholem's life is harder to delineate. Things change gradually during the 1930s. It is impossible to point at one event or one cause, but it is clear that from Scholem's perspective radically changed during this time period. In Palestine, the conflict between Arabs and Jews slowly escalated and even erupted in brutal violence on several instances. In Germany, the Nazi party came into power, sucking Europe into a deadly spiral of war that put Jews everywhere on the European continent and beyond it in terrible danger. Scholem reacted to this unfolding of events. It would have been strange if he had not. This second transition is no less radical than the first one, even if the ideological changes that took place during this period were gradual and left only few written traces.

Scholem's two transitions—from Berlin to Jerusalem and from fringe to mainstream—must be taken into account not only in order to have a fuller picture of his biography but, more important, in order to understand the stories Scholem told through his historiography. The first major event in Scholem's historiographical discussion is the formation and reception of the Lurianic Kabbalah. And it is, I have argued, inexorably attached to the views, hopes, and visions he had as a young man propagandizing and struggling among the Zionist youth movements in Berlin. In Scholem's telling, the Lurianic Kabbalah comprises an ideology. It was perhaps the single most influential ideology of the Jewish people. And like the ideology he propagated before and during World War I, it entailed a vision of an anarchic, free, yet obedient community that works in concert and individually to make the world a better place and bring a utopian state into existence.

Although many years passed between the time he was active in the youth movements and the time he first penned his Lurianic myth, the two episodes, I argue belong together. This too may not be altogether surprising. Scholem, it seems, had one vision of utopia, which he held throughout his life. It was a notion of a community, of *Gemeinschaft* that can withstand the pressures of history and human existence. He developed this vision when he was a young activist in the circles of Zionist youth movements in Berlin before the "Great War." And he then used this vision when he cobbled together the sources of the Lurianic myth. Subsequently, every time Scholem discussed the myth he reverted to the utopian image that he developed in his youth and that, so it seems, was deeply ingrained in his being. The Lurianic myth, it might be noted here again, was the only myth that Scholem fully narrated even as he argued that the Kabbalah was nothing but the mythological undercurrent of Jewish history.

The second, more complex historiographical issue taken up in these pages has to do with Scholem's discussions of the history of the Sabbatean movement, theology, and ideology. Indeed, nowhere is his scholarship more sensitive to change than in this aspect of his work. A comparison of Scholem's most comprehensive studies of Sabbateanism shows the shifting tendencies and alliances that characterize the second and third phase in his life. Scholem took up the study of Sabbatean history in the later 1920s, that is, when he was powerfully engaged in a public debate about messianism and Zionism. In this debate, he stood firmly on the secular side. Zionism, he forcefully argued, is not and should never be a messianic movement. Such a tendency would necessarily lead to nothing less than the destruction of the Zionist project. Scholem's early study on Sabbateanism was therefore a wager in this debate. It meant to prove that any attempt to realize a utopian undertaking in the world ends, by necessity, in calamity.

His subsequent comprehensive studies of Sabbateanism were less poignant. In his most famous essay, "Redemption through Sin," Scholem is clearly outraged by the moral standard of the Sabbatean believers, even if his fascination with their lurid practices is not difficult to discern. And yet he draws no explicit political parallels. Scholem is still critical of Sabbateanism in the chapter devoted to it in *Major Trends*, but he seems also to be more understanding. Here, Sabbateanism is described as the product of large, unavoidable historical circumstances and not the result of actions and decision undertaken by individuals. In his final word on the matter, his biography of Sabbatai Zevi, Scholem says hardly anything about the theology that so enraged him only two decades earlier. In the 1940s and 1950s Scholem's political zeal has waned all but completely. And subsequently, in his discussion of Sabbateanism he largely abstained from the issues that, according to his previous analysis, make the Sabbatean system of belief so radical and outstanding. This, I have argued, does not seem to be a coincidence.

Scholem's historiography, thus, seems to closely cohere with the political and historical context. This is the first and most substantial finding of this biographical study. This finding is further corroborated by a close reading of Scholem's most symbolic article: his piece on the Star of David, published shortly after Israel received its independence in 1948. However, there is another important facet to Scholem's life that this study unveils.

For most of his life, Scholem was an outsider who exercised only very limited influence over the world around him. During his lifetime, Scholem experienced many personal and professional disappointments and real losses. This may not be unknown among scholars. Nevertheless, the more human and humble image represented in the chapters above starkly contradicts the image Scholem still enjoys today in the eyes of a wider public. For many, he is still a commanding figure of great influence and import. But he reached this stature only much later in life. As a young man, he suffered greatly.

In 1915 and just short of his graduation, Scholem was expelled from high school for disseminating what was deemed to be antiwar propaganda. In hindsight, Scholem was able to clothe the entire episode in the colors of youthful confrontation and principled resistance. But this was long after he had gained universal recognition for his scholarly achievements and after the impressions of the "Great War" had faded in the light of the subsequent world war. At the time, Scholem's actions appeared to have cost him his future. Under any circumstance, it is difficult to explain to one's father the reasons for being expelled from school. But Scholem had to tell his father that he was expelled for circulating a letter arguing against the participation of Jews in the war. To make things worse, Scholem had to face a future without matriculation, effectively barred from ever entering the university. While he eventually found a way to take these exams,[4] he could not have foreseen this when he was expelled.

Scholem was not only expelled from school but also made to leave his house. The constant tension with his father over political issues erupted in 1917, after Scholem's older brother was arrested for demonstrating against the war while in uniform. As a result of an argument at home, Arthur Scholem expelled his youngest son from his house and denied him further financial support. Reminiscing on these events, Scholem portrayed a struggle in which a young man had stood up firmly and calmly for his principles against his somewhat unreasonable father and was subsequently proven right. "When I raised a mild objection to one of my father's assertions, he flew into rage and said he had now had enough of the two of us, that Social Democracy and Zionism were all the same, anti-German activity which he would no longer tolerate in his house, and that he never wanted to see me again."[5] Almost needless to say, Scholem never divulged anything of his own emotional reaction, although it is not hard to guess. On May 12, 1917, Scholem received the following letter

4. Scholem, *From Berlin to Jerusalem*, 61.
5. Ibid., 84.

from his father: "I have decided to cut off all support for you. Bear in mind the following: you have until the first of March to leave my house, and you will be forbidden to enter it again without my permission. On March first, I will transfer 100 marks to your account . . . Anything more than this you cannot expect of me . . . Whether I agree to finance your further studies after the war depends upon your future behavior."[6] This could not have been other than a most chastening experience for the young Scholem.

Scholem's expulsion occurred alongside another even more worrisome crisis that befell the Scholem family. As noted, Gershom Scholem's older brother Werner, to whom he was deeply attached, was arrested for demonstrating at an antiwar rally in Berlin while in uniform. He was initially charged with treason, which carried a severe penalty. This event took place shortly after he had returned home wounded from the front in Serbia. Werner's arrest instigated the quarrel that culminated in Arthur's decision to cut off his youngest son. Again, observed at a distance of many years these events form the background to Scholem's story and seem to mesh into the general unrest of Scholem's youth. However, Werner's service on the front, his war injury, his release, and his arrest must have been a source of untold anxiety and anguish to his family. The effect of these events on all those involved should not be discounted in light of Scholem's cool-headed account, focused on the conflict between the youngest son and his father and delivered many years later.

Werner Scholem was eventually released from prison, but his fate continued to cause great concern in the years to come. After the end of World War I, Werner experienced a short, turbulent period of political activity as a member of various socialist and communist groups, parties, and organizations.[7] At the height of his political career, between 1924 and 1928, he served as a representative of the Communist party of Germany in the Reichstag, the German parliament. However, as he was both Jewish and a communist, he was an obvious target for the Nazi regime. Werner was arrested in 1933 and murdered in Buchenwald concentration camp seven years later. Ample evidence is to be found in Scholem's correspondence, especially that with his mother, of the frustration, apprehension, and despair that these events instilled in other members of the family. "It's downright unpleasant here," Scholem's mother, Betty, wrote on June 18, 1933, "the business about Werner's ostensible release has

6. *Gershom Scholem: A Life in Letters*, 41.
7. Mirjam Zadoff, *Der rote Hiob*, esp. 111–200.

really finished me off. Furthermore, it's impossible to find an attorney. Everyone we've asked has declined after hearing the word 'politics'!"[8]

Scholem's brother was not the only one among Scholem's small circle of close friends to die prematurely in tragic circumstances. His childhood friend Edgar Bloom was killed in battle in World War I. Walter Benjamin, his most significant friend, took his own life in Portbou, a small and remote village on the border between France and Spain, during his flight from the intensifying war and persecution in Europe. It would appear that Scholem lost something more than a friend on the day Walter Benjamin died. Benjamin was only one of a number of individuals in Scholem's immediate circle who took their own lives, albeit in radically different circumstances. Among these it is important to mention Paul Celan, who committed suicide in 1970, Peter Szondi, who took his life in 1971, and Joseph Weiss, who killed himself in 1969. Weiss was Scholem's favorite student and a friend with whom he had maintained a close relationship for almost thirty years. His death was a terrible blow to Scholem.[9]

The mass murder of Jews and the destruction of the European Jewish world at the hands of the Nazis left a deep and indelible imprint on Scholem's life. Living in Jerusalem, Scholem was himself safe, but he experienced the persecution of the Nazi regime as a rather personal affair. Firsthand accounts of events in Berlin reached Jerusalem with the sudden influx of German immigrants, some of whom Scholem knew personally. They were friends, friends of friends, relatives, and neighbors, who had become refugees overnight and came knocking on Scholem's door in Jerusalem, as he had once when he immigrated. Scholem was well informed of the catastrophe, and it rendered him mute. "At the time of the catastrophe," he wrote to Ben Zion Dinur, "there are no teachings [*Thora*] . . . the one standing at the eye of the storm must always be silent."[10]

Although Scholem was well informed of the events in Europe, his first visit to the continent after the war left a lasting impression on him. In 1946 Scholem was sent on a search and rescue mission on behalf of Jewish Cultural Reconstruction (JCR) and the Hebrew University. The JCR's objective was to locate, sort, and ship to the United States and to Palestine the books pillaged by the Nazi army from Jewish institutions all over Europe. It is an ironic twist of fate that while Jews were systematically murdered, their libraries were at least

8. Scholem, *Gershom Scholem: A Life in letters*, 283.

9. Noam Zadoff, *Gershom Scholem and Joseph Weiss: Correspondence*.

10. Noam Zadoff, "Zion's Self-Engulfing Light." See also the discussion of this letter in chapter 6 above.

partially salvaged. The books were first shipped from the areas of German occupation to Germany and were later placed in several large warehouses, including one in Offenbach am Main, in order to protect them from the Allies' bombings.[11] Scholem traveled to Offenbach in order to examine and classify the many thousands of books in the depot, which had been placed randomly in crates and stacked to the ceiling. On this trip Scholem also visited Paris, Berlin, Frankfurt, and Prague. He thus observed at first hand the ruins of the spiritual and material landscape of his youth, people scattered across the land, destitution, and military occupation. In the Offenbach Depot Scholem sorted books whose original owners had been murdered, their bodies placed in unmarked graves or cremated and scattered to the wind. This trip, as Noam Zadoff observes, marks a turning point in Scholem's life.[12] World War II, which had wrought unimaginable destruction on Jewish life, claimed the lives of Werner Scholem and Walter Benjamin, and turned Berlin into rubble, weighed heavily on Scholem's mind. It therefore may be no coincidence that Scholem, who expressed his opinion on almost everything relating to the Jewish people, hardly ever spoke about the Holocaust.

Rather than the authoritative figure on all things Jewish and the esteemed intellectual whose personal ties spanned the globe, it is this more complex Scholem, buffeted by the violent winds of history, that I have set out to portray in the chapters of this book. I have tried to show that, like Walter Benjamin's famous angel of history, Scholem constantly turned to face the past because he could not keep his eyes on the catastrophe of the present. In describing this tormented Scholem, I have sought to offer, first and foremost, a more complex understanding of the man who exerts such a decisive hold on the contemporary imagination. This is an evaluation that, I believe, corresponds with the person rather than with an invented image, even if Scholem himself profoundly contributed to the creation of this image. But more important, I hope that this more complex image of the man will draw attention to a somewhat overlooked aspect of his work.

This humane image of Scholem—as a man who was swayed by the violent currents of historical change, and who experienced many moments of

---

11. Elisabeth Gallas, *"Das Leichenhaus der Bücher": Kulturrestitution und jüdisches Geschichtsdenken nach 1945* (Göttingen: Vandenhoeck & Ruprecht, 2013), 9–26.

12. Noam Zadoff, "Reise in die Vergangenheit, Entwurf einer neuen Zukunft: Gershom Scholems Reise nach Deutschland im Jahre 1946," *Münchner Beiträge zur jüdische Geschichte und Kultur* 2 (2007): 67–80.

difficulty and defeat—opens up the subject to be consider last, namely, the discrepancy between the man and his image. To be sure, Scholem contributed to this discrepancy in his writing. As an indication and example, one can take the difference between his authoritative rhetoric and the enigmas and complexities presented by his writings. The very first sentence of Scholem's seminal study on Sabbateanism, "Redemption through Sin," is a commanding statement. "No chapter in the history of the Jewish people during the last several hundred years has been shrouded in mystery as that of the Sabbatean movement."[13] The question whether or not this is true is beside the point in this context. What I seek to point out is how Scholem charges his essays with a sense of urgency, and how he places himself in a position of authority over an extraordinarily wide field of knowledge. This is not an isolated example. At the very beginning of his essay titled "The Crisis of Tradition in Jewish Messianism," Scholem writes: "There are three ways in which tradition evolves and develops in history."[14] And the first sentence of "Towards an Understanding of the Messianic Idea in Judaism" declares: "Any discussion of the problems related to Messianism is a delicate matter, for it is here that the essential conflict between Judaism and Christianity has developed and continues to exist."[15] The poise, confidence, and charisma that Scholem generates through these statements are unmistakable.

By contrast to these gestures of certitude and authority, the actual arguments Scholem advances in his articles and books are intensely complex and often quite equivocal. The essay "Towards an Understanding of the Messianic Idea in Judaism" is a telling example. As noted in chapter 4 above, Scholem was not the first to write about the messianic idea in Judaism.[16] In fact, the phrase was coined by the historian Joseph Klausner, with whom Scholem sharply disagreed. The reader may well assume that twenty-two years after writing his revolutionary study of the Sabbatean movement "Redemption through Sin," Scholem would now finally divulge the secret of Jewish messianism in a succinct, general, and compelling way that would directly confront Klausner and his interpretation of the messianic idea. Scholem indeed discusses messianism, and his text is relatively succinct. Nevertheless, the article hardly

13. Scholem, "Redemption through Sin," 78.

14. Ibid., 49.

15. Ibid., 1.

16. See also Moshe Idel, "Messianic Scholars: On Early Israeli Scholarship, Politics and Messianism," *Modern Judaism* 32, no. 1 (2012): 22–53.

mentions Klausner, nor does it offer a critique of his interpretation of the messianic idea. Scholem's discussion of the messianic idea in this work is rather surprising and somewhat unsatisfying.

It turns out that messianism is not, according to Scholem, an idea but a historical event. When a messiah actually appears on the stage of history, he incorporates in his actions the different elements and ideas that exist within the tradition and applies them according to the needs of the actual historical situation. Therefore, it is the historical hour and the specific nature of the Messiah that determine the nature of the messianic event, rather than some particular idea or another. Succinctly put, messianism, according to Scholem, is the historical manifestation of different and at times even contradicting elements, a product of human hope and the Jewish tradition. Thus, in what appears to be his most important essay on the messianic idea, Scholem makes an almost outrageous claim. The messianic idea in Judaism, he argues, capitulates in the face of historical circumstances and is therefore worthy of only limited philosophical attention.

Whatever Scholem's ideas about the history of messianic movements, the discrepancy between his gestures of authority and the substantive and conceptual suggestions he offers is clearly evident in this essay. The title of the essay as well as its initial section creates an undeniable impression of certainty, suggesting that the following pages will finally put the vexing problem of messianism in Judaism to rest. Finally, someone will explain how messianism operates within the Jewish religion, which is at once driven by messianic ambitions and stubbornly resistant to the messianic message of Jesus of Nazareth. Yet Scholem's actual discussion is almost infuriatingly complex. Instead of a bottom line and albeit his provocative openings, what Scholem mostly offers is more consideration.

The discrepancy between Scholem's posture of authority and the substantial political implications of his discoveries likewise emerges in the very last section of his magnum opus *Major Trends in Jewish Mysticism*. As noted in chapter 5 above, in the very last section of his book Scholem discusses the question of the continuity of the mystical tradition by recounting a Hasidic tale. And as we have seen, at the concluding moment of the tale, just when Scholem seems poised to reveal to his readers the fundamental lesson of Jewish mystical history, he falls silent, leaving all the questions in abeyance. Scholem's masterpiece ends on a rather equivocal note. "To speak of the mystical course," Scholem declares, "is the task of prophets not of professors."[17] This summation places Scholem squarely in the role of professor, who can

17. Scholem, *Major Trends*, 350.

therefore volunteer no assessment of whether mysticism may continue to exist even in conditions of modernity. Yet this statement also may appear somewhat disingenuous. It seems implausible that the preeminent scholar of the mystical tradition, a political activist, and a singularly charismatic intellectual could have nothing to say about this issue.

Scholem's reluctance to address the contemporary spiritual, social, and political significance of mysticism at the end of his most important work leaves his readers, I would suggest, more perplexed than satisfied. These perplexities became an invitation to further interpretation. Broadly speaking, the discrepancy in Scholem's historiography (between gesture and political substance) can be interpreted in two different ways. One can argue that Scholem's gestures of certainty are genuine. Not only did Scholem understand the political poignancy of his scholarly work but also his choice to hide its meaning from his readers was part of a larger albeit hidden project. In order to substantiate this line of argumentation one must seek out a deeper reading of Scholem's works, one that penetrates the literal meaning of the text and unveils its hidden message. There, it would seem, in the interpreted version lies the truth about the relation between mysticism, messianism, and Sabbateanism and present-day Jewish politics and society. Alternatively, one could argue that Scholem said precisely what he meant and that his vexing reluctance to discuss the politics of mysticism in Judaism was based on ignorance. Scholem, it would then follow, failed to discuss in his writing how Jewish mysticism was to continue because he simply did not know. Or in other words, he claimed to be a mere historian because he genuinely felt that he was not a prophet. If this is true, the discrepancies in Scholem's historiographical texts are not part of a calculated attempt to conceal a more controversial truth but rather exactly what they appear to be: an indication of perplexity and puzzlement.

The interpretation of Scholem's life and work presented throughout this book tends towards the latter solution. Scholem never found sufficient answers to the questions that he had posed himself. I am not suggesting that he failed to describe accurately the history of the Sabbatean movement, or that he failed to identify the author of a certain manuscript. In his scholarly work Scholem was fruitful and prolific. Yet the central issues that drove his lifelong endeavor—his belief in the possibility of a Jewish national rejuvenation and his hope for personal spiritual fulfillment—remained largely unresolved. As a young man and an activist Scholem appeared to be very certain about the possibility of solving the problem of exile. He called his answer Zion. But as we have seen in chapter 2, Scholem's idea of Zion was somewhat vague, even though he discussed it in stern and pathos-filled language. I would furthermore suggest that Scholem's frequent psychological crises and his ongoing conflicts with peers and superiors indicate that he himself was aware of the shortcomings of his Zionist ideology. He must have known, for example, that the silent introversion that he advocated to the members of the Zionist youth movement in his resignation letter[18] could serve as a badly needed critique but not as a practical political action plan.

As a political activist in Palestine Scholem did not harbor any illusions. He was well aware that a nation taking its first steps on the stage of world history must reckon with the reality that it encountered through diligent effort that could never quite fulfill itself. He never believed that the binational parliamentary democracy he advocated would annul the conflict between Arabs and Jews, nor did he believe that a negotiated solution could settle the Jewish, Arab, and British claims once and for all. In other words, he totally rejected the notion that Zionism could function as a messianic movement or that it was motivated by messianic aspirations. After all, he had discovered, Jerusalem was not to become Zion, at least not in the foreseeable future. He thus eventually accepted what he considered to be the verdict of history. He viewed the creation of the Jewish state as a misfortune, but nevertheless felt that this was probably the best of all possible solutions. He ultimately grew to identify himself with the State of Israel, but as the interviews he gave late in his life clearly indicate, he never thought that it was perfect.

As was his choice to become a Zionist, Scholem's decision to study the Jewish mystical tradition was motivated by a search for answers. While he never said so explicitly, this conclusion seems unavoidable. In the opening line of his letter of 1937 to Zalman Schocken titled "A Candid Word about the True Motives of My Kabbalistic Studies," Scholem writes: "In no way did I become a 'Kabbalist' inadvertently." And later he adds, "It seemed to me that here, beyond the perceptions of my generation, existed a realm of associations, which had to touch on our most human experiences."[19] Scholem does not explain what these "most human" experiences were, but one may assume that he was referring, albeit not exclusively, to the experience of being in exile. The Kabbalah, the search for an inner spiritual tradition within Judaism, was surely but another aspect of Scholem's quest for a spiritual place to call home.

Yet it appears that even his study of the mystical tradition never quite provided Scholem with the kind of answers he had hoped for. In his otherwise rather presumptuous letter to Schocken, Scholem expresses a certain skep-

18. Scholem, "Farewell."
19. Quoted in Biale, *Counter-history.*

ticism about the outcome of his search. "To penetrate it [the misty wall of history] is the task I set for myself. Will I get stuck in the mist, will I, so to say, suffer a 'professorial death'?"[20] Did Scholem ever fulfill the task he took on himself, did he successfully "penetrate the mist," and if so, at what cost? He never told us. To be sure, Scholem was not an ordinary university professor, even if he acquired many of the profession's traits. As noted, he took great care to avoid taking a firm stance on the major issue that had originally led him to the Kabbalah. He never divulged how the realm of associations created in the vast literature of the Kabbalah might touch upon the contemporary human condition, and he often skirted discussion of the political implications of the mystical past. These issues, he maintained at the very end of *Major Trends*, were better left to prophets and should not be taken up by university professors such as him.

*

Throughout his life and in his work Scholem confronted the most basic conundrums of modern life. He wrote extensively about religion and politics, homecoming and exile, hope and disappointment. As a young man Scholem seems to have sensed that his answers were insufficient, and as he grew older he knew that this was indeed the case. Mysticism could offer no real remedy in a reality that was essentially devoid of a divine presence. And Zionism could not fulfill the spiritual hopes that Scholem had had for it. In the end, he clearly saw that history had the upper hand. He was aware that his hopes to extract from it traces of authentic spirituality had proved successful only to a very limited degree. Zionism, too, was transformed by momentous events that far exceeded his reach. The actual events of world history thus quelled Scholem's yearning for magic and mystery and rendered his Zionist hopes for a better human society obsolete. He thus learned at first hand how aspirations are hollowed out by time. For this reason, I believe, he carefully avoided offering any solutions to the questions that plagued him and that motivated his writing.

Scholem remains interesting and influential to this day, I would argue, not because of the solutions he offered but because the questions that motivated him are ever present in his historiography and in his autobiographical writing. He chose Zionism and the Jewish mystical tradition in order to find a solution to a life stranded in exile. He failed to find what he was looking for, but he never stopped seeking. And although he knew that his path had led him

20. Ibid., 76.

to establish a rather precarious home, he never grew tired of discussing it. Scholem's ongoing quest for answers and for a place to call home informs his two stories. Furthermore, it is precisely because they are told thus, as quests, that they remain vital today. This is what I have tried to show throughout the book.

With his historiography largely disproved and his famous memoir shown to be partial, Gershom Scholem stands before us as the author of a great odyssey. It began in Berlin and ended not in some imaginary Ithaca but in modern-day Jerusalem. Jerusalem today is an imperfect place. One must squint in the blazing sun to find in it traces of spirituality. Nevertheless, some people call it home. This is not because they love it so dearly, but because they consider it better than anything else in this world. This is the case with regard to Gershom Scholem, who kept his aspirations alive even after he realized that they would never be fulfilled. It is because of people like him that Jerusalem is more than what it seems. Like Scholem, the city has no redemptive power, yet as when reading his works, a sense of yearning for political, social, and spiritual redemption is still palpable when walking the city's streets.

Jerusalem 2016

INDEX

Note: Page numbers in italics indicate figures.

Wagner, Richard, 50

Wailing Wall events: Arab-Jewish relations following, 105–6; riots following, 106–7, 106n30, 106–7n31, 108, 115–16, 129, 131, 166, 169, 172–73

Wandervogel, 31–32

Wasserstrom, Steven, 24n66

Weidner, Daniel, 6, 23, 52n95, 113n43, 133n15; *Gershom Scholem: politisches, esoterisches und historiographisches Schreiben* (Gershom Scholem: Political, Esoteric, and Historiographical Writings), 21–22

Weiss, Joseph, 1–2, 3, 84, 207

Weizmann, Chaim, 177, 177–78n22, 179, 184

Weltsch, Robert, 133, 173

Wershuvsky, Chaim, 159–60

Wilhelm, Kaiser, 42

Wissenschaft des Judentums, 92

Wood, James: *How Fiction Works*, 18–19

World War I, 39, 43n63, 55–57, 55n105, 179, 201–2, 203; alienation during, 40; Scholem's polemic against, 35, 38, 39–47, 43–46, 45, 55–56, 55n105, 101, 131, 202

World War II, 149, 165, 168, 179, 182–83, 201–2

writing, ethical value of, 19

yearning, proletariat of, 34–39

Yishuv, the, 101–4, 106–8, 107–8n33, 108n37, 117, 117n56, 174, 187, 190

youth movements, 26, 29, 31–34, 31n14, 39, 65; German, 31–32, 65, 92, 101; Jewish, 32–34, 35, 41, 46–47, 49, 55, 59, 59n120, 92 (*see also* Zionist youth movement); Orthodox, 32–34; Zionist, 35, 40–47, 59–61, 66, 89, 95, 101, 109–10, 114–15, 168, 178, 181, 203, 212

Zadoff, Noam, 131, 208; *From Berlin to Jerusalem and Back: Gershom Scholem between Israel and Germany*, 23

Zion, 45–46, 49; dream of, 97–100; idea of, 28–31, 34, 37–38, 55, 59–60, 89–90, 94–95, 101, 111–15, 175, 185, 211–12; utopian ideal of, 37–38

Zionism, 4, 8–9, 21, 23, 55, 81, 87, 92, 175, 205, 213; anti-Semitism and, 185–87, 188; Arendt and, 181–95, 187n44; in Berlin, Germany, 48, 48n77; chauvinistic, 182; cultural, 178, 184; disappointment with, 109–15; as an escape from alienation, 185; Europe and, 44–45; exile and, 37–38, 45–47, 59–61, 163; futurity and, 165; history of mysticism and, 163–67; the Holocaust and, 187; imperialism and, 113–14, 129; internal debate within, 185; Jewish intellectuals and, 184–85; Jewish modernity and, 184–85; Jewish mysticism and, 130, 162–65; the Jewish state and, 171–72, 177–81; Kabbalah studies and, 130n6; language and, 116–18; mainstream view of, 25, 168–97, 190, 212; meaning of, 28; as "measure of all things," 37–38; messianism and, 115–17, 120–22, 124, 129, 140–41, 204; movement in exile, 113–15; mysticism and, 163–67; myth of rejuvenation and, 28–31; Nazism and, 191–92; Palestine and, 94–123, 128–29, 165–66, 186–87; politics and, 94–123, 149, 184; renewal and, 163–64; as revolt against culture of exile, 37; role of, 162, 163–64; Sabbateanism and, 9, 12, 16, 129–31, 132, 140, 162, 164–66, 176, 176n17, 196; Scholem's disappointment with, 25; socialism and, 35–37, 35n28, 38; as a spiritual movement, 178; spiritual rejuvenation and, 163–67, 178; the Star of David and, 197; turn to, 31–34; universalism of, 16; Zionist establishment, 168–69, 170–71, 173, 174, 177, 178; Zionist intellectuals, 173n7. *See also* Zionist movement

Zionist Association of Germany, 43, 98

Zionist Congress, 168, 178; Basel, 1897, 171, 178–79

Zionist General Council in Tel Aviv, 106

Zionist movement, 118, 128–29, 131, 170–71, 173–74, 177–79; Brith Shalom and, 107–8n33; "cult of Palestinian Zionists," 113–15; division into two parts, 113–15; evolvement of, 183–85;

Zionist movement (*cont.*)
the Holocaust and, 179–80; the Jewish state
and, 178–80; mainstream view of, 189; Nazis
and, 194; political consciousness and, 184;
reorientation in the 1930s and 1940s, 179–80;
Zionist Labor movement, 115–16, 184; Zionist youth movement, 26, 29, 31, 31n14, 34, 35,
40, 41–47, 59–61, 109–10, 114–15

Zionist Organization of America, 171; Atlantic
City conference, 182–83
Zionist press, 168
Zionist youth movement, 66, 89, 95, 101, 168,
178, 203, 212; Buber and, 41–45; Scholem's
polemic against, 59–61, 181
Zohar, the (Book of Splendor), 67, 151, 163
Zweig, Arnold, 133